LEGO MINDSTORMS NXT 2.0

The King's Treasure

James Floyd Kelly

Apress®

Lego Mindstorms NXT 2.0: The King's Treasure

ISBN-13 (pbk): 978-1-4302-2491-4

ISBN-13 (electronic): 978-1-4302-2492-1

Printed and bound in the United States of America 9 8 7 6 5 4 3 2 1

Lead Editor: Jonathan Gennick
Technical Reviewers: Adam Tester, Fay Rhodes
Editorial Board: Clay Andres, Steve Anglin, Mark Beckner, Ewan Buckingham, Tony Campbell, Gary Cornell, Jonathan Gennick, Michelle Lowman, Matthew Moodie, Jeffrey Pepper, Frank Pohlmann, Ben Renow-Clarke, Dominic Shakeshaft, Matt Wade, Tom Welsh
Coordinating Editor: Jim Markham
Copy Editor: Seth Kline
Compositor: Mary Sudul
Indexer: Ann Rogers/Ron Strauss
Artist: April Milne

Distributed to the book trade worldwide by Springer-Verlag New York, Inc., 233 Spring Street, 6th Floor, New York, NY 10013. Phone 1-800-SPRINGER, fax 201-348-4505, e-mail orders-ny@springer-sbm.com, or visit http://www.springeronline.com.

For information on translations, please contact Apress directly at 2855 Telegraph Avenue, Suite 600, Berkeley, CA 94705. Phone 510-549-5930, fax 510-549-5939, e-mail info@apress.com, or visit http://www.apress.com.

Apress and friends of ED books may be purchased in bulk for academic, corporate, or promotional use. eBook versions and licenses are also available for most titles. For more information, reference our Special Bulk Sales–eBook Licensing web page at http://www.apress.com/info/bulksales.

For Kristie B. and Canvin – thanks for everything

Contents

■About the Author ix

■About the CAD Reviewer x

■About the Technical Reviewer xi

■Acknowledgments xii

■Introduction xiii

■Chapter 1: Turns and Tricks 1

    Day 1: King Ixtua's Treasure Repository, 2:13 p.m. 1

    The Maze Challenge 4

    Evan's Solution 6

■Chapter 2: Mazerunner—Planning and Design 9

    The MazeRunner 9

    The Robot Description 11

    The Task List 12

    Limitations/Constraints 13

    Mindstorm 15

    Sketches 17

■Chapter 3: MazeBot—Build It 19

    Never Be Afraid to Experiment 20

    Step by Step CAD Instructions – MazeBot 21

■Chapter 4: MazeRunner—Program It 41

    Some Experience Required 41

    Into the Maze 46

    Out of the Tunnel 55

Left Turn and Right Turn Calculations 58

Simulating the Challenge 59

■ Chapter 5: Swing and Switch **61**

Day 4: King Ixtua Treasure Repository, 9:14 a.m. 61

Don't Look Down 62

The Monkey's Swing Challenge 63

Evan's Solution 64

■ Chapter 6: RopeSwinger—Design and Planning **65**

Getting Started 65

The Robot Description 65

The Task List 66

Limitations and Constraints 68

Mindstorm 68

Sketches 70

■ Chapter 7: RopeSwinger—Build It **73**

Never Be Afraid to Experiment 74

Step by Step CAD Instructions – RopeSwinger 75

■ Chapter 8: RopeSwinger—Program It **113**

Swing Swing 113

Pulling the Lever 117

■ Chapter 9: Hook and Pull **125**

Day 5: King Ixtua's Treasure Repository, 8:39 a.m. 125

Watch Your Step 126

Tricky Tupaxu 127

The Four Warriors 128

Hooks and Doors 129

Evan's Solution 131

■ Chapter 10: RingTosser—Design and Planning **133**

The RingTosser 133

The Robot Description 133

The Task List 134

Limitations and Constraints 136

Mindstorm 136

Sketches 138

■**Chapter 11: RingTosser—Build It** **141**

Step by Step CAD Instructions – RingTosser 143

■**Chapter 12: RingTosser—Program It** **179**

It Starts with Rolling 179

Building the Challenge Area 187

■**Chapter 13: Rock and Roll** **201**

Day 6: King Ixtua Treasure Repository, 9:27 a.m. 201

The Story Wall 202

An Uphill Battle 202

The Ramp of the Warriors 203

The Ramp Room 205

Evan's Solution 206

■**Chapter 14: RampRider—Design and Planning** **207**

The RampRider 207

The Robot Description 207

The Task List 209

Limitations and Constraints 210

Mindstorm 210

Sketches 212

■**Chapter 15: RampRider—Build It** **213**

Step by Step CAD Instructions – RampRider 217

■**Chapter 16: RampRider—Program It** **235**

Multiple Statues 235

The Ramp Challenge Setup 244

■**Chapter 17: Grab and Release** **247**

Day 7: King Ixtua's Treasure Repository, 8:41 a.m. 247

Tupaxu's Story 248

The King's Throne 250

Evan's Solution 251

■**Chapter 18: ZipLiner—Design and Planning** **253**

The ZipLiner 253

The Robot Description 253

The Task List 254

Limitations and Constraints 256

Mindstorm 256

Sketches 258

■**Chapter 19: ZipLiner—Build It** **261**

Step by Step CAD Instructions – ZipLiner 263

■**Chapter 20: ZipLiner—Program It** **291**

Hold On! 291

The Zip Line Challenge Setup 295

■**Chapter 21: Treasure and Discovery** **303**

Day 8: King Ixtua Treasure Repository, 7:02 a.m. 303

Qau's Challenge 304

The King's Legacy 304

Qau's Teacher 305

■**Design Journal** **307**

■**Index** **317**

About the Author

James Floyd Kelly is a freelance writer living in Atlanta, Georgia, with degrees in English and Industrial Engineering. A long-time LEGO MINDSTORMS developer, he is editor-in-chief of the world's most popular NXT blog, *thenxtstep.com*, which continues to draw an estimated 40,000+ readers monthly, and is a regular contributor to the LEGO MINDSTORMS development team. James Kelly has written on topics including robotics, building custom computers and free software. When not writing, he can be found spending time with his wife and young son exploring all sorts of places and things.

About the CAD Creator

 For **Christopher R. Smith** (a.k.a. Littlehorn), exploration is an important interest and with an attention to the details he leaves nothing unexplored. He believes that everything is possible and our world is what we make of it. He enjoys building with LEGO elements, CAD'ing building instructions, and being part of the MINDSTORMS community as an MDP and MCP for LEGO, as well as, having fun with his fellow bloggers of The NXT Step . Chris spent a decade as a Senior Quality Assurance Inspector in the Shuttle Avionics Integration Laboratory at NASA's Johnson Space Center in Houston, Texas. His innovations were recognized by NASA with a prestigious Space Act Award. He would like to thank his wife, Veena, and his children, Revi and Benjamin, for their support and inspiration.

About the Technical Reviewers

 **Adam Tester** has fostered a passion for the creative power of LEGOs since childhood, and was very excited at the chance to help contribute to this book. Adam is an Aeronautics student at Embry-Riddle Aeronautical University, enjoys skiing, mountain-biking and video games, and is commissioning as a pilot for the Air Force in May 2010.

 **Fay Rhodes**, a member of the MINDSTORMS Community Partners panel, is author of the LEGO MINDSTORMS NXT Zoo! and the LEGO MINDSTORMS NXT Robots Alive! Endangered Species. She was is a contributor to the original LEGO MINDSTORMS NXT Idea Book.

Acknowledgments

Writing the sequel to LEGO MINDSTORMS NXT 2.0: The Mayan Adventure was no easy task. This book was hard work! Much of the thanks must go to the team at Apress for all their hard work. Starting with Dominic Shakeshaft, Jonathan Gennick, and James Markham, and Seth Kline, the team continued to grow with the book… readers should turn to the second page of the book and take a long look at the names of all those involved in getting this book completed. It's a long list, isn't it? If you like the book, please email Apress and let them know – everyone loves to hear that their work is appreciated.

Two special individuals who have my gratitude are Adam Tester and Fay Rhodes. Adam and Fay were my technical editors, checking my instructions, my programs, and basically catching my mistakes. Robot building and programming is complicated, and I appreciate their diligence in helping me test the five robots and challenges found in these pages.

I'm very proud of the building instructions in this book –I was able to get my good friend Christopher Smith to convert the photographs of my robots into CAD images. Chris does amazing work, and my editors were always telling me how impressed they were with the results he provided. Thanks, Chris… for all the hard work.

I'd also like to thank all the teachers, parents, and students who have emailed me, written letters, and tracked me down at various events to let me know how much they enjoyed The Mayan Adventure. You're the reason this book was written. I hope you enjoy The King's Treasure, and I'd love to hear from you about your experiences with the challenges found in this book; you can email me at jktechwriter@gmail.com.

Finally, I have to thank Ashley. This book was one of three I was writing simultaneously, and she was very understanding and patient with me during some very tight deadlines. Ashley, you're the best.

Introduction

Welcome to *LEGO MINDSTORMS NXT 2.0: The King's Treasure*. Yes, it's the sequel to *LEGO MINDSTORMS NXT: The Mayan Adventure*, but no previous experience with that book is required to use or enjoy this book. Please be aware that The Mayan Adventure used the LEGO MINDSTORMS NXT 1.0 kit which was released in 2006. The LEGO MINDSTORMS NXT 2.0 kit was released in August 2009 and this book uses that kit and its components for all the specific robots used in this book. Owners of the NXT 1.0 kit can still enjoy the story and challenges found in this book, but there will be some modifications that the reader must perform if using the NXT 1.0 kit.

Readers of *LEGO MINDSTORMS NXT: The Mayan Adventure* will be able to pick up where that story ended – a map to King Ixtua's treasure repository was found in his tomb and Evan and his archaeologist uncle are off on another adventure to find the king's treasure. Feel free to jump straight to chapter one and get started!)

For Those New to NXT

I don't like to make assumptions, but since you're holding this book, I'm guessing that you are either an owner of the new LEGO MINDSTORMS NXT 2.0 robotics kit or are interested in this robotics kit and what can be done with it.

This book is fairly unique, and I'll tell you why. For the earlier version of MINDSTORMS (called MINDSTORMS Robotics Invention System, or RIS for short), numerous books were written, most of which focus on building rather extravagant robots, hacking the MINDSTORMS processor (called the Brick), and doing other wild things with the product. And the books were great! Many of them showed you, step by step, how to build and program very unique creations. But after reading them, I felt that a few things were missing.

The first thing I noticed was a minimal amount of "where to start" type information. The first time you open up a MINDSTORMS robotics kit, you might feel a little overwhelmed at the sheer number of pieces (almost *all* of them small) in the box. You get an instruction manual and some sample robots to build, but there is very little information for those new designers who are asking "How do I start designing a robot?"

The second item I found lacking was incentive. There are lots of robots that can be built, but many MINDSTORMS owners get stuck trying to come up with a problem to solve. "What should I build?" is a frequently asked question. There are robotics competitions, with fixed tasks to complete and well-defined conditions for winning, but what if you're not into competitions or lack access to them? Where can a person find challenges to take on and accomplish?

The last gap involves training. Many of the books on the market are great at telling you how to build and program robots, but many times the explanations aren't really explanations—they're instructions: "Put this piece here" and "Drop that there." What is missing are the reasons for doing something (or, at least, the authors' reasons).

With *The King's Treasure*, I've tried to fill in these gaps as follows:

- To answer the question "How do I start designing a robot?" I've provided something called a Design Journal worksheet. This is a worksheet that I use (and encourage you to use) to demonstrate the development of the book's robots, using a step-by-step method. It's not the only method out there, but it's my hope that you will find it useful as a way to keep your thoughts organized and to help you move forward in a constructive way.

- As for lack of incentive, I've divided the book into five sections, each of which involves a challenge. Each section has part of a fictional storyline that sets up a *reason* for building a robot. The story is fictional, but the challenges give you plenty of encouragement to experiment and develop your own robots.

- And when it comes to training, I provide solutions to the five challenges by walking you through the development of my robots, their construction, and their programming. I give you some "Do this" and "Do that," but always with an explanation.

I don't use a lot of fancy, technical terms. There are some in there (it's unavoidable when dealing with programming), but I think you'll find that the book is written in an easy-to-follow way and, hopefully, you'll also find the process fun.

If you're completely unfamiliar with NXT, you really should install the NXT-G software (the CD that comes with the kit) and go through the included tutorials. These tutorials will teach you the basics of how to use the software as well as give you some basic construction skills. To get the most out of this book, you do need to at least be comfortable with using the NXT components, opening the NXT-G software, creating and saving programs, and uploading programs to your robot. If you're comfortable with this short list, then you're almost ready to start . . .

How This Book Is Organized

As I mentioned earlier, I've divided the book into five sections. Each section is further divided into four chapters. The fictional storyline starts in Chapter 1, continues in Chapters 5, 9, 13, and 17, and concludes in Chapter 21. The storyline is where you find the details of a particular challenge (for that section); these details are important because they help you to determine the robot's objectives.

Chapters 2, 6, 10, 14, and 18 are what I call the "theory" chapters. Don't let that word scare you, though. When I say theory chapters, I simply mean that these chapters give you plenty to think about—what does the robot need to do, what can it *not* do, what parts should be used, and what parts should *not* be used. I use the Design Journal page in these theory chapters, and I've provided five blank copies in the back of the book for you to follow along with me (or use them to develop your own robots).

Chapters 3, 7, 11, 15, and 19 are the building instructions for the robots. In each chapter, you'll find a set of photos that walks you through building my version of the robot. You can follow my steps and build the exact same robots I include in the book, or you can come up with your own creations. (If you find you're missing a part or something just doesn't snap together properly, the best part about Lego robots is that there's always a workaround—another way to connect something or a combination of parts that can be used as a substitute. Don't stress about it—use your creativity and find an alternative solution!)

Chapters 4, 8, 12, 16, and 20 provide the programming instructions. I use *plenty* of screenshots to show you how to configure each block that is used in the NXT-G programming language. If you have used my building instructions, you can also use the programming instructions. These chapters also include instructions for you on how to set up a test environment for testing your robots and see if they can complete the challenges.

Who Is This Book For?

It doesn't matter if you are 10 years old or 50, building robots is fun. This book is for everyone who wants to build some new MINDSTORMS NXT 2.0 robots and have fun. I don't expect you to be a programming guru—I'm certainly not. I also don't expect you to have advanced degrees in robotics, engineering, or computer science. Let's all remember that LEGO MINDSTORMS NXT 2.0 is, ultimately, a LEGO product. It's a TOY! It's supposed to be fun, not stressful.

If you're a kid, this book can be a great way to get your mom or dad interested in your hobby. And if you're a parent, this book can be a great way to have some fun with your kids. I think you'll see that it's fun to create challenges for yourself (or someone else) and then try to build some great robots to overcome those challenges.

What You Need to Use This Book

The only things you need besides this book are a LEGO MINDSTORMS NXT 2.0 robotics kit and a computer to run the software and upload programs to your robots. There are currently three versions of the MINDSTORMS NXT kit—the retail versions 1.0 and 2.0, that you can buy online or in stores, and the education version that LEGO sells to teachers, schools, and individuals. There are differences in the types of parts that come in the three kit versions, so please be aware that all the robots in this book have been built with the retail 2.0 version. If you own the NXT 1.0 or education versions, that's okay. It just means that if you find I'm using a part that you don't have, you'll have to improvise. Don't let that bother you—just look at it as another challenge to overcome and something new to learn.

Extras for This Book

Extra Design Journal pages can be downloaded from the Source Code page on the Apress Web site, at http://www.apress.com.

If you have comments, pictures to share, or questions about The King's Treasure, please visit the special forum discussion Web page created just for the book.

http://thenxtstep.com/smf/

Click on the Book Discussions section and then click on The King's Treasure to participate."

■ ■ ■

CHAPTER 1

Turns and Tricks

Location: Southwest Guatemala

102 miles SW of Guatemala City

Coordinates: 14º 04' N / 90º 09' W

Weather Conditions: 98 degrees Fahrenheit, Humidity 60%

Day 1: King Ixtua's Treasure Repository, 2:13 p.m.

Evan slowly crawled forward, feeling the rocks scratch his stomach through his favorite tee shirt. *Make that my* former *favorite shirt*, he thought, hearing a slight rip as it snagged on a sharp rock. He stared down the vertical shaft for a few seconds, then shook his head and groaned.

"What's wrong, nephew?" asked Dr. Phillip Hicks. "You're not afraid of heights, are you?"

Evan rolled over on his back and tried to block with his hand the sunlight that filtered through the leaves and large branches of the jungle's canopy. Evan's uncle smiled down, offered a hand, and pulled him to his feet.

"We've already been down there a dozen times," said Uncle Phillip. "It's a piece of cake. You'll be harnessed in. Don't worry."

"How deep is the descent?" asked Evan. His hands were sweaty.

"About sixty feet," replied Dr. Hicks, turning and walking down the slight hill in the direction of the supply tent. "Come on, let's go find Erin and get you fitted with a harness. My other assistant, Tag, is already down there waiting for you."

Evan sighed deeply as he walked down the trail. *I've waited almost two years for this chance*, he thought.

Two summers earlier, Evan had flown down to Guatemala to spend some time with his archaeologist uncle during the excavation of a newly discovered tomb. Evan had brought along his robotics kit because he'd anticipated being bored to tears and wanted something to help pass the time. Rather than boredom, Evan had instead found himself assisting his uncle's team by building a handful of robots to access some impossible tomb locations that were filled with obstacles and traps. In the end, they had successfully entered the king's tomb and found many treasures, including a scroll containing the location of the king's treasure repository.

Evan ducked under the supply tent's flap. Sitting on a chair in the center of the tent was Erin, his uncle's current assistant. Evan had been sad to hear that Max and Grace, Uncle Phillip's two previous assistants, had graduated college and were now directing their own excavations in other parts of Guatemala; it was Erin who had picked him up from the airport and driven him to the current excavation site. She was nice and had asked dozens of questions about his trip, his family, and the robotics kit sitting in the back of the truck with his other luggage. Not much was different between King Ixtua's tomb and his treasure repository, she had told him. His robotics kit was going to be needed once again.

Erin waved him over.

"Are you ready for this?" she asked, pointing to an adjacent chair.

Evan nodded. "Yes, but let's do this quick before I change my mind," he replied.

Uncle Phillip dragged a chair over and joined them. "The legend of King Ixtua is completely true," he said. "If you remember, the tomb builder, Tupaxu, built in all sorts of traps to keep out tomb robbers. King Ixtua was fond of monkeys, and had dozens of trainers. Tupaxu took advantage of that and made access to the tomb almost impossible for humans. Only trained monkeys could navigate some of the tight spaces and unlock special areas of the tomb. We're expecting the treasure repository to be just as tricky. Tupaxu built it in the caves beneath that hillside out there."

Erin handed Evan a climbing harness and pointed out two loops for him to step through. "Now, tighten those straps there until they're snug. Make it tight. You don't want to slip out," she said with a smile.

Evan pulled and tugged on the straps. "You're going to have to cut this harness off," he replied.

Uncle Phillip smiled. "Good. Come over here and let me show you a few final things before we send you down." He walked over to a small wood table that looked as if it would collapse any minute under the weight of the equipment boxes stacked on top.

Erin waved. "See you at the bottom, Evan," she said as she disappeared under the tent flap.

Evan joined his uncle at the table. A variety of items were scattered on the tabletop. "A week before you arrived, we located the entrance to the caves and lowered down some video cameras. The entry room is small and can only hold four or five people at a time. This is Tag's sketch and measurements," Dr. Hicks said, indicating a small drawing (see Figure 1-1).

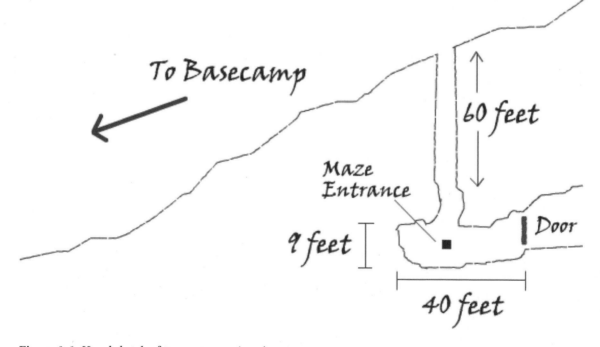

Figure 1-1. Hand sketch of treasure repository's entry room

"This," said Uncle Phillip as he held up a small remote control box, "is all that's left of my attempt at gaining access to the second chamber. We purchased two remote control cars with wireless video cameras before we flew down. Both cars were lost in a small tunnel in the entry room." He tossed the remote control on the table and then pointed at a handful of photographs from his shirt pocket.

"From those photographs, and based on where we lost the cars, we've been able to sketch out a rough estimate of the tunnel. Best of all, it seems to match a faded sketch we were able to retrieve from a scroll found in King Ixtua's tomb," said Dr. Hicks. He pointed at another hand sketch on the table (see Figure 1-2).

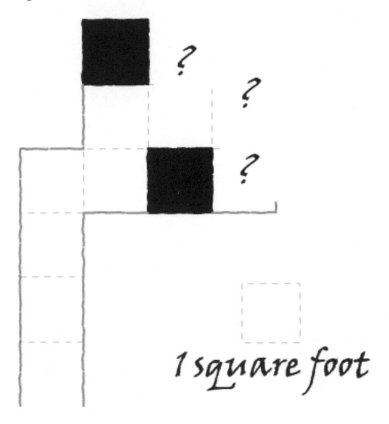

Figure 1-2. Known portions of the entry room's maze

"We know from the scroll we found in King Ixtua's library that the First Chamber can only be accessed when a pressure plate is triggered in that little maze. It will unlock the door in the entry room. We also know that Tupaxu surrounded the path to the pressure plate with a deep pit. Both our remote control cars fell off the path in the tunnel. We determined that the hole is about fifty feet deep. We calculated that based on when the car fell in the hole and when the video stopped broadcasting. Apparently, the cars and video cameras weren't designed to survive that kind of fall."

"I guess not," replied Evan. "But my robots aren't going to survive a fifty foot fall either."

Uncle Phillip nodded. "No, but from what I remember of your designs from a couple years ago, your robots have the advantage of sensors and can be programmed to think for themselves, right? I think we can safely assume that this sketch from the scroll is an accurate depiction of the proper path for your robot to take."

"Yes, sir," answered Evan. "But I won't know for certain until I go and take a look."

Uncle Phillip gripped Evan's shoulder. "Well, let's not hold Tag up any longer. It's time to go take a look for yourself. Come on."

The Maze Challenge

Evan closed his eyes as he stepped off of the firm soil. Thick line running through his harness kept him from falling into the shaft below him. The line fed through a large pulley wheel above his head and then to an electric wench about twenty feet from the shaft opening.

"Ready?" asked Uncle Philip, tapping the top of Evan's helmet. "You'll be fine."

Evan nodded and opened his eyes. The wench operator pushed a button, and Evan felt a short jolt as he began to descend. He closed his eyes again.

"I'll see you when you get back up!" yelled Evan's uncle.

Evan had been told the descent would take about one minute, but when his feet finally touched bottom, he was certain it had been much longer.

"Hey there!" said a voice.

Evan opened his eyes and was blinded by a bright light. He reached up and covered his eyes with his hands.

"Oops! Sorry about that," said the voice. "Forgot to switch off my helmet light."

Evan rubbed his eyes. "You must be Tag," he said.

"That's me," said Tag, grabbing and shaking Evan's hand. "Nice to finally meet you, Evan."

"Same here," said Evan, looking around. "Wow!"

Tag nodded. "Yep. Impressive, isn't it? Hand cut stone… it probably took Tupaxu's team months to enlarge this particular cave."

Two large standing halogen lights lit up the small chamber. The ceiling was no more than eight or nine feet high, and Mayan glyphs were carved into every inch of the walls.

"Look at all those glyphs," said Evan. "Do we know what they say?"

Tag walked over to the East wall of the cave and pointed at a section of glyphs that were slightly larger than the rest.

"Tupaxu was a smart man. He knew he wouldn't be around forever, so he left instructions for accessing the tomb here. But the instructions are vague in some areas. We're going to have to be very careful."

Evan smiled. "Uncle Philip said the team lost some remote control vehicles. Sorry about that," he said.

Tag nodded. "Look here on the North wall," he said, pointing at an opening (see Figure 1-3).

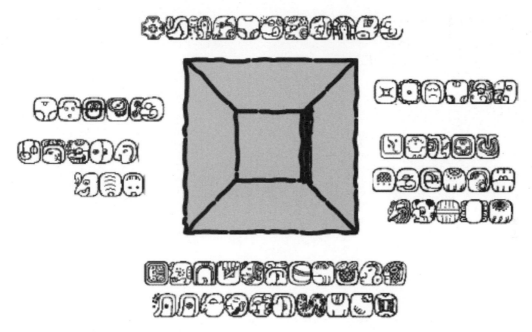

Figure 1-3. Entrance to the maze in the entry room

Evan thought back to the first entrance of King Ixtua's tomb. Two years ago, he had sent a robot down a small, rectangular hole to open a locked door. Here, in the middle of the North wall, was an almost identical hole with glyphs surrounding it.

"Uncle Philip showed me a drawing," said Evan. "It looks like the first tunnel entrance we found two years ago, but that one didn't have any traps."

"Nope. Completely different," replied Tag. "This hole does go back a few feet, but after that it twists and turns and the path is completely surrounded by a deep pit that we weren't expecting. It's a nicely designed maze."

Tag turned on his helmet light and looked into the tunnel. Evan could see the light hit a wall a few feet ahead and darkness to the right and left.

Tag pulled a piece of paper from his pocket and unfolded it. "This is a photocopy of the original sketch we found. This circle indicates the pressure plate to unlock the door to the second chamber."

Tag's helmet light allowed Evan to see the complete maze (see Figure 1-4).

Figure 1-4. Pressure plate location indicated in scroll found in King Ixtua's tomb

Evan pointed at the map. "Are we certain that this is the correct path?"

Tag sighed. "No, but there has to be at least one path to the pressure plate that doesn't go over any of the pits, right? Our tests with the remote control cars verify at least the first few feet after this first right turn."

"But even with this map the trick will be staying on that path without my robot falling into a pit," replied Evan. "Is the maze floor fairly level?"

"It sure is," said Tag. "There are some minor bumps and cracks in the rock, but the floor appears to be level and solid. Well, at least where there's no pits to fall into."

Evan scratched his head and looked closer at Tag's map.

"You already have an idea, don't you?" asked Tag.

Evan looked at Tag and smiled.

Evan's Solution

Tag and Erin watched as Evan opened his robotics kit on the worktable. The clear container sounded like a medicine man's rattle; they could see small plastic parts of all shapes and colors sorted into little compartments under the translucent container lid.

"The two basic problems here," said Evan, "are that we don't know where the actual pressure plate is located, and the robot will need to find the edges of the path to avoid falling off."

Evan opened the container, reached in, and pulled out a small rectangular object.

"I recognize that," said Uncle Philip. "That's the controller for the robot, right?"

Evan nodded. "Yes, sir. This is the Mindstorms NXT Intelligent Brick. It will hold the program that I'm going to write to give the robot some decision-making abilities. It will also send and receive signals from some other items in the kit."

Evan handed the Brick to Erin and pulled a few more items from the container.

"And these are some motors and sensors. It'll require a combination of all of these things to get the robot safely to the pressure plate," said Evan.

Erin and Tag took the sensors and motors from Evan and carefully inspected the parts.

"They're light," said Erin. "I was expecting metal."

Tag nodded in agreement.

"All the parts are made of plastic," replied Evan. "But when the parts are connected, the robot will be stable and fairly rugged."

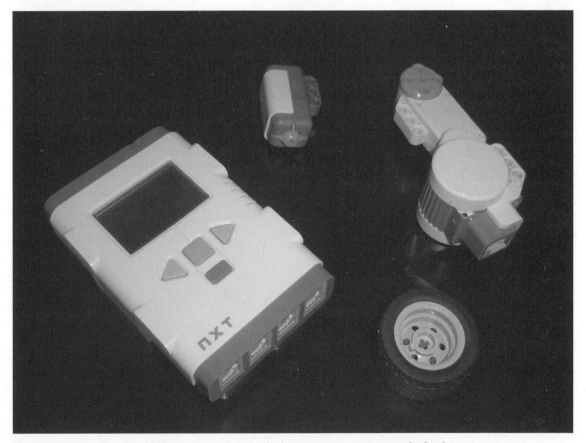

Figure 1-5. Evan's robot kit has many parts, including motors, sensors, and wheels.

Uncle Philip leaned closer to the Evan and looked in the container. "So, do you have an idea of how to tackle this maze problem? Our remote control cars weren't very successful."

Evan picked up his small notebook and opened it. Inside were a handful of photocopied pages he had brought along. He pulled one out and held it up for the group to see.

"This is a Design Journal worksheet. I use them to help me design my robots. I think I've got enough information from seeing the maze entrance and Tag's sketches to get started. It'll probably take me two or three hours to build and test something."

Tag smiled. "Dr. Hicks, I've got some more measurements I need to take down in the entry room. If you don't mind, I'm going to head back down until Evan is ready."

"Go ahead," Evan's uncle replied. "Erin and I need to translate more of the glyphs from the photos you took down there. They may be important if Evan can get us into the First Chamber."

Tag nodded at Evan. "Good luck," he said, ducking under the tent flap.

Uncle Philip and Erin stood and stretched.

"By the way," said Evan. "How many chambers are there?"

Uncle Philip looked at Erin. "Yes, have we confirmed that number yet?"

Erin nodded. "Just like King Ixtua's tomb, this treasure repository has four chambers. Tupaxu seems to like the number four, doesn't he? All the scrolls I've translated so far indicate that the king's treasure is stored in the Fourth Chamber."

Evan pulled his laptop from his backpack. "I wonder if there are any other similarities between King Ixtua's tomb and his treasure repository," said Evan.

Uncle Philip patted Evan's shoulder. "Well, the only way we'll find that out is if we let you get started. Call me if you need anything."

"Yes, sir," replied Evan. He watched Erin and his Uncle duck out of the tent. "Hey, Uncle Philip?"

Evan's uncle stopped and looked back. "Yeah?"

"Thanks for inviting me," said Evan.

Uncle Philip smiled. "You're part of the team, Evan. We're glad you're here. See you in a bit."

Evan pressed the power button on his laptop and pulled a pen from his backpack. "Okay, time to figure this puzzle out…"

The story continues in Chapter 5…

CHAPTER 2

■ ■ ■

MazeRunner—Planning and Design

In this chapter you're going to learn (drum-roll, please—cue the announcer) . . .

A PLANNING AND DESIGN PROCESS!

Please don't let the words scare you. Yes, "planning and design process" sounds boring, but I promise that you'll have fun with this chapter. I know you're ready to start putting pieces together to build a bot, but if you take some time and go through these P&D chapters, you'll be building and programming your own robots in less time, with fewer mistakes.

So, let's get started. That door to the First Chamber is still locked, and you're going to need the MazeRunner to open it.

■ **Note** If you've already read *LEGO MINDSTORMS NXT: The Mayan Adventure,*[1] this chapter is going to be very familiar to you; much of the text is identical, as a matter of fact. Feel free to skip to Chapter 3 if you like, but if you're a bit rusty on the use of the Design Journal worksheet, going through this material again may be useful.

The MazeRunner

You may already have begun thinking about a design for your MazeRunner. It may or may not share some similarities to the one shown in Figure 2-1. That's okay—you may have a much better design in mind, so feel free to build your own version of the robot, but do follow along carefully with the steps in this chapter.

---

[1] Jim Kelly, *LEGO MINDSTORMS NXT: The Mayan Adventure* (Berkeley, CA: Apress, 2006)

Figure 2-1. The MazeRunner

Now, are you wondering how that little robot is going to open the door that leads to the First Chamber? You're going to answer that question by following along using a copy of Evan's Design Journal worksheet.

■ **Note** There are five blank Design Journal worksheets in the back of this book that you can cut out. You're going to use them to design the robots in this book *and* robots of your own. If you need more pages, you can find a file titled DesignJournal.pdf in the Source Code area of the Apress Web site (http://www.apress.com) that you can use to print more pages.

At the top of the Design Journal worksheet you'll see the words Robot Name. Go ahead and write **MazeRunner** in the box, and pat yourself on the back. The Planning and Design Process has begun. (You could write something else, such as **RobotThatNavigatesMazeAndUnlocksDoor**, but you might run out of space.)

The Robot Description

Okay, now that you've named your robot, it's time to describe it. No, I'm not talking about "Short, grey and white, with wheels." What is this robot supposed to do? At this point, I hope you've read Chapter 1. If not, I'll wait as you go back and read it. Okay, have you finished it? Good. Now, what is this robot supposed to do? Don't say it, write it.

Look on your Design Journal worksheet, and you'll see Robot Description and a large blank box. Don't be shy here. This is where to try your hardest to accurately describe what this robot will do for you. Look back to Figure 1-4 in Chapter 1 if you need a reminder about the obstacles that MazeRunner will face. Let me show you what I wrote down, and you can compare it to your description, okay? Here goes (see Figure 2-2).

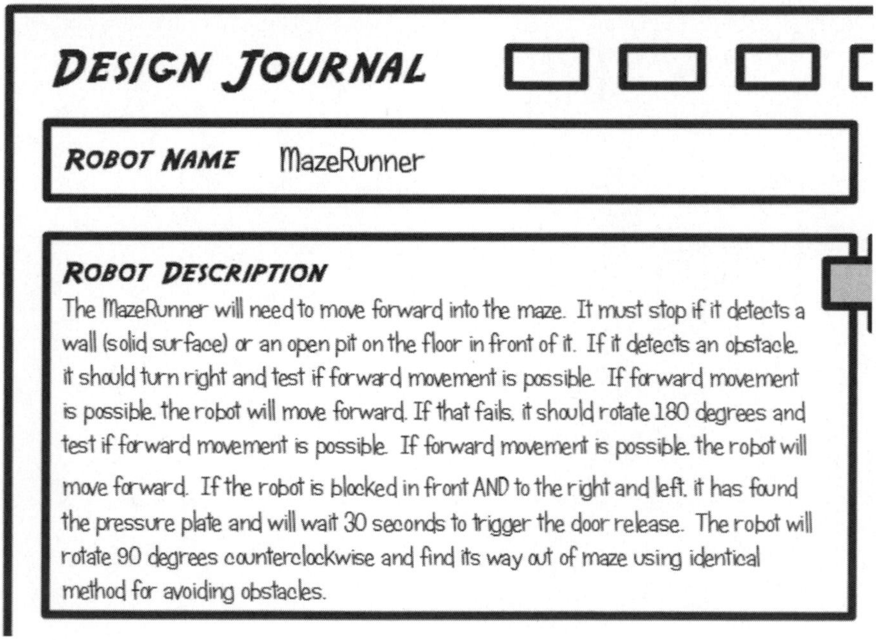

Figure 2-2. Robot description

If your description isn't exactly like mine, that's okay. What *is* important is that you got the major points: Move forward until the path's edge is encountered. Turn left and move forward again until the next edge is detected, and so on. Trust me—without an accurate description of the robot, it will be more difficult to build (in Chapter 3) and program (in Chapter 4). Don't worry if your description missed something; you'll get better at this, I promise. You're going to have more opportunities to write robot descriptions later in the book. By the time you're finished, you'll be an expert.

So, what's next, you ask? Okay, I'll tell you—you're going to take the description you wrote and break it down into small, single-item tasks.

The Task List

On your Design Journal worksheet, locate the Task List section. This section is where you're going to list each individual task that the robot must perform. The *good news* is that if you wrote down a detailed description (see the previous section) then this section is almost already done.

What do I mean by "individual task?" An individual task is something such as "Walk forward five feet" or "Turn doorknob." Something like "Press the button and turn the wheel" is not an individual task. Your goal is to list the actions your robot will perform, one at a time. Take a look at my Task List (see Figure 2-3).

Figure 2-3. The MazeRunner Task List

Compare your Task List to mine. Were you able to break down the robot description into individual tasks? These individual tasks will help you in many ways, including assembling the correct form for your bot, picking the appropriate sensors to be used, and later when you're programming the bot.

I'll give you a small preview of how we'll use the task list later. Look at steps 1 and 4—both are testing to see if forward movement is possible. Are you already thinking about how to do this? You've got options, of course. There's the Ultrasonic sensor that can be programmed to stop the robot when it detects an object in front of it (the wall). And what about the Color sensor? This type of sensor can easily tell the robot when the color beneath it changes; this could be useful in locating the path's edge and the pit in front of the robot. I hope you can see that the Task List can be helpful when you start thinking about the NXT components you'll need to complete a job. For now, let's leave the Task List and move on to the next section of the Design Journal.

Limitations/Constraints

You're going to encounter one obstacle quickly when you begin to design your robots using the LEGO MINDSTORMS NXT 2.0 kit. What is it? It's the number of parts in your kit.

It would be nice if you had access to an unlimited number of sensors, motors, connectors, beams, and other components. But for this book, and the robot designs included in it, I'm not making any assumptions about your collection of parts except that you have the LEGO MINDSTORMS NXT 2.0 kit.

When you begin to design your robots, you need to be aware of limitations (or constraints) such as this one. Limitations and/or constraints can come from many different places. Besides the number of parts in your robotics kit, you need to keep in mind things such as the following:

- Robot size and weight (tall, short, heavy, light, wide, thin, square, circular)

- Weather and lighting conditions (outdoors, indoors, artificial light, no light)

- Floor or surface conditions (soft, hard, wet, empty like a pit trap, and so on)

- Movement requirements (up, down, left, right, forward, backward, diagonal)

There may be some constraints that you won't encounter until you begin building and testing your robots. Don't worry if this happens. Your main goal at this point should be to write down any limitations that come immediately to mind. Just look back at your Robot Description and Task List and the environment or objects where the robot will interact. Do any constraints come to mind? Write them down on your Design Journal worksheet in the Limitations/Constraints area.

Take a look at Figure 2-4. I've written down a few sentences that describe what I think are some major constraints for the MazeRunner. Remember, there may be other constraints that won't show up until we begin testing our design. The important part is to try and identify any obvious constraints before you begin to design and build your bot.

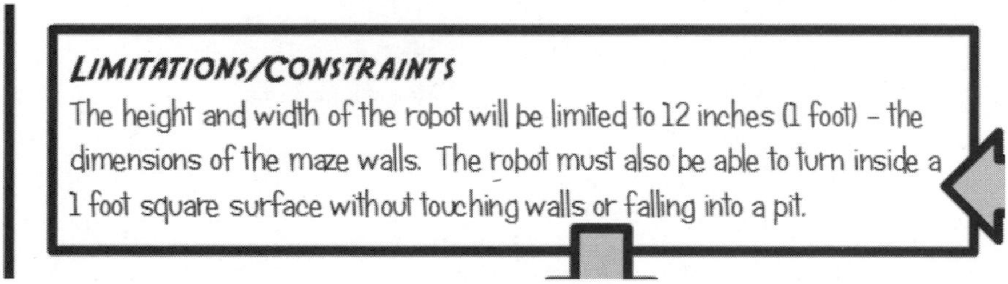

LIMITATIONS/CONSTRAINTS

The height and width of the robot will be limited to 12 inches (1 foot) – the dimensions of the maze walls. The robot must also be able to turn inside a 1 foot square surface without touching walls or falling into a pit.

Figure 2-4. The MazeRunner has a few constraints to consider.

The constraints for the MazeRunner aren't too difficult to work around. Let's take a look at the challenge and see how these constraints will affect the robot design.

■ **Caution** The following pages contain information about the actual location of the pressure plate and all the pit traps. If you do not wish to see this information, skip the challenge setup information. You will need someone to set up the MazeRunner Challenge for you if you do not wish to know the location of the pits and the pressure plate. The MazeRunner Challenge setup instructions can be found in Chapter 4.

First, the robot will enter the maze that has a fixed height and width. The robot you build cannot be too wide or too tall or it simply won't fit into the tunnel. We know the measurement of the tunnel is 12 inches tall and 12 inches wide, so we'll keep that in mind when we begin to design.

The second constraint is a little trickier. Take a look at Figure 2-5. This is an overhead view of the maze, and it shows the final location of the pressure plate and all the pit traps.

= 1 square foot

Figure 2-5. The MazeRunner has to avoid pits and walls to find the pressure plate.

The robot will proceed down the three foot long tunnel before entering the maze and must stop before it hits the rock wall. When it stops, it must turn right and move forward. However, it must then stop before it falls into the first pit trap. Every time the robot is turning, we'll have to be careful to give it sufficient space to turn and not bump into the wall or fall into a pit.

There are numerous methods for building and programming a robot to make a right-angle turn, and I encourage you to experiment with other methods. But how will the robot perform these right-angle (or 90 degree) turns with enough room to avoid bumping the walls or falling into the pits? Glad you asked.

Ideally, we would like the robot to stop a certain distance from the wall before turning right, and the best place for the robot to stop would be with its center point directly above the center point of the one foot square space. I don't want this to get too complicated, so just be aware that during the building and programming of the MazeRunner, we'll be tinkering and tweaking to get the bot to perform well in a corner.

■ **Note** During the building and programming of the MazeRunner, you'll perform many tests. During this phase, you'll test many of the bot's functions—forward speed, stopping speed, detecting the wall, detecting a pit, stopping at a proper distance, and more. I'll cover this in more detail in Chapter 4.

One constraint I didn't list is more of a condition that might affect the robot. The surface of the tunnel is stone. It's a flat rough surface, not made of sand. I'm mentioning this constraint only to demonstrate that you must always be aware of the external conditions the robot will face. Because the surface is flat and rough, we should be able to use the rubber wheels to move the robot, because they'll have a good grip on the surface of the tunnel. But this might not always be possible. A wet surface can sometimes cause plastic or thin wheels to simply spin without getting traction, keeping the robot from moving. And what if the robot doesn't have a surface to roll or walk across? I'll answer that question in Chapter 6.

Try to always keep an open mind when thinking about the obstacles your robot will face. Examine the robot's environment, its tasks, and its overall goal as you start to brainstorm about how you'll solve the problem. And that's what you're going to do next. You're going to brainstorm about this bot's design, components, and overall appearance in this next Design Journal section—Mindstorm.

Mindstorm

Convenient name for this section, huh? The LEGO MINDSTORMS NXT 2.0 robotics kit uses that unique word, "Mindstorms." For us, to mindstorm (or brainstorm) is our chance to use our creativity and start developing ideas for how we will design and build this bot. This is an easy section to complete. What I want you to do is simply write down your questions, observations, and ideas that have been popping into your head since you became aware of the challenge. There are no incorrect items to place in this section except for sketches—those come last. So, to get you started, take a look at Figure 2-6. You'll see some of my initial thoughts on this challenge, the MazeRunner, and the direction I want to take for my initial design.

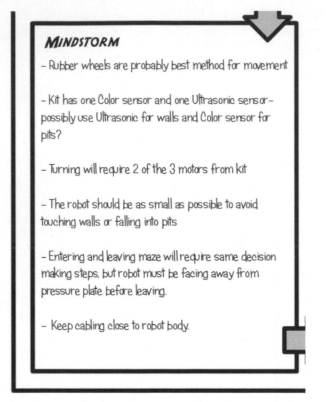

Figure 2-6. The Mindstorm section contains my initial thoughts.

I'm not going to cover all my Mindstorm items here, but I would like to mention a couple and explain how and why I wrote them.

One of my observations was "Turning will require 2 of the 3 motors from kit." This might seem like common sense, but then again, maybe not. In order for a bot to turn, it has to have a force that makes it turn. Two wheels, connected to a single motor, only give forward and backward motion. For the bot to turn left and right, it requires another motor. By spinning one motor (and its wheel) in one direction and spinning the other motor in the reverse direction, we can cause the bot to turn. This can also be accomplished simply by locking the second motor in place and keeping it from spinning. One wheel will spin, the other wheel will not spin, and the bot will turn.

Finally, after the MazeRunner finds the pressure plate and waits for 30 seconds, it will need to make a special turn in order to prepare to exit the maze. Look back to Figure 2-5 for a moment where the robot will stop when it finds the pressure plate. After the 30 second wait is over, it is still facing towards the pit. It needs to rotate 180 degrees – only then will the robot be facing in the direction it came from and be able to leave the exit. If you follow the logic described in the Task List, you can see that the robot will find its way out of the maze just as easily as it found the pressure plate!

Your main objective here should be simply to have some fun and write down some of your initial thoughts on what you'd like to do with your bot design. You might have to take a completely different direction after some testing. You might find you exhaust your supply of a particular component. What you write down isn't going to lock you in to a particular design. You can change the design anytime—you can even start over completely. Print out another Design Journal worksheet and try a different design. It's supposed to be fun, so make it fun. Go crazy with your ideas—the crazier, the better!

Now you're done with the Robot Description and the Task List is full. You've identified some Limitations/Constraints and your Mindstorm items section is overflowing with your thoughts and observations. It's now time to finish up with the Design Journal's final section—Sketches.

Sketches

When I draw stick figure people, they tend to have very short legs and very long arms. I still color outside the lines with crayons. I guess what I'm trying to say is that if you're a professional artist, you don't have to worry about any competition from me.

However, I can draw shapes that are fairly close to squares, circles, rectangles, and triangles. And that's good enough for what I'm going to ask you to do in this section. I want to give you some suggestions before starting on the building of your bot, and I'm going to show you how I took my own advice with my sketches for the MazeRunner.

I'm going to reference some of the ideas I wrote down in the Mindstorm section and show you how I came up with the size and shape of the MazeRunner. First, I'll start with the shape. Take a look at Figure 2-7 and notice that I started with a basic shape to help determine the placement of sensors, motors, and other parts.

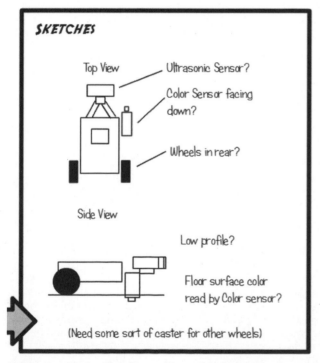

Figure 2-7. In the Sketches section, start by placing basic shapes.

I started with a small, stubby-shaped box that represents the Intelligent Brick. I know I want to use wheels, but I'm not sure yet whether to put the wheels on the front or back of the MazeRunner, and I'll try to create some sort of caster so the robot turns a little easier. I also need to decide between a Touch sensor or the Ultrasonic sensor for detecting an approaching wall. If I use the Touch sensor, it will need to be placed far in front of the bot, possibly on a long neck or pole, to allow it time to stop the bot and give it room to turn. But if I use the Ultrasonic Sensor I can place it closer to the bot's body, because it can detect a wall or obstacle from a distance and doesn't require an impact with the wall or obstacle. Because my goal is to keep the MazeRunner as short in length as possible, I'm going to use the Ultrasonic sensor to detect walls. I also plan to use the Color sensors to detect the presence of the floor. When the Color sensors stop detecting the floor and moves over the edge, I'll know the MazeRunner is close to falling off and must move back a small distance.

So, let me summarize where the MazeRunner is right now.

My MazeRunner requires two motors (for turning), the Ultrasonic sensor for detecting walls, the Color sensors to detect the pit traps, and the Intelligent Brick. Unless I want the Brick to scrape the ground while it moves, I'll need to give it one or two extra wheels. I'll try to save some weight and keep the size down by using three wheels or some form of caster wheel.

I'm envisioning using the Intelligent Brick as the main body. Two motors, one on each side of the Brick, will spin the two wheels used for forward and backward motion and for turning. I'm going to mount the Ultrasonic Sensor close to the front of the bot to detect the wall. I'll try to configure a small caster that will pivot to make the bot's turning a little smoother and give less resistance. I'll test various placements of the Color sensors in front of the robot so they find the pit traps before the robot gets too close to a pit's edge.

What do your sketches look like? Have you taken a different approach to the design of the MazeRunner? Remember, there is no *right* or *wrong* solution. If your MazeRunner reaches the end of the tunnel, lands on the pressure plate, and then returns to the tunnel entrance, you've succeeded in opening the tomb door.

In Chapter 3 I'm going to walk you through the assembly of my version of the MazeRunner. Feel free to change it up! Put a Touch sensor in front to detect walls and see if you can find a way to use the Ultrasonic sensor to detect the pit traps. Try giving it a different number of wheels. Chapter 4 will show you how to program the MazeRunner; at the end of the chapter I'll also give you some ideas on how to set up the challenge and test your bot.

Now, let's go and build the MazeRunner!

CHAPTER 3

▪▪▪

MazeBot—Build It

Before you begin building the MazeRunner, take a look at Figure 3-1. This is my version of the MazeRunner, but you can certainly design and build your own version without going through this chapter.

Keep in mind as you build this robot that this is a symmetrical robot. That means that the left side (what you see in the figure) is a mirror image of what you'll see on the right side. As you're building, when you see the instructions showing some pieces inserted on the left side, sometimes you won't see the matching part(s) that you should insert on the right side as well.

Notice the arrow in the figure? Underneath those two odd looking pieces are the two small spheres (called Zamor spheres) that function as caster wheels. When you're done building the MazeRunner, just place one small sphere under each "shell" and you're ready to move on to Chapter 4 where you'll program the robot. Have fun!

Figure 3-1. *Evan's version of the MazeRunner*

Never Be Afraid to Experiment

I've tried to provide enough detail in each figure for you to discern what parts are used and where those parts are placed. If you find that what you're holding in your hands doesn't quite look like the picture, do the following:

1. Take a deep breath.

2. Remember this is supposed to be fun.

3. Go back to the previous step and confirm you've made it that far.

4. Look at the current step, and examine the figure's details for clues to where components should be placed. Try tricks like counting holes to determine where two or more parts connect or skipping ahead a few figures to try and see the parts from another angle.

5. When in doubt, take your best guess and move forward.

Enjoy the building process and realize that if your final bot doesn't look *exactly* like the one in this chapter, that's okay. Remember: getting the bot to work and solving the challenge is your main goal.

■ **Note** If you modify or try to create your own version of the MazeRunner (or any other bot in this book), please take a picture and e-mail it to me. I would enjoy seeing your final bot in action. I've included my e-mail address in the Introduction.

And now, on to the construction of the MazeRunner!

Step by Step CAD Instructions – MazeBot

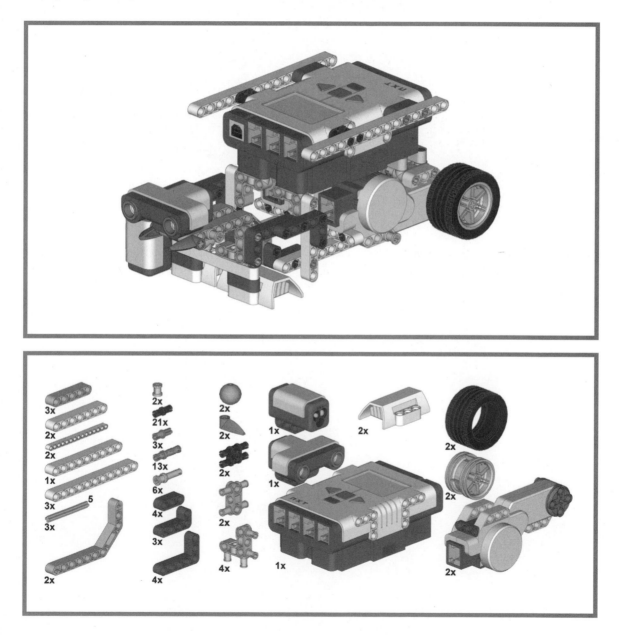

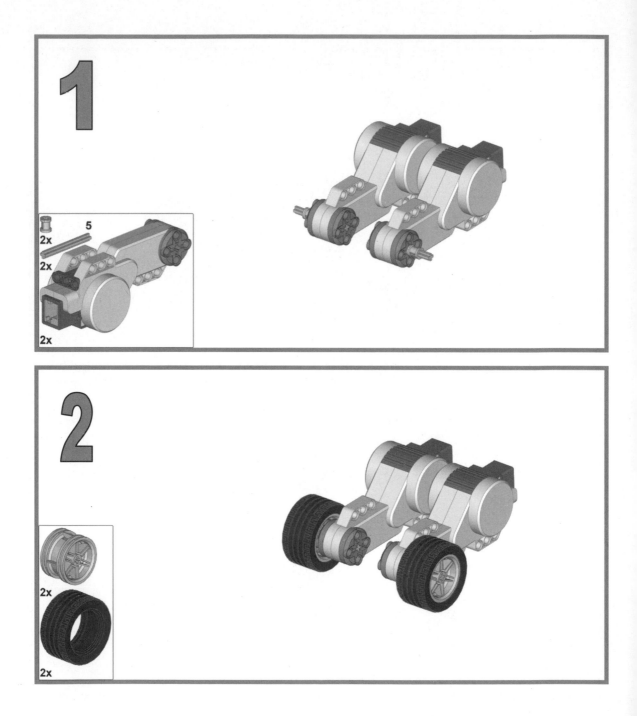

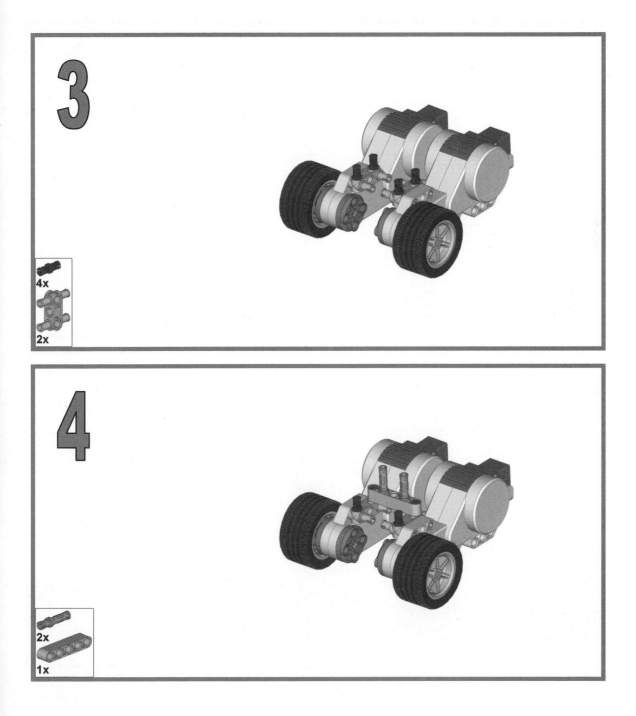

5

2x

6

Rotate

7

4x

8

1x

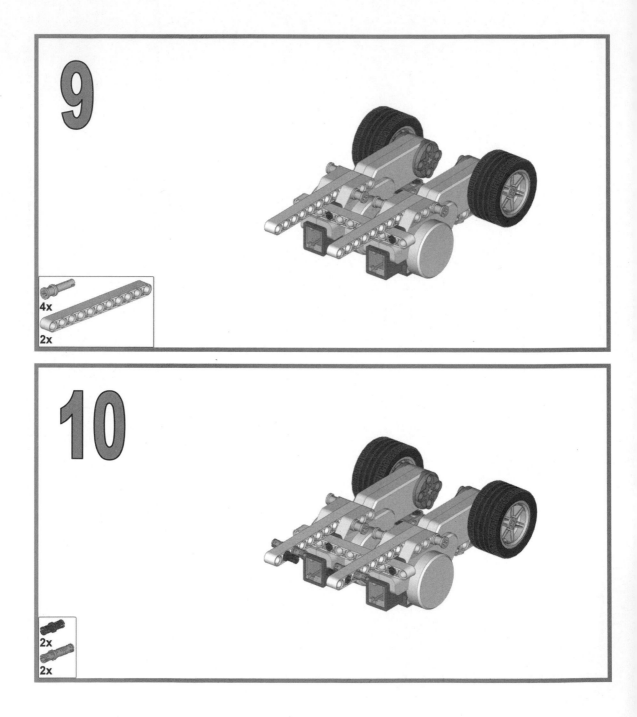

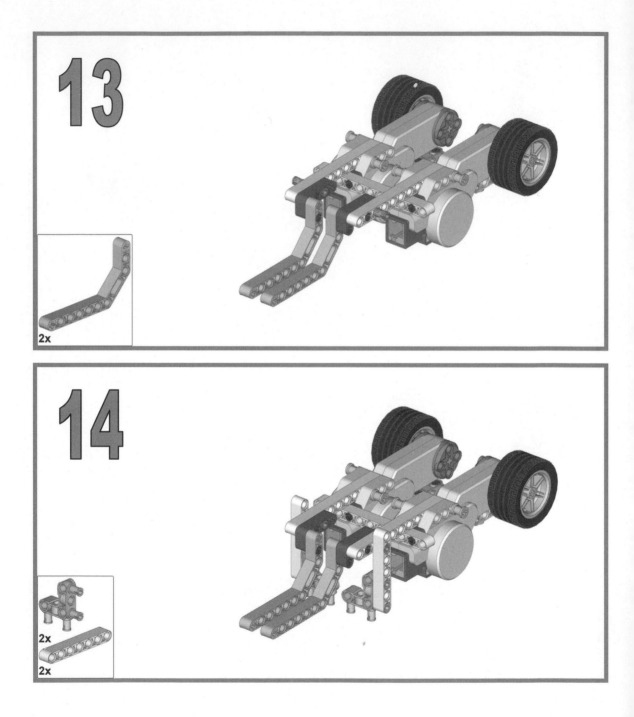

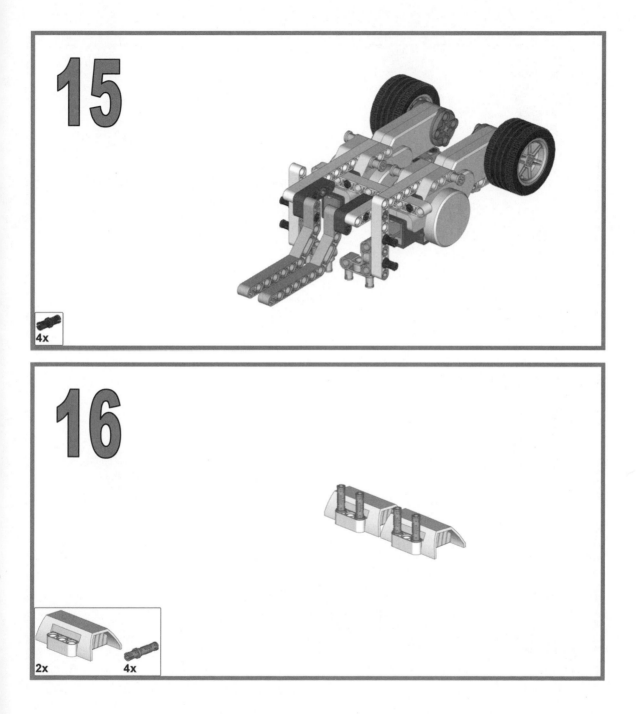

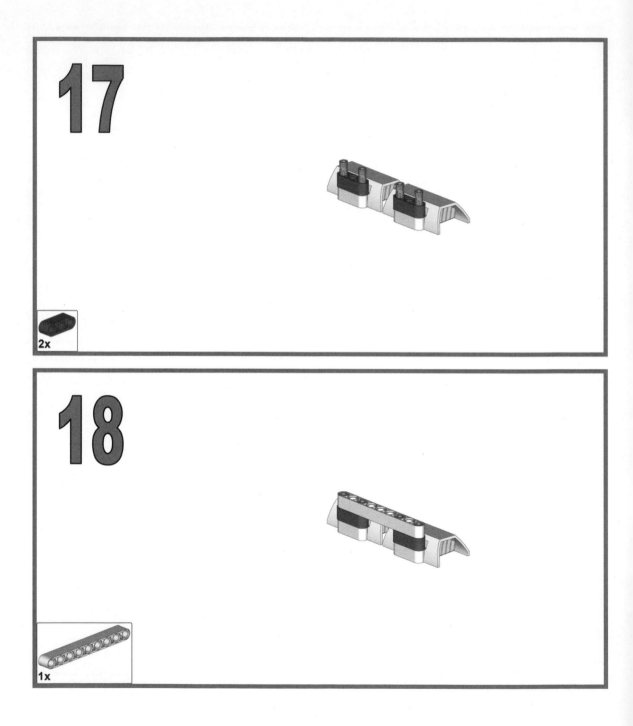

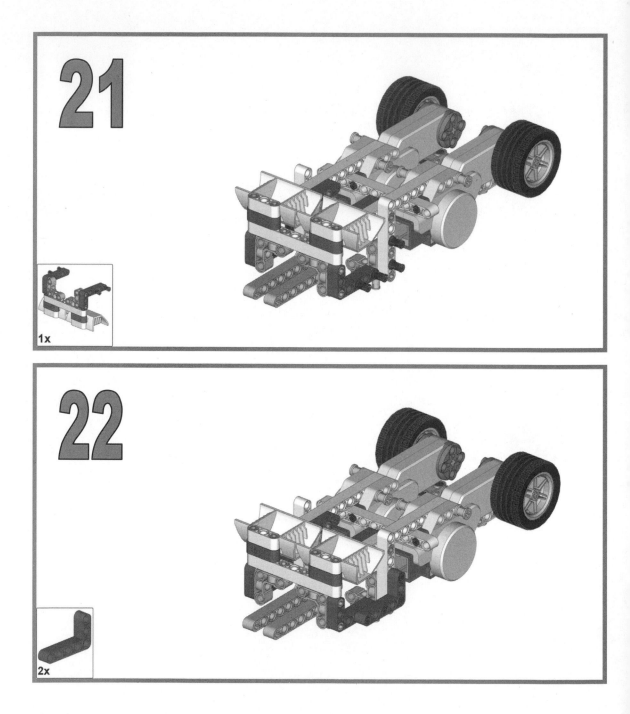

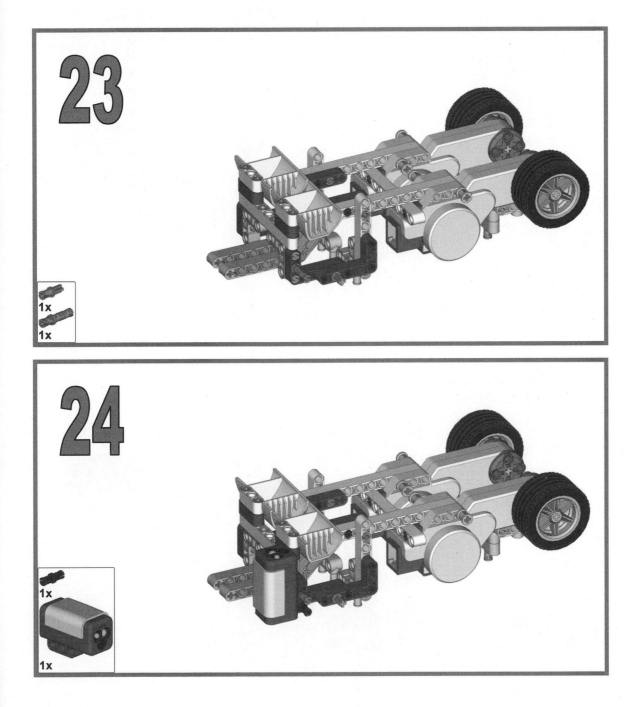

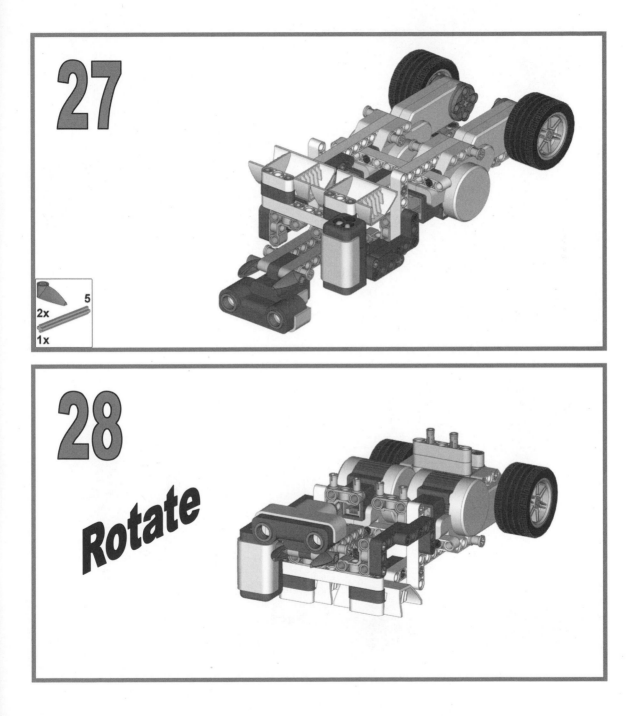

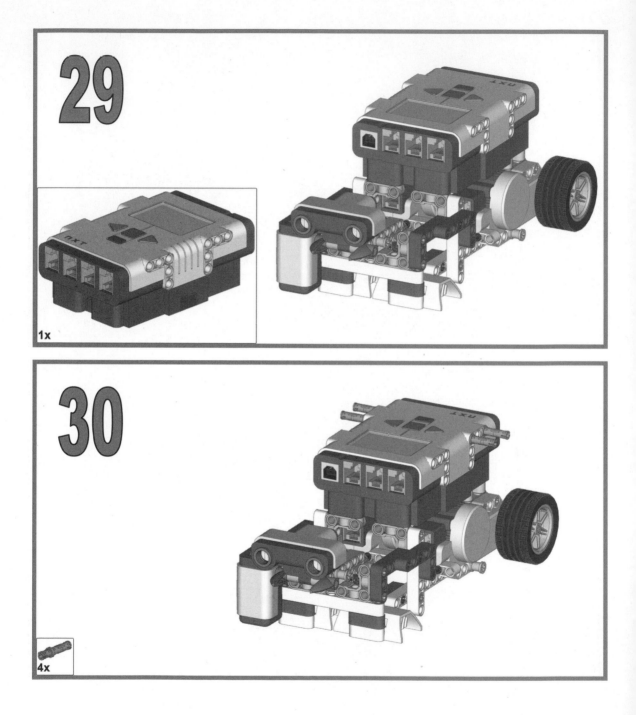

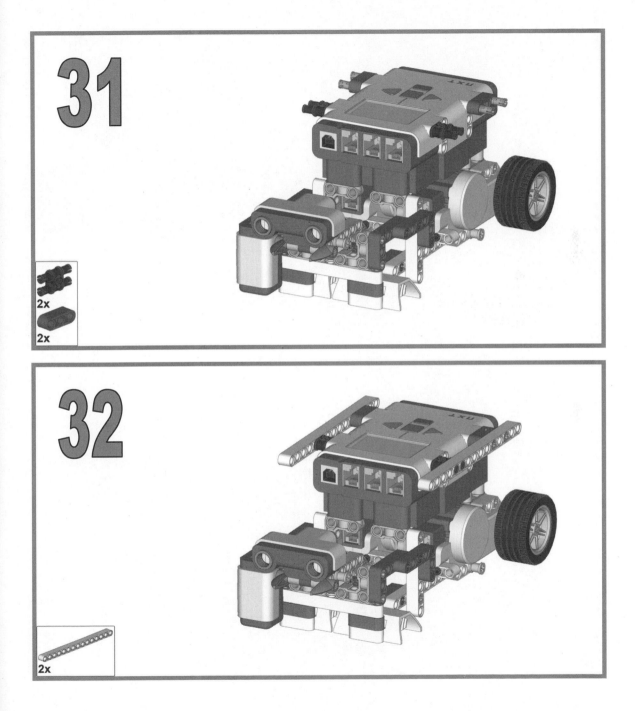

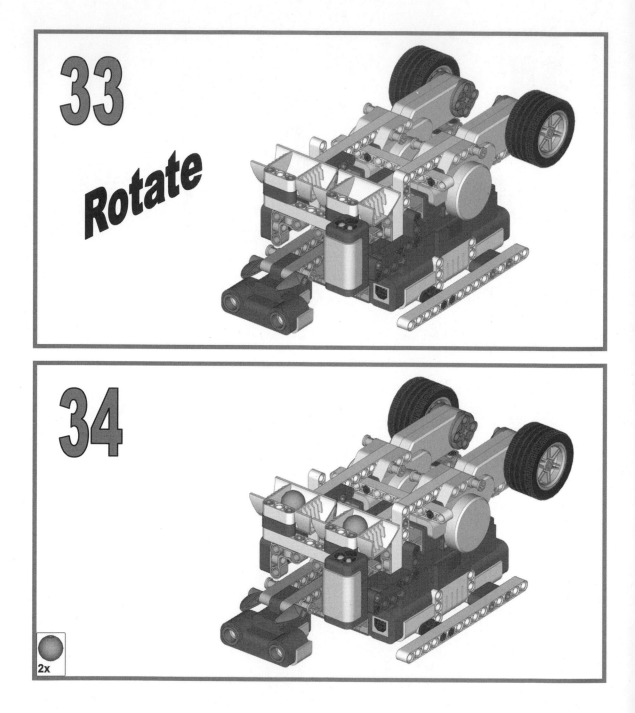

33

Rotate

34

2x

35

Rotate

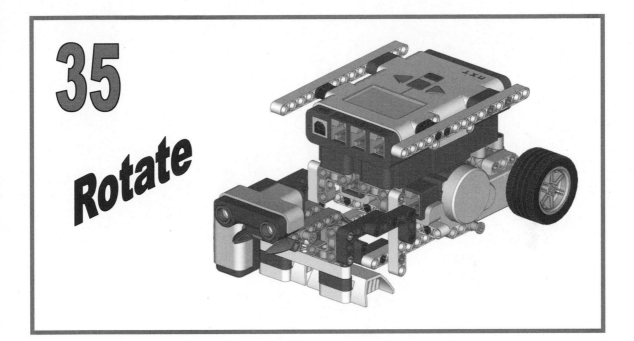

CHAPTER 4

■ ■ ■

MazeRunner—Program It

In this chapter you're going to use your Design Journal worksheet to help you create the program that sends the MazeRunner into the maze (and back), triggering the pressure plate that will allow entry into the next chamber of King Ixtua's treasure repository.

Some Experience Required

This chapter isn't about teaching you the basics of the software. Included with the LEGO MINDSTORMS NXT 2.0 software is a collection of software tutorials. At this point, I'm making the assumption that you've built the bots included with the LEGO MINDSTORMS NXT 2.0 kit and you've gone through the tutorials for programming the bots. During these tutorials, you received some basic skills in selecting programming blocks, dropping them into the workspace, and configuring the blocks.

In this chapter, I'm going to show you how to use your completed Design Journal worksheet for the MazeRunner to help you construct the program, block by block. So go ahead and open up the LEGO MINDSTORMS NXT software (see Figure 4-1).

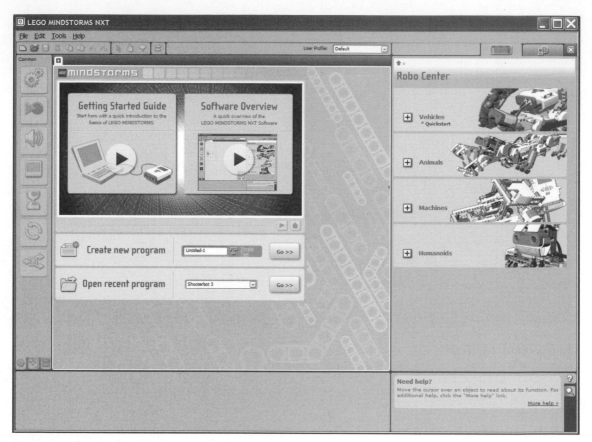

Figure 4-1. *The LEGO MINDSTORMS NXT 2.0 software*

Type MazeRunner into the blank text field labeled Create New Program, then click the Go button (see Figure 4-2).

Figure 4-2. *Enter a name for the new program and click Go.*

■ **Note** To have more workspace visible on your screen, close the RoboCenter area on the far right by clicking the smaller red X (to the right of the small icon that looks like two red cartoon people) in the upper-right corner of the software.

Now, before we start dropping blocks all over the place, we need to think about what this program is supposed to do. Remember the Task List from the Design Journal? This is where that Task List is going to come in handy (see Figure 4-3).

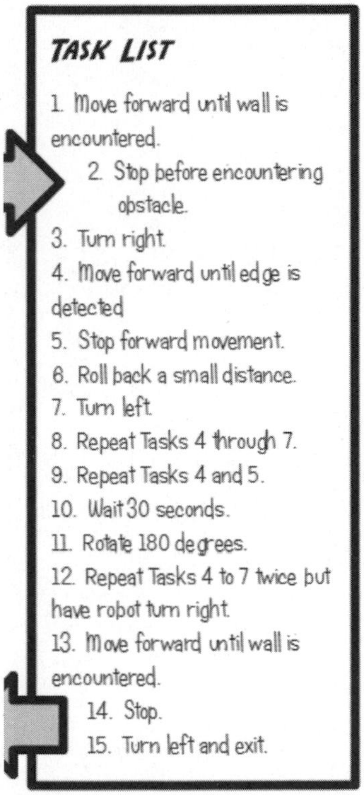

TASK LIST

1. Move forward until wall is encountered.

    2. Stop before encountering obstacle.

3. Turn right.

4. Move forward until edge is detected.

5. Stop forward movement.

6. Roll back a small distance.

7. Turn left.

8. Repeat Tasks 4 through 7.

9. Repeat Tasks 4 and 5.

10. Wait 30 seconds.

11. Rotate 180 degrees.

12. Repeat Tasks 4 to 7 twice but have robot turn right.

13. Move forward until wall is encountered.

    14. Stop.

    15. Turn left and exit.

Figure 4-3. The Task List will help us organize our program.

We're going to use each of the numbered items from the Task List to determine what types of programming blocks to place on the workspace. Like the construction of the actual MazeRunner, there are also numerous ways to program the bot. As you experiment with the LEGO MINDSTORMS NXT software, you'll probably discover new (and better) methods for programming. You might find a way to shorten the program so it takes less memory space in the Intelligent Brick. Or you might choose to switch out the Ultrasonic Sensor with the Touch Sensor, which requires slightly different programming blocks. My point is this: there's no *perfect* method for programming the MazeRunner. With that in mind, let's do a little planning before dropping some blocks.

Figure 4-4 shows the basic MOVE block and its configuration panel. If you've worked your way through building and programming the sample robots that come with the LEGO MINDSTORMS NXT 2.0 kit, then you're probably already familiar with this block; it's one of those blocks you'll be using over and over again.

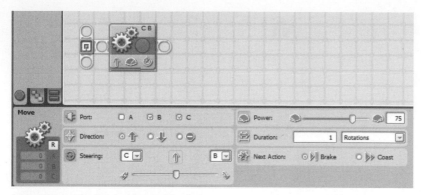

Figure 4-4. The basic MOVE block

■ **Note** You can drag and drop a MOVE block from different locations. One is located on the COMMON palette, and the other MOVE block can be found on the COMPLETE palette. In this chapter, I'm not going to point out every place for you to grab a block. In most instances, just look around on the COMMON and COMPLETE palettes and you'll find the necessary blocks. This will help to familiarize you with all the other programming blocks available. If you find one you're not familiar with, drop it on the workspace and play around with it for a few minutes . . . there's no rush.

We'll configure the MOVE block a little later. For now, let's move to the next Task List item: "Stop before encountering obstacle." Obviously, this task would use a Touch Sensor or Ultrasonic Sensor. The MazeRunner in Chapter 3 uses the Ultrasonic Sensor, so we know we'll be configuring it later.

One interesting thing to note is that the bot will make one right turn followed by two left turns during its travel to trigger the pressure plate. How did I come up with these numbers? Take a look at Figure 4-5 and you'll see the turns.

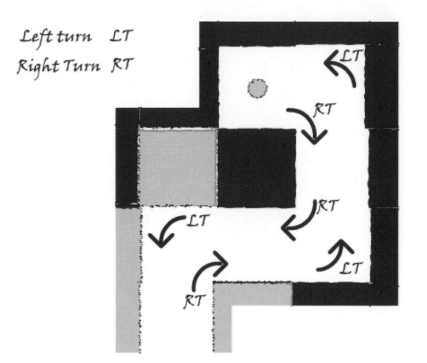

Figure 4-5. The MazeRunner will make one right turn and two left turns to find the trigger.

After the robot has reached the end of the maze and turned completely around, it will make two right turns and one left turn on its way out of the tunnel (see Figure 4-5).

Now, why is this important? Because when you're programming, it pays to reduce the amount of work you need to do. And the LEGO MINDSTORMS NXT software comes with a useful block we're going to use here that will save us some time. That block is the LOOP block (see Figure 4-6). A LOOP block saves us time because any blocks placed inside it can be executed more than once, depending on the LOOP block's settings. More on this later.

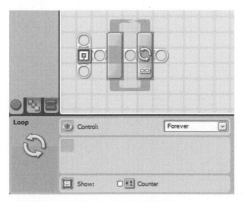

Figure 4-6. The basic LOOP block

The final block I want to discuss is the WAIT block (see Figure 4-7). When the MazeRunner reaches the trigger, I want it to stay there for 30 seconds, just to make sure the pressure plate is triggered. The WAIT block is the key to doing that.

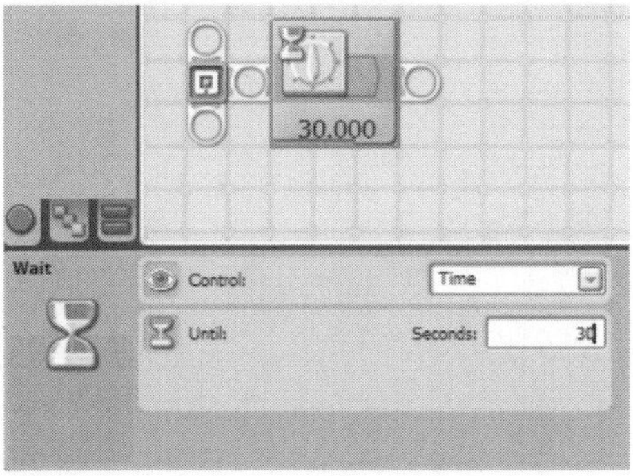

Figure 4-7. *The basic WAIT block*

With these four blocks, plus a few more you'll learn about shortly, you have all you need to program the MazeRunner to perform its duties.

Into the Maze

To save some time, I want you to look at the Task List again. I'm going to group some of the tasks together like this:

(Group) Detect Edge, Stop, Roll Back Small Distance, Make Turn

By grouping certain tasks together, I can place those blocks and then copy and paste them without having to drag and drop blocks again. I'll be using this technique a handful of times throughout the chapter and will tell you when I've done so.

Now, let's build this program. What I'll be doing for the remainder of the chapter is tell you in small bits what the robot will do,and then show you a succession of blocks to place and configure. I will show you the order of the blocks as well as the configurations you should make in each block's configuration panel.

Our MazeRunner's first action is to enter the tunnel and use its Ultrasonic sensor to search for the wall. When it finds the wall, we want it to stop and turn right. So, let's start by dropping in a MOVE block to get the robot rolling. We'll set it to roll forward an Unlimited amount and at a low speed (Power set to 30). Figure 4-8 shows our MOVE block.

■ **Note** For Direction, I've selected the downward pointing arrow – this was discovered in testing as the proper directional setting for forward movement. You may need to change this if you build a different version of the MazeRunner.

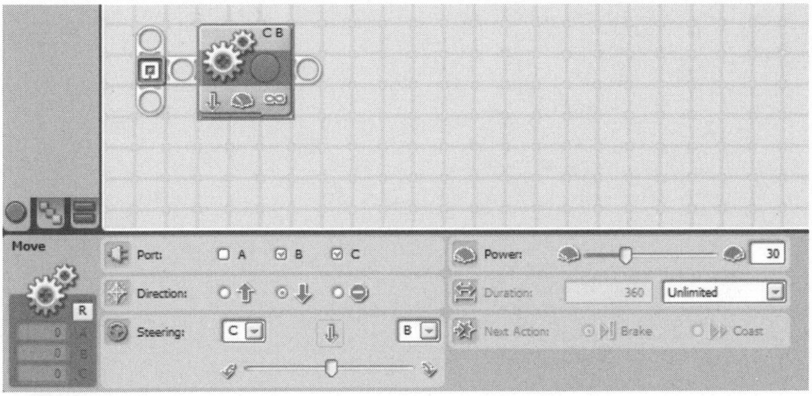

Figure 4-8. You'll start with the MOVE block.

Next, we want the robot to keep moving until the Ultrasonic sensor detects the wall. I've set a distance of less than 4 inches for testing. This number may change during the testing phase at the end of the chapter. Once the wall is detected, we want the motors to stop, so I'll drop in a WAIT block configured to use the Ultrasonic sensor, as shown in Figure 4-9.

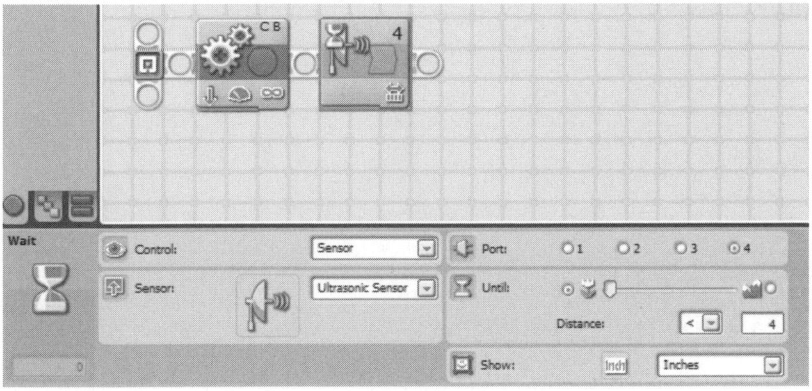

Figure 4-9. The configuration panel for WAIT-Ultrasonic block

Once the Ultrasonic sensor detects the wall, a new MOVE block is needed to stop the motors as shown in Figure 4-10.

■ **Note** At the end of this chapter, I'll cover testing of the MazeRunner. The setting of four inches might not be correct for your MazeRunner. You'll have to test different sensitivities of the Ultrasonic Sensor to determine the proper distance for the Ultrasonic Sensor to break the WAIT block and stop the forward movement.

47

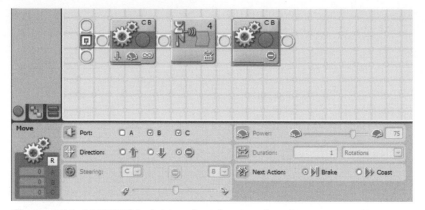

Figure 4-10. A MOVE block is used to also stop the motors.

And now the MazeRunner needs to make a right turn. I drop in another MOVE block and configure it as shown in Figure 4-11. Notice that I've dragged the Steering selection all the way to the right and configured the motors to rotate 320 degrees. The number you use for the Duration will very likely be different than mine. All sorts of things can affect this, including the surface material the robot drives on, the distance between the two wheels, and the Power setting. I use a Power setting of 30 to make the robot turn slowly—this helps with accuracy.

■ **Note** To find the actual values you'll need to turn right and left, skip to the end of this chapter and look for the section labeled "Left and Right Turn Calculations."

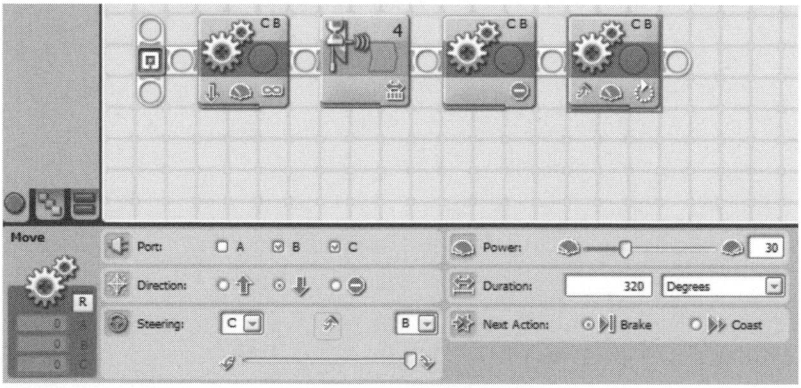

Figure 4-11. Use a MOVE block to make a right turn.

And now the MazeRunner is ready to start using the Color sensor to find the edges of the path so it can make the proper turns to find the pressure plate.

For the next few blocks, I want to introduce you to the concept of nesting. Putting a LOOP block inside another LOOP block is called nesting and we're going to use this concept with the MazeRunner.

To do this, drop a LOOP block first and configure it as shown in Figure 4-12. It's configured to loop twice—any blocks found inside, including other LOOP blocks, will execute twice (or more for a nested LOOP block).

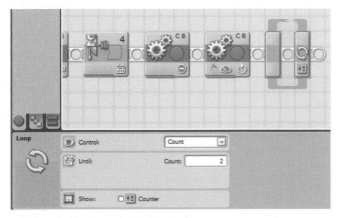

Figure 4-12. Place a LOOP block and configure it for a count of 2.

Why a count of two? Remember earlier when we talked about how the MazeRunner would make two left turns before finding the pressure plate? Those two left turns are going to happen based on the blocks we place inside this LOOP block. Refer back to the Task List and you'll see that the robot will move forward until the edge is encountered, roll back a short distance, and then turn left. All three of these actions will happen twice, so we'll program these movements inside this outer LOOP block.

I use the term "outer" because there will be an "inner" LOOP block that you can see dropped inside the outer LOOP block and configured as shown in Figure 4-13.

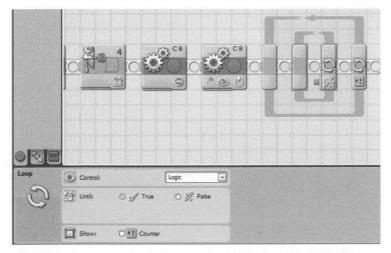

Figure 4-13. A nested LOOP block will test for the path's edge.

This inner LOOP block will run continuously until a True logic signal is sent to it. What's a logic signal? Sensors (and motors) can send a True or False signal to a LOOP block (and other blocks) based on their condition. For the Color sensor, we want it to send a True signal to the LOOP block when it detects a change in color (that is, when the sensor goes from detecting the surface/ground to detecting no ground – the pit). But first, we need to put the MazeRunner in motion. Simply drop another MOVE block into the "inner" LOOP block and configure it to run Unlimited as shown in Figure 4-14.

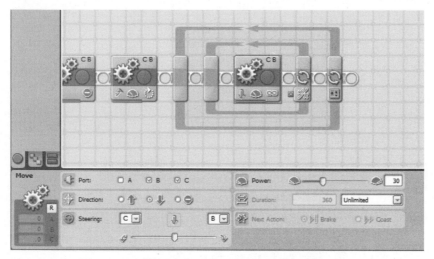

Figure 4-14. This MOVE block starts the robot moving forward.

You already saw how a WAIT block configured to use the Ultrasonic sensor was used to let the motors run until the wall was detected. Here, as the "inner" loop continually runs, a sensor block (for the Color sensor) will be checking to see if it detects the edge. (For my simulation of this challenge, I used blue painter's tape to represent the edges of the path – see the section "Simulating the Challenge" at the end of this chapter.) I've dropped in the Color sensor block and configured it as shown in Figure 4-15. Your configuration of the sensor may be different depending on the color you use to represent the pit.

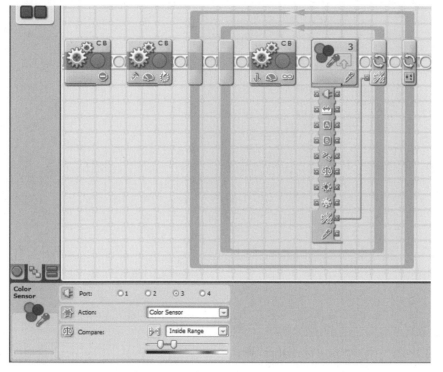

Figure 4-15. Place a Color sensor block to look for the path's edge.

There's a lot happening in Figure 4-15, so let me explain a few things. First, click on the lower left corner of the Color sensor block to expand its data port. Click on the second plug from the bottom (if you hover your mouse pointer over it, it will say 'Yes/No') and drag a green data wire to the plug coming out of the "inner" LOOP block. You'll also notice that in the configuration panel, I've dragged the two small bars in the Compare section so that they border the blue color – one is to the left of the blue and the other is to the right. Depending on the color you use to simulate the edge of the path, you will need to move these to pick your color.

Now, let's summarize what's happening in the outer LOOP block. Once the robot has found the wall and turned right, it executes the outer LOOP block. The first thing inside that loop that executes is the inner LOOP block. A MOVE block starts the robot rolling forward and the Color sensor is looking for the blue painter's tape I used. As long as it doesn't detect the color blue, it continues to send a False logic signal to the inner LOOP block and that block keeps looping and looping. But once it encounters the blue tape, the Color sensor sends a True signal to the inner LOOP block and that loop ends! What happens next? We need the robot to stop and then roll back a short distance and then turn left. So, let's drop in two MOVE blocks just after the inner loop block and configure it as shown in Figure 4-16. The first one is simply configured to stop the motors (see Figure 4-10 for the panel settings) and the second MOVE block has the robot pull back a short distance.

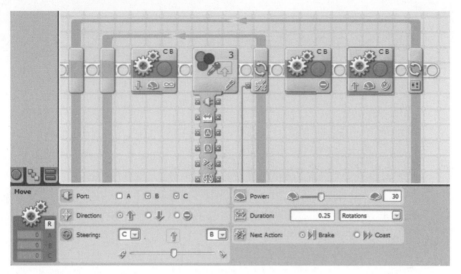

Figure 4-16. This MOVE block will force the robot to reverse direction a small distance.

Finally, I need to add in another MOVE block that will force the MazeRunner to turn left. That block and its configuration panel are shown in Figure 4-17. Remember that the number you configure for the Distance value may be different than mine—you'll have to obtain this number by testing your robot.

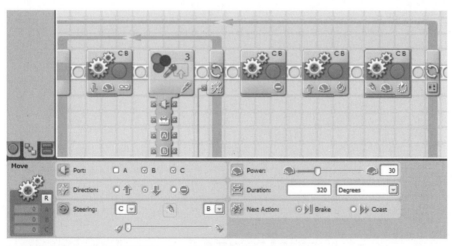

Figure 4-17. Add a MOVE block to make the final left turn.

Now, keep in mind that the outer LOOP block will run twice. The MazeRunner will perform the previous movements again—it will approach the next path edge, stop, pull back a bit, and then turn left. At this point it should be facing the pressure plate. All that's left now is to send the robot forward until the Color sensor detects the pit's edge (or blue tape) and then pull back the robot a bit. To do this, drop in another LOOP block and configure it as shown in Figure 4-18.

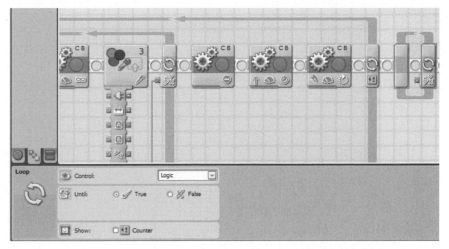

Figure 4-18. Another LOOP block will get the robot to the pressure plate.

Inside this LOOP block we'll once again have the robot rolling forward slowly until the Color Sensor sends a True signal to the LOOP block to end the loop. Figure 4-19 shows these two blocks dropped inside the LOOP block and the configuration panel for the Color sensor. (For the MOVE block, set its Duration to Unlimited, Power to 30, and direction to Forward.)

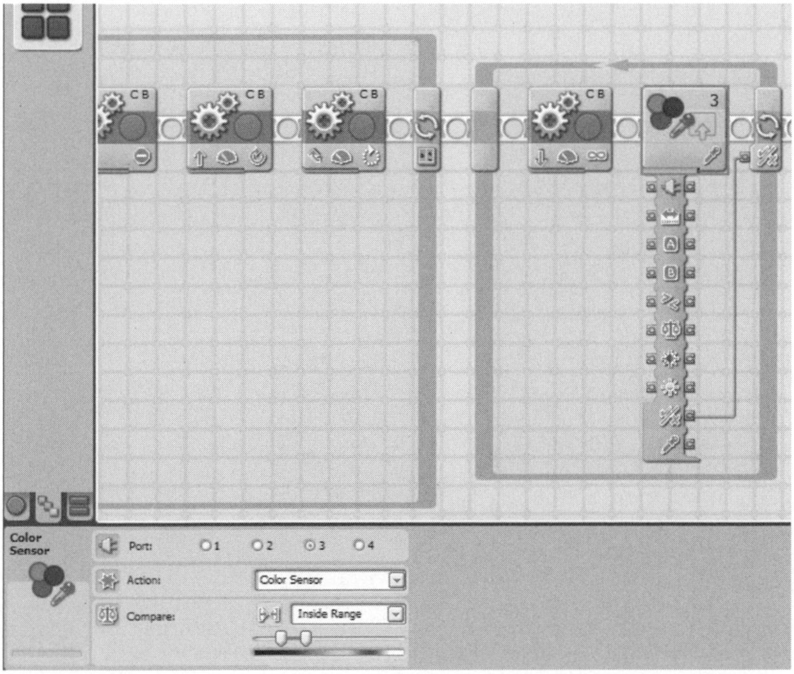

Figure 4-19. The Color sensor block will detect the edge just past the pressure plate.

At this point, we now want the robot to stop, back up a bit, wait for 30 seconds, and then rotate 180 degrees. Drop in a MOVE block configured to stop the motors, another MOVE block to back the robot up about 0.25 rotations (1/4 rotation), and then drop in a WAIT block and configure it as shown in Figure 4-20. (Feel free to reduce the wait from 30 seconds to 5 or 6 to speed things up a bit.)

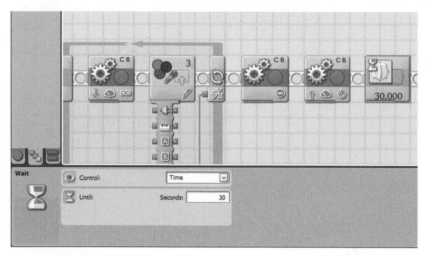

Figure 4-20. The WAIT block will have the robot pause and sit on the pressure plate.

Finally, before the robot begins its exit of the maze, drop in a MOVE block and configure it to turn in the opposite direction. This block and its configuration panel settings are shown in Figure 4-21. The Duration value for your robot may be different, so obtain this value during the testing phase.

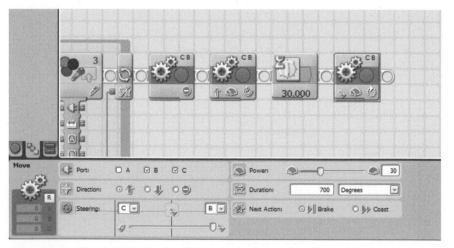

Figure 4-21. This MOVE block will turn the robot to face the opposite direction.

Out of the Tunnel

Now it's time to get the MazeRunner out of the maze. You're going to be surprised at how easy this is. Think about it—exiting the maze is pretty much the same as entering it, except that you'll be making opposite turns. Whereas you make a single right turn and two left turns to find the pressure plate, now you're going to make two right turns to leave the pressure plate and then a single left turn to leave the maze.

You may think this will involve a lot of dragging and dropping of blocks, but not really. You only need to click and hold your mouse button and drag a selection window around all the LOOP blocks shown in Figure 4-22. Release the mouse button and then hit Ctrl+C to copy all those blocks to your computer's clipboard. (The selection window is blue-green in color; you can see it surrounding all the blocks in Figure 4-22.)

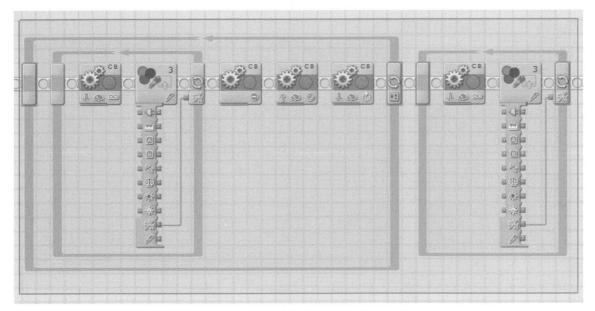

Figure 4-22. Drag a selection window around all these blocks and use Ctrl+C to copy them.

Next, drag your work area (click the Hand toolbar button— also called the Pan Tool—on the toolbar at the top of the software) so the very end of the program beam is visible, as shown in Figure 4-23.

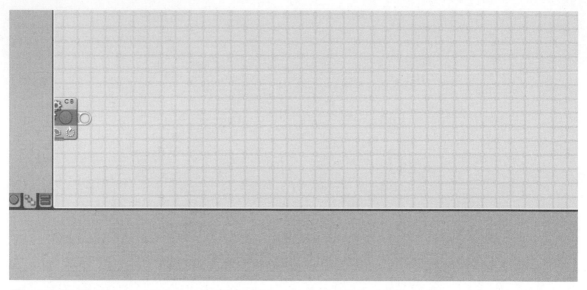

Figure 4-23. Move your program so the end of the program beam is visible.

Now press Ctrl+V to paste the collection of blocks onto the screen. Click the Arrow tool on the toolbar once and then click and hold the pasted blocks so you can drag them around. Move the mouse pointer to the end of the program beam shown in Figure 4-23 and release the mouse button. (After you press Ctrl+V, the blocks will slightly faded in color to indicate they need to be dragged and dropped onto the program beam.)

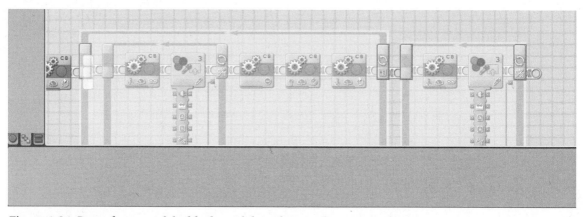

Figure 4-24. Paste the copy of the blocks and drag them to the program beam.

Once pasted, you will need to go in and modify the fourth MOVE block in the outer LOOP block so it makes a right turn instead of a left. This is easy—just click that block and change the Direction arrow setting, as shown in Figure 4-25.

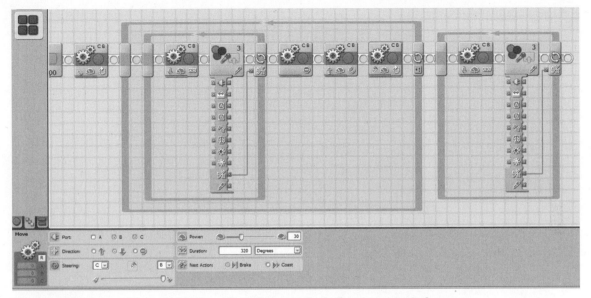

Figure 4-25. The newly pasted blocks will get the robot to the last turn to exit the maze.

At this point, the robot is ready to make the last turn (a left turn) so it can exit the maze. So, we'll have the motors stop, back up the robot a short distance, make the left turn, and then keep rolling forward for a specified amount of time. Do all this by dropping in a MOVE block configured to stop the motors, a MOVE block to back the robot up .25 rotations, another MOVE block to rotate the robot to the left, and then a final MOVE block configured to run the motors for an Unlimited Duration. The WAIT block at the end is configured for 10 seconds, plenty of time for the robot to roll three feet. Figure 4-26 shows the remaining five blocks, including the configuration panel for the WAIT block.

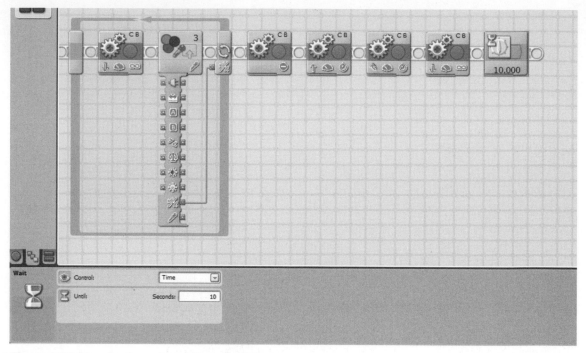

Figure 4-26. Stop, back up, turn left, and exit the maze.

Left Turn and Right Turn Calculations

For almost every robot that you build and program, you'll need it to make turns – left turns, right turns, 180 degree turns, and everything in between. Fortunately, LEGO has built a tool right into the Intelligent Brick that will allow you to find the values for various turns that your robots need to make. As you rotate your robot, a value can be made to display on the screen that tells you exactly how many rotations, degrees, or turns that a motor has made. To use it, start by turning on the Intelligent Brick.

Using the Brick's right or left button, scroll through the list of options until you find View. Press the orange select button on the Brick and, using the right or left buttons, scroll through this list until you find Motor degrees. Once again, press the orange select button.

Now, you're going need to select the port to monitor. Motor B will make the first turn, so use the left or right button to scroll and find Port B. Select it and you'll notice a small box on the LCD screen with the number 0 (zero) in it. Just for grins, turn the wheel on motor B and watch what happens on the screen. That number tells you how many degrees the motor turns. If you turn the motor forward, you'll get a positive number (1 and climbing). If you turn the motor backward, you'll get a negative number (-1 and dropping). Press the orange select button to reset the degree counter.

Next, place the MazeRunner on a flat surface and press the orange select button to reset the counte, and manually turn the MazeRunner 90 degrees to the left. For best results, try to keep the wheel for motor C from rotating. Just twist and turn the MazeRunner left so that the wheel on motor B turns. When you're done, take a look at the LCD screen. Your results might vary, but for my MazeRunner I got a reading of 320. Now do the same thing for Port C. A true right turn, done the same way, should give you the same result (or very close).

The number you get for motor B and motor C is the number you'll enter for the Duration setting for the various MOVE blocks used to turn the MazeRunner.

Keep in mind that your MazeRunner will be different from every other MazeRunner—some motors are little more stiff, some less stiff. My rubber wheels might behave a little differently on a wood floor versus a cement floor. Battery levels will be different. There are so many factors that can affect how your MazeRunner operates. Don't get frustrated . . . just tweak and tweak and then tweak some more.

At this point, you'll have to do some testing to determine that the right and left turns are as close to 90 degree turns as possible. Don't take risks—if the bot is off by a few degrees, you'll take the risk that your bot might not go straight and get stuck somewhere where you can't reach it. You want the bot to turn as close to 90 degrees as possible and then move forward on a straight path. Tweak the individual Duration settings until you're happy that the bot is turning left and right correctly.

Simulating the Challenge

Obviously we don't want to test our robots on a high surface where they could fall off and get damaged. In order to simulate this challenge, I recommend using blue painter's tape to outline the path the robot must navigate, but any color will work as long as it is different than the surface color. You can see a picture of my setup in Figure 4-27.

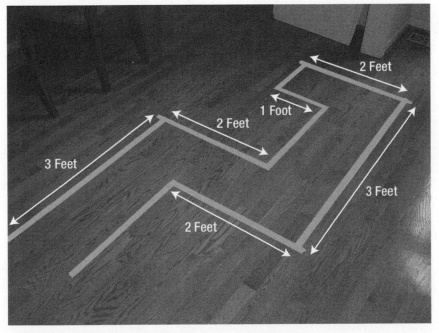

Figure 4-27. Use blue painter's tape to outline the path.

Next, I placed a box as shown in Figure 4-28 to act as the wall the MazeRunner must detect before making its turn to enter the maze.

Figure 4-28. A box can act as the wall the robot's Ultrasonic sensor must detect.

I found through testing that the MazeRunner does not do well on carpet. A hard surface is best (I have wooden floors) but I was also able to run the test on a cement floor and a large plastic-top table.

Every robot behaves differently – motors can be configured for different power and speeds, battery strength can be high or low, and the spheres used as caster wheels in my MazeRunner occasionally don't roll 100% accurately. Take it all in stride – run as many tests as you can to tweak all the various settings and, when you're confident your robot is ready, run an official test and see if you can get your robot into the maze, trigger the pressure plate, and then get safely out of the maze and ready for the next challenge. Good luck!

CHAPTER 5

■ ■ ■

Swing and Switch

Location: Southwest Guatemala

102 miles SW of Guatemala City

Coordinates: 14º 04' N / 90º 09' W

Weather Conditions: 87 degrees Fahrenheit, Humidity 50%

Day 4: King Ixtua Treasure Repository, 9:14 a.m.

Evan knew the moment his robot triggered the pressure plate. A loud crack was heard from behind the wooden door just a few feet from where he stood. Erin, Tag, Uncle Phillip, and Evan all jumped at the loud sound.

"I hope that's a good sound," said Evan.

"It is," replied Uncle Philip. "I've seen this kind of locked door before. Tupaxu used a large wooden beam to block access to the room. That snap we heard was a small mechanism that breaks a wooden peg holding the beam in place. We should be able to open the door without triggering any traps."

"Nice job programming that robot," said Erin. "I think I hear it coming back."

Tag shone his flashlight into the maze's entrance. Evan could hear the motors even before the robot turned left at the final corner. It rolled straight towards him. Evan reached in, pulled the robot out, and turned it off to save the batteries.

"Amazing," said Tag. "Every archaeology team should have a robot kit like that."

Uncle Phillip, examining the wooden door, turned to Evan. "I agree. At the next archaeology conference I attend, I'm considering giving a talk on the use of this little robot kit in future expeditions. Great job, Evan."

Evan smiled. "Thanks."

"Okay, let's get this door open," said Uncle Phillip. "Tag, give me a hand here, please."

With four people, lighting equipment, and some video and photography equipment set up, the room felt extremely cramped to Evan. He hoped the next room offered more space to move around. He watched as Tag and Uncle Phillip pushed hard against the slowly opening door.

When the door was fully open, Tag took one of the tripod halogen lights from the first chamber and moved it into the doorway. Evan was anxious to see what awaited the team on the other side.

Erin nudged Evan. "This is the worst part. Waiting," she said with a smile.

Tag took a few steps back and let Dr. Hicks move into the doorway.

Evan watched his uncle look left, then right, and then pull and read something from his shirt pocket. Dr. Hicks removed his Florida State University cap and scratched his head.

"You've got to be kidding me," Evan heard his uncle mutter.

Don't Look Down

"Be careful," said Uncle Phillip, moving back from the doorway. "Don't step into the room."

Evan waited his turn, letting Tag move into the doorway. He walked away shaking his head. Erin was next.

"I'm not sure what I'm seeing here," she said. "But I'm definitely not seeing a floor."

"Take a look at the ceiling," replied Dr. Hicks.

Evan shuffled his feet, anxious to take a look.

Erin looked up, nodded, and then turned to Evan. "Your turn."

Still holding his robot, Evan moved to the doorway, careful to avoid knocking the halogen light over, and looked into the room beyond (see Figure 5-1).

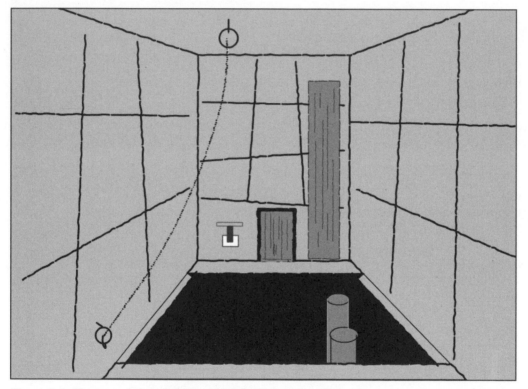

Figure 5-1. *The second chamber has a high ceiling and no floor.*

Evan groaned and took a few steps back. "I hate heights."

"Tupaxu definitely knew how to build some tricky rooms, didn't he?" asked Uncle Phillip.

Evan took another look at the room. The most obvious feature was the huge pit instead of a floor. Two large stone pillars jutted up from the pit, their round surfaces large enough for someone to stand on, but you'd have to jump four feet to the first one.

On the other side of the huge open pit was a door. A lever of some sort was to the left of the door and a tall, odd looking plank, approximately twenty feet tall leaned against the wall to the right of the door.

Evan also noticed a rotting piece of rope that was tied to a ring on the left wall. The other end of the rope was tied to a ring in the ceiling.

"Sorry, Uncle Phillip, but I'm not swinging across any pit," said Evan with a weak smile. He walked back into the entry room and sat down on the floor next to his uncle. "I *really* hate heights," Evan repeated to himself.

Uncle Phillip nodded. "Don't worry, Evan. I don't think that rope would hold our weight anyway."

Tag and Erin peered through the doorway again. Evan looked up and saw them shaking their heads. Apparently the team was in agreement that this was not a room that Tupaxu meant for anyone to cross.

"Unbelievable," said Erin. "I'm not quite sure what to make of this."

Dr. Hicks scratched his head. "I have an idea, but I need to go up and check one of the scrolls first. Tag, would you please take some measurements of the room using the laser distance finder and some digital pictures? Join us up top when you're done."

Uncle Phillip patted Evan on the back and stood up. "I can see we're going to be needing your robot kit again, Evan. Let's head up."

The Monkey's Swing Challenge

Inside the equipment tent, Uncle Phillip pointed to his sketch of the room (see Figure 5-2). "This is an interesting challenge that Tupaxu wrote about in one of the scrolls we found in King Ixtua's library. In a nutshell, one of the king's trained monkeys would swing across, pull the lever, and the wooden bridge would lower for a person to cross the pit."

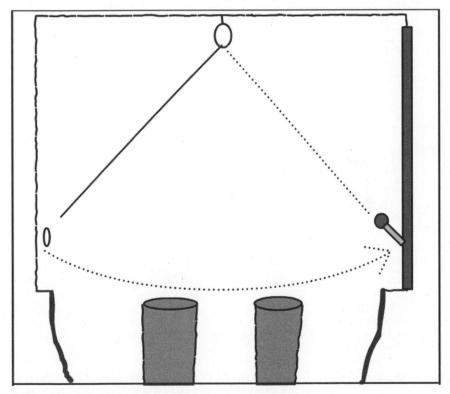

Figure 5-2. *Side view of the room with measurements.*

Tag pointed at the drawing. "Why don't we just build our own bridge and lay it across these pillars?"

"Why even go that far? Can't we just throw a rope to loop it over the lever and pull?" asked Erin.

Dr. Hicks smiled. "Tupaxu was no dummy. In his description of the chamber, he notes that the pillars have supports we cannot see. The supports are added only if the lever is pulled. If we tried to build a bridge to the other side, the pillars would collapse under any weight applied to them. No. We need to get that lever pulled first," replied Dr. Hicks.

Evan squirmed in his chair. "What about Erin's suggestion? Can't we just try to lasso the lever and pull it down?" he asked.

"Once again, Tupaxu has anticipated that trick," said Uncle Phillip. "See this rope that's tied to the ring at the top of the ceiling? When the monkey would swing over, it was trained to take the loop at the end of the rope and slide it on to the lever's handle. When the lever is pulled down, the rope pulls the ring in the ceiling. If the lever is pulled and not the ring, the large stones that make up the sides of this room collapse and the room is destroyed."

"Okay," said Erin. "We won't be doing that!"

Tag nodded. "I think we'd end up pulling the lever off the wall rather than down, anyway," he replied.

Uncle Phillip turned to Evan. "I hate to keep putting pressure on you to solve our problems, but Tupaxu was a real genius when it came to traps. Without your robots, we may have to stop here and have something specially engineered… and expensive. Any ideas?"

"No pressure," said Tag with a grin.

Evan's Solution

A few hours later, Evan called for the group to return to the tent. Although he had yet to build anything, he'd completed his Design Journal worksheet and had some ideas.

"First, is there any chance we could rig up two lengths of thin rope or twine with a hook on each end to latch on to the ring?" asked Evan. "The rope that's still hanging there is falling apart from age."

Everyone turned to Tag, who nodded. "I've got plenty of strong twine, and I can make some hooks easily enough. It's about twenty feet from the door's entry to the ring, but I think I can rig something up with some tent poles and tape to get them there. Why?'

Evan smiled. "Well, I've been thinking about this problem, and the only solution I've been able to come up with involves building a robot to do exactly what the monkey was trained to do. If my basic understanding of pendulums is correct, I'm going to build a robot that swings!"

The story continues in Chapter 9…

■ ■ ■

CHAPTER 6

RopeSwinger—Design and Planning

For your next challenge, you need to get a robot across that chasm to pull a lever to release the bridge. Building it might be a bit tricky, but I'm going to lead you through the design process. Once again, we'll be using the Design Journal worksheet to help us get a better idea of what's involved in this challenge and how to solve it.

Getting Started

Grab a blank Design Journal worksheet. In the Robot Name box, write **RopeSwinger** (you can obviously come up with your own name, if you like.) Once you've got your robot name, let's move on to the Robot Description.

■ **Note** There are four blank Design Journal pages left in the back of this book (if you used one for Chapter 2). If you need more pages, feel free to make photocopies of the Design Journal page, or visit the Code/Download area of the Apress web site [www.apress.com] to download the page in PDF format.

The Robot Description

Remember, your Robot Description doesn't need to be extremely long and complicated. Keep it simple and uncluttered. The goal here isn't to describe the robot as "slightly heavy, a mixture of sensors, three motors, and a bunch of beams." This section is where you try to accurately describe the overall process the robot will follow.

Ask yourself the question, "What is this robot supposed to do?" and start writing inside the Robot Description box. Write "visually." Picture your robot going through the actions to perform what you believe needs to be done to solve this challenge (refer to Chapter 5 if you need a reminder). Now compare what you wrote down to my Robot Description in Figure 6-1.

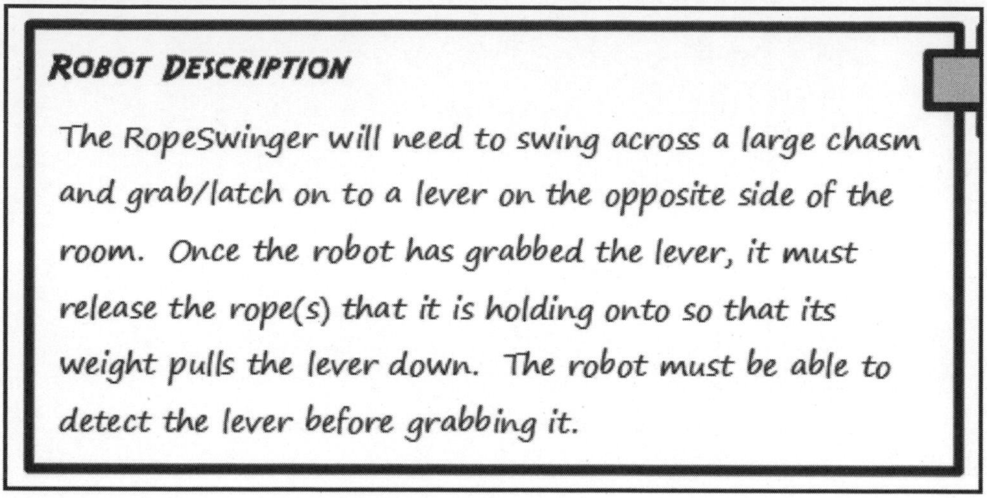

ROBOT DESCRIPTION

The RopeSwinger will need to swing across a large chasm and grab/latch on to a lever on the opposite side of the room. Once the robot has grabbed the lever, it must release the rope(s) that it is holding onto so that its weight pulls the lever down. The robot must be able to detect the lever before grabbing it.

Figure 6-1. The RopeSwinger's Robot Description.

Don't worry if your Robot Description doesn't match mine exactly, but there are a handful of observations you should have made about this challenge. First, this robot will indeed be crossing a distance minus wheels or tracks. The key word for me is "swing"—the NXT robots are too heavy to fly across, and throwing it across the room isn't a good idea.

Your Robot Description should also make note of the need to grab on to the lever and then release the rope or twine that it is using to swing across the room. Finally, although we're not sure yet about which sensor to use, it's likely you'll need one to detect the wall or lever, so make sure that's in your description. Now, let's tackle the Task List.

The Task List

The Task List, if you remember, takes your Robot Description and breaks it down into smaller, more detailed functions the robot must perform—move back, spin, or pick up key, for example. Look back to your Design Journal page's Robot Description and fill out the Task List, making sure to keep each step as simple as possible. Figure 6-2 shows how I've broken down the robot's tasks.

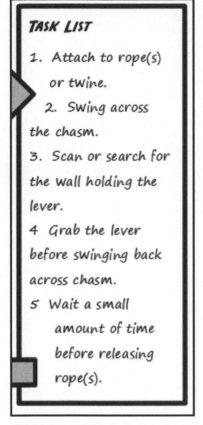

TASK LIST

1. Attach to rope(s) or twine.

2. Swing across the chasm.

3. Scan or search for the wall holding the lever.

4 Grab the lever before swinging back across chasm.

5 Wait a small amount of time before releasing rope(s).

Figure 6-2. The RopeSwinger's Task List is almost identical to the Robot Description.

I believe that the Task List is the most important section on the Design Journal worksheet because each of the tasks will affect the design of your bot. Each item is an action item, so each action must be paired up with a physical assembly that will either perform the action or assist with the performance of that action. Have you ever heard the phrase "form follows function?" This means that the shape of an item (its form) is usually determined by what it will do (its function). Your robot is no different. For your RopeSwinger to perform its duties, you must keep its main job in mind while you are designing it.

Now, let's take a closer look at your Task List. Make certain that it matches the Robot Description as closely as possible and that every step is present. If your Robot Description is complete, your Task List items should be, too.

Notice in my Task List that the first thing is to make sure the robot is securely attached to the rope or twine it will use to swing across the room. I'm not sure yet how I'll do this, but whatever method I use, it must be safe enough for the robot to swing across and not fall off. "Attach" is a vague word, but it will help me when it comes time to begin building and testing—my robot must be able to hold on tight!

The next item on the task list is the fun part. The robot will simply swing across the room. It doesn't get any easier—hold the robot (that's attached somehow to the string), start the program, and release the robot. The swinging part is easy, but what happens on the other side of the room can make my robot's job difficult.

Once the robot is swinging across the room, it needs a way to find the lever. Because the lever is attached to a large, flat surface (the wall), I have two possible choices here—the Ultrasonic sensor and a Touch sensor. The Touch sensor requires direct contact to trigger the robot to grab the lever. The Ultrasonic sensor can detect the wall well before it reaches it but will need some fine-tuning to get the sensitivity correct. Either way, scanning for the wall has to happen for the robot to make a timely grab for the lever.

Finally, once the robot "discovers" the wall, it needs to make a grab for the lever and hold on! If it misses, it should have enough momentum built up to swing back across the chasm for me to grab and try again. (Just to be safe, maybe I'll rig up some sort of "butterfly catcher" to reach out and grab it—just in case.)

Once the robot does grab the lever, it needs to release the rope. Doing so will allow the weight of the robot to pull down on the lever (we hope). So I'll have to come up with some mechanism to release the string/twine once the robot has grabbed the lever. This is going to be fun!

Limitations and Constraints

Don't spend too long thinking over this section because, truthfully, until you start building, you really can't imagine all the limitations that you are going to run into. Just visualize the RopeSwinger swinging across the chasm—do you see any trouble ahead? Take a look at Figure 6-3 to see what I came up with for the Limitations/Constraints box.

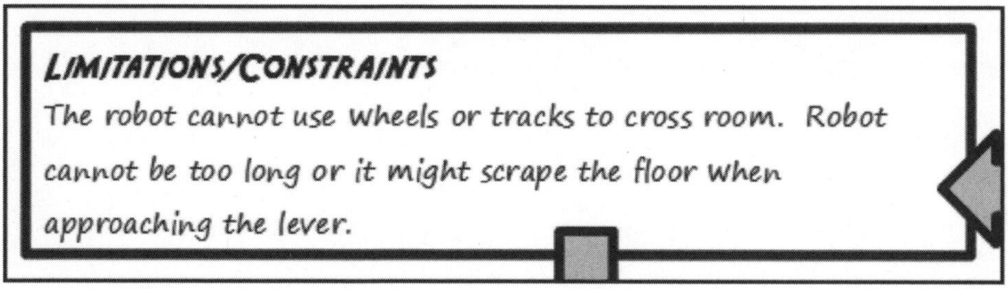

LIMITATIONS/CONSTRAINTS
The robot cannot use wheels or tracks to cross room. Robot cannot be too long or it might scrape the floor when approaching the lever.

Figure 6-3. The RopeSwinger does have some limitations to overcome.

The biggest constraint I could imagine is one we're already well aware of—this robot can't use wheels or track to cross the room. No big deal, as I've already determined that swinging across is the best solution. But it's the other constraint I was able to think of that could be critical. I can't let the robot crash into the floor.

When this challenge starts, I'll be holding the robot in my hands on one side of the room. When I release it, it will swing across, making an arc shape. I need to make certain that at no point during the swinging the robot scrapes across the floor. As I build and test this robot, I'll need to keep this in mind and keep the height/length of my robot to a minimum.

You might encounter more constraints as the project moves forward. Or maybe you've come up with a constraint or two not mentioned here. Perfect. Keep them in mind when designing your own version of the RopeSwinger.

Mindstorm

This is my favorite part of the process before I actually start building. Remember, there are no right or wrong ideas. Just find a comfortable chair and start thinking about your bot. You've probably already got a ton of ideas floating around in your head; this is the time to put the best of them down on paper. And if you think you're not that creative, let me make another suggestion.

Sometimes I have difficulty "getting creative." I might be tired or just not in the mood to do some heavy thinking. If this happens to you, especially now that you're trying to get your RopeSwinger design started, it can be frustrating. When I find that my creative energies are not at full strength, I play a game called "Won't Work."

With "Won't Work," instead of focusing on solutions to the challenge, you're going to think about solutions that (ta-da!) won't work. The idea is that if you're not feeling creative (typically considered a positive emotion), you can be anti-creative. (Okay, I made up that word, but it does work. Trust me.) By thinking about things that won't work, I typically begin to start finding things that *will* work . . . and then I'm thinking creatively. Here are a couple of examples of my "Won't Work" session:

1. If I put the robot on a single piece of string, it will start to spin and may not be able to grab the lever.

2. I can't put the Ultrasonic or Touch Sensor in front of the robot because it will hit the wall or lever.

Hopefully, you're beginning to develop an idea for the design of your RopeSwinger and how it will work.

Take a look at Figure 6-4 and you'll see the ideas I've written down for the Mindstorm section of the Design Journal page.

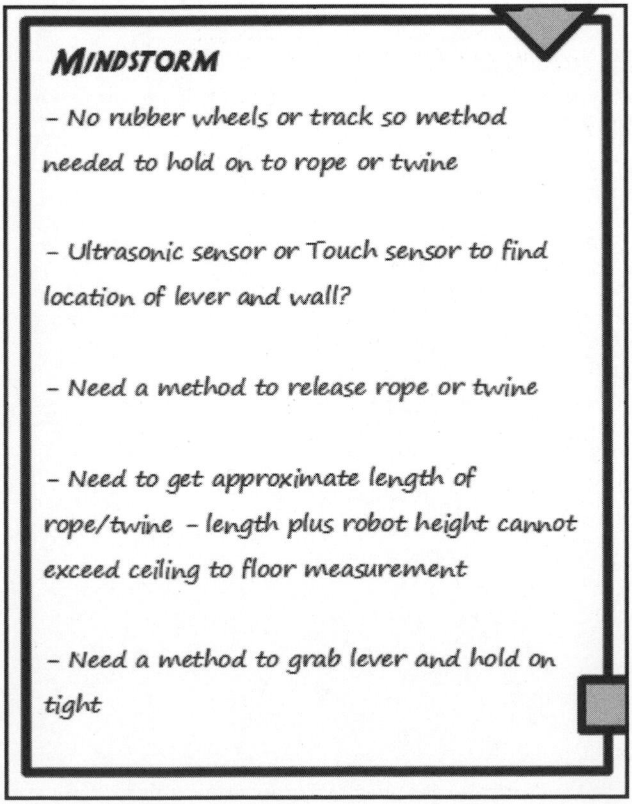

MINDSTORM

- No rubber wheels or track so method needed to hold on to rope or twine

- Ultrasonic sensor or Touch sensor to find location of lever and wall?

- Need a method to release rope or twine

- Need to get approximate length of rope/twine - length plus robot height cannot exceed ceiling to floor measurement

- Need a method to grab lever and hold on tight

Figure 6-4. The Mindstorm section will help you to complete your RopeSwinger design.

The first item I really need to address is how I'm going to have my robot hold on to the string or twine. I need a good method for making sure that my robot doesn't release the string too early. I can't tie the robot to the string, so I'll need some way for my robot to "let go"—this will probably involve the use of a motor. Think about how your hand holds a balloon on a string. I can pinch the string between two fingers or I could tie a small loop and fit it over my closed pinkie – when I open my pinkie, the loop will slip off and the balloon will fly away. Hmmm… that's an idea.

As for whether to use the Ultrasonic sensor or Touch sensor, I'm leaning towards the Ultrasonic. Why? Well, I can tweak the Ultrasonic sensor's sensitivity during testing and make certain it triggers the grabbing mechanism I'll design at the right time—not too soon and not too late. The Touch sensor, on the other hand, requires that my robot impacts the wall or the lever; I'd rather avoid that option. Now I just need to decide where to place the Ultrasonic sensor so it can best detect the approaching wall.

The fourth observation I've listed in the Mindstorm box reminds me that I need to take some measurements of my challenge area (described in Chapter 8). There are a lot of factors involved here that will affect your robot design: how high the ceiling is (where the string is tied to), the distance the lever is from the floor, and the distance from the ceiling to the floor. Unless you have a real chasm to test with (and I don't recommend this), you'll probably be running the challenge in a room with a real floor; you'll need to let the string hang straight down from the ceiling and attach your robot to make sure it won't scrape the floor as it swings across the room!

The final Mindstorm item involves grabbing on to the lever. All kinds of complicated grabbing mechanisms come to mind, but keeping it simple here will be the best. If I were swinging across, I'd just use my hands – wrap my fingers around the lever and hold on. So I'll try and come up with something similar for my robot.

Now it's time to take everything you've collected—Robot Description, Task List, Limitations/Constraints, and Mindstorm information—and come up with a sketch (or two or three) that represents a possible shape and design for your robot.

Sketches

What I like about this last section of the worksheet is that I've never seen two people come up with the same solution. There are always variations, even if they're slight, that make each person's robot concept unique. The idea you have in your mind for the RopeSwinger is probably nothing like the one I have developed, but they probably share some similarities.

I know that my robot needs a way to grab the lever and to release the string. I'll be using two different mechanisms here, so this will probably involve the use of two motors. I know the NXT Brick will be in there somewhere, but what about the Ultrasonic sensor? Where will I place the "hands" that will grab the lever?

I tend to draw using basic shapes like rectangles, squares, and circles, so my sketches will consist of components drawn using their most basic shapes (the grabbing mechanism, for example, is nothing but two claw shapes). Figure 6-8 shows my initial sketches for the RopeSwinger.

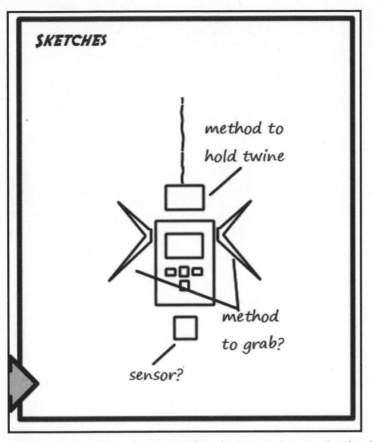

Figure 6-5. I use basic shapes to define the RopeSwinger in the Sketches area.

As you can see, I've got a few concepts to test out when I start building. I might find a way to hold on to the string but give the "grabbers" room to operate. It seems like it will be easy enough to locate the mechanism that will hold the string at the top, but I really won't know until I start building.

Should I place the Ultrasonic sensor at the top or bottom? Well, if I place the string holding mechanism at the top, that really only leaves me the bottom. But I think this will work great because when the robot begins to approach the lever, the Ultrasonic sensor will be the closest point on the robot to the wall! (As this vertical design swings towards the wall, those items near the bottom will be just slightly closer due to the arc of the swinging robot.)

I'm anxious to start building and testing, and I'm sure you are, too. Chapter 7 will show you the final design I came up with and Chapter 8 will walk you through the challenge's program. Keep reading to build my RopeSwinger, or take a giant leap and come up with your own version!

CHAPTER 7

■ ■ ■

RopeSwinger—Build It

Before you begin building the RopeSwinger, take a look at Figure 7-1. This is my version of the RopeSwinger, but you can certainly design and build your own version without going through this chapter.

Keep in mind as you build this robot that it is almost 99% symmetrical. That means that the left side (what you see in the figure) is a mirror image of what you'll see on the right side. As you're building, when you see the instructions showing some pieces inserted on the left side, sometimes you won't see the matching part(s) you should insert on the right side.

Figure 7-1. Evan's version of the RopeSwinger

73

Never Be Afraid to Experiment

I've tried to provide enough detail in each figure for you to discern what parts are used and where those parts are placed. If you find that what you're holding in your hands doesn't quite look like the picture, do the following:

1. Take a deep breath.

2. Remember this is supposed to be fun.

3. Go back to the previous step and confirm you've made it that far.

4. Look at the current step, and examine the figure's details for clues to where components should be placed. Try tricks like counting holes to determine where two or more parts connect or skipping ahead a few figures to try and see the parts from another angle.

5. When in doubt, take your best guess and move forward.

Enjoy the building process and realize that if your final bot doesn't look *exactly* like the one in this chapter, that's okay. Remember: getting the bot to work and solving the challenge is your main goal.

■ **Note** If you modify or try to create your own version of the RopeSwinger (or any other bot in this book), please take a picture and e-mail it to me. I would enjoy seeing your final bot in action. I've included my e-mail address in the Introduction.

And now, on to the construction of the RopeSwinger!

Step by Step CAD Instructions – RopeSwinger

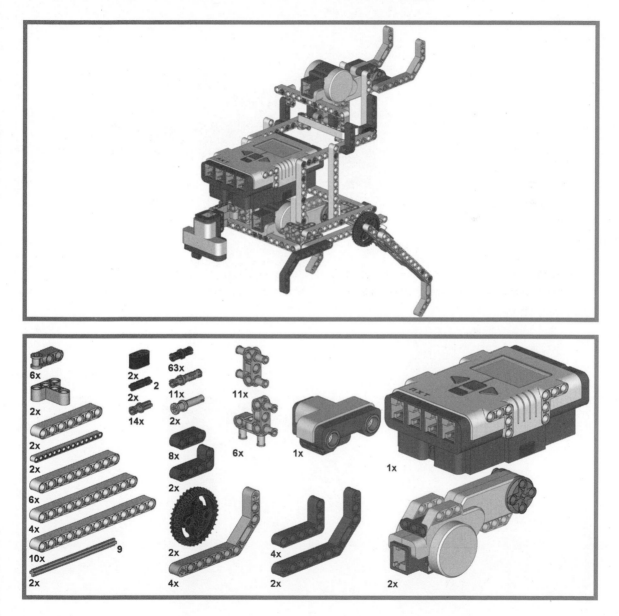

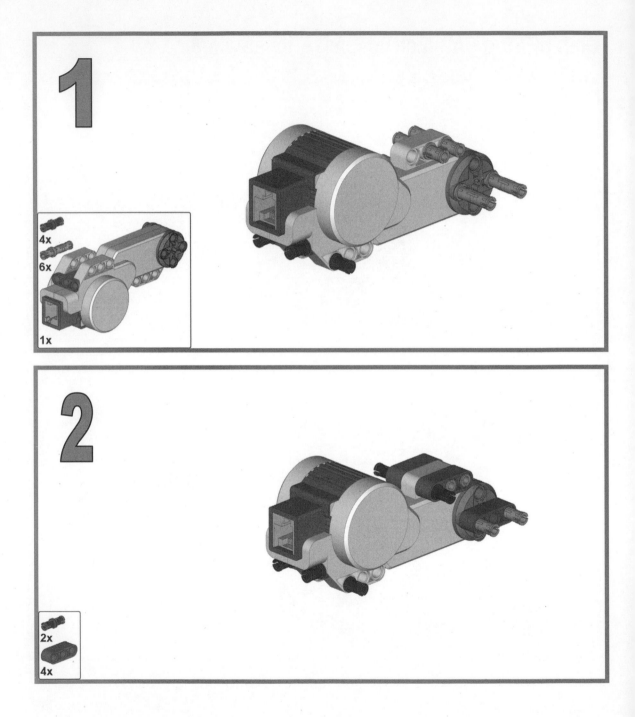

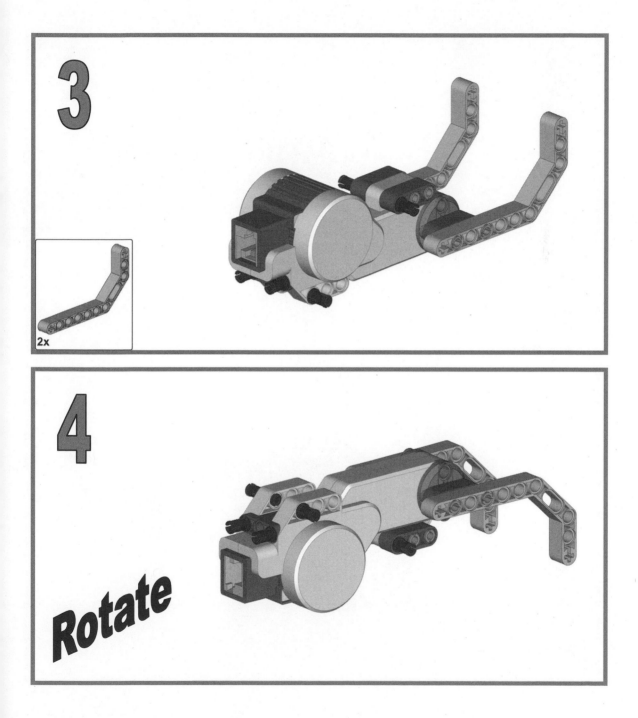

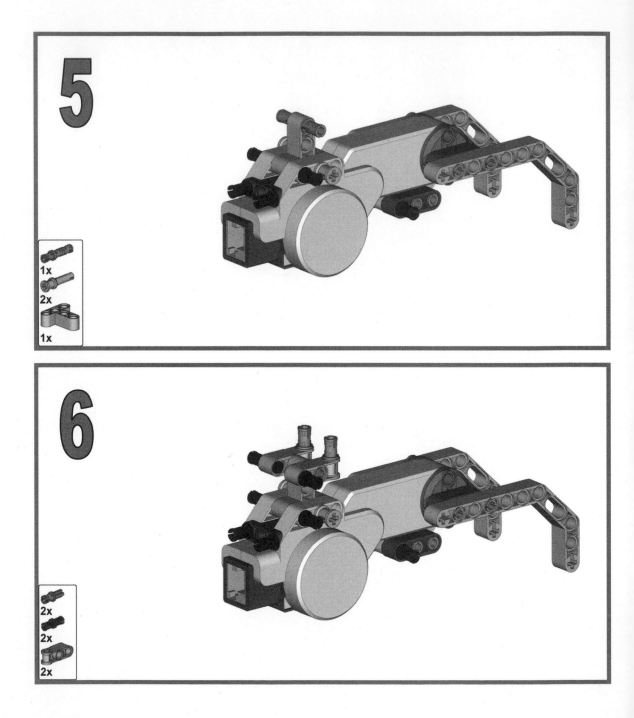

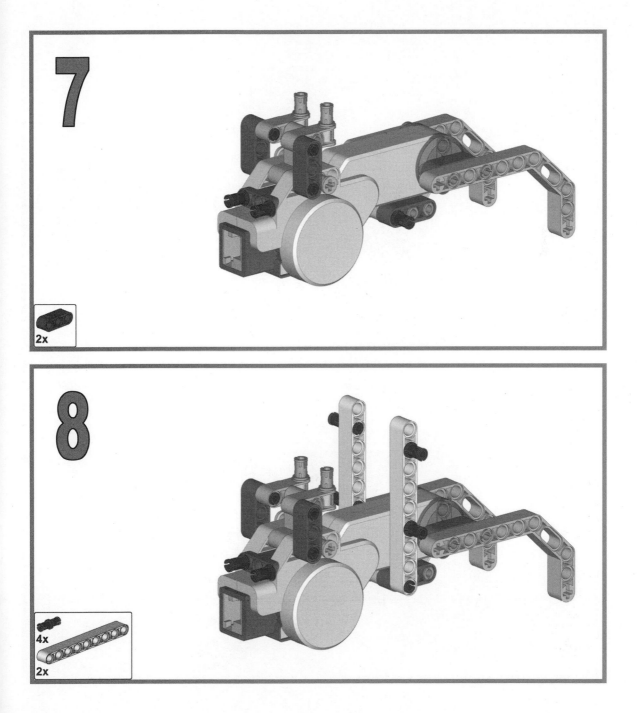

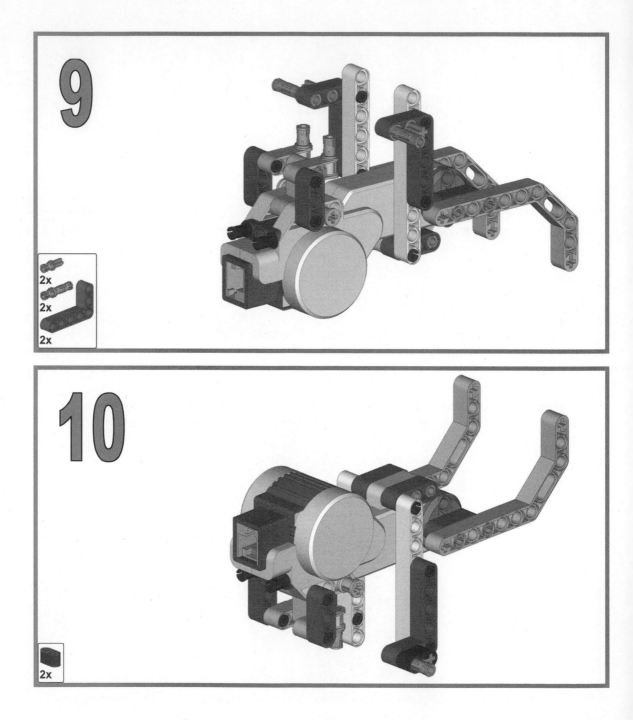

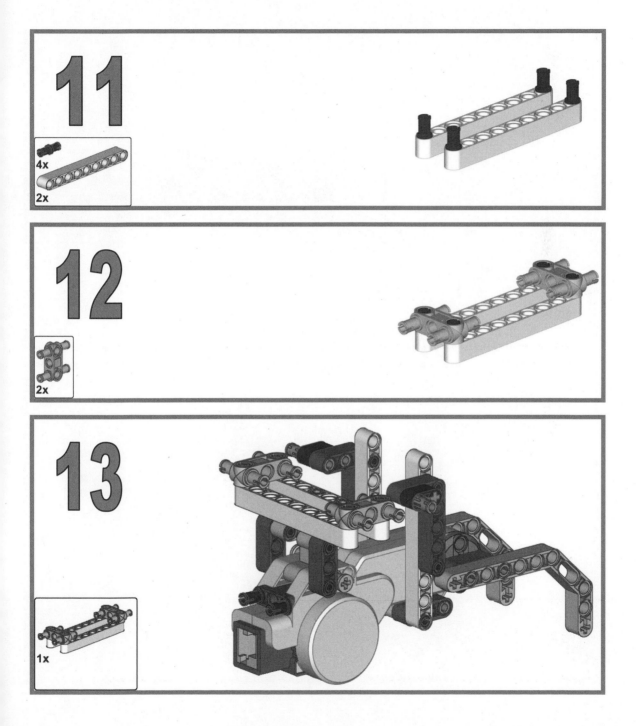

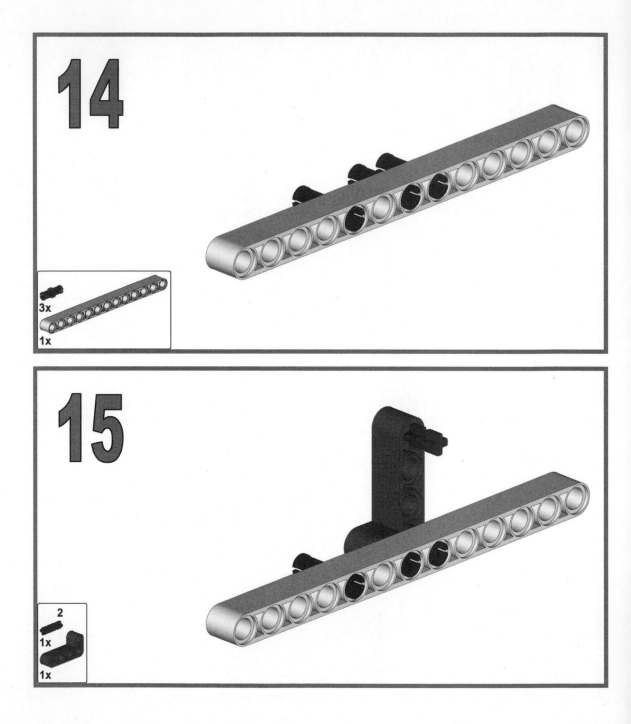

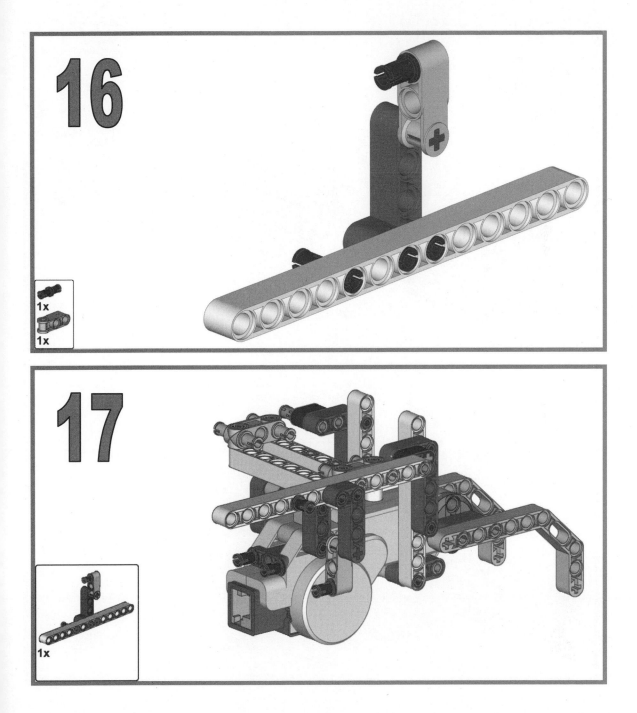

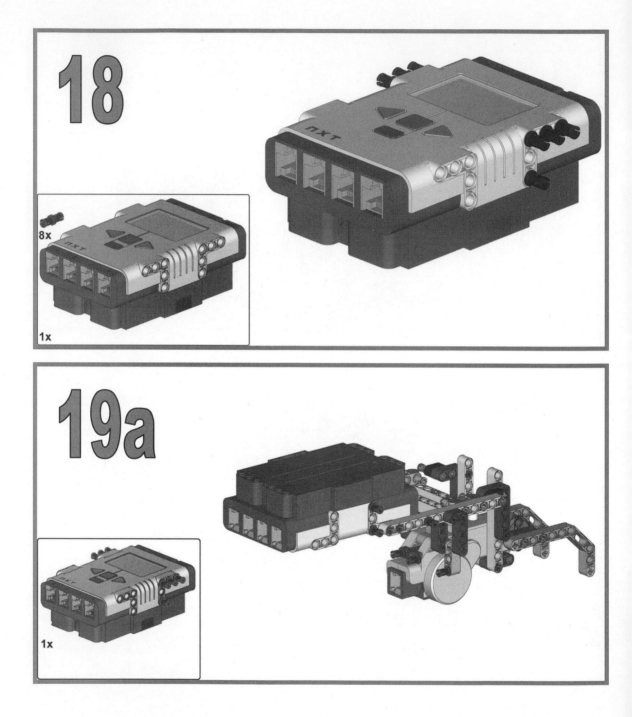

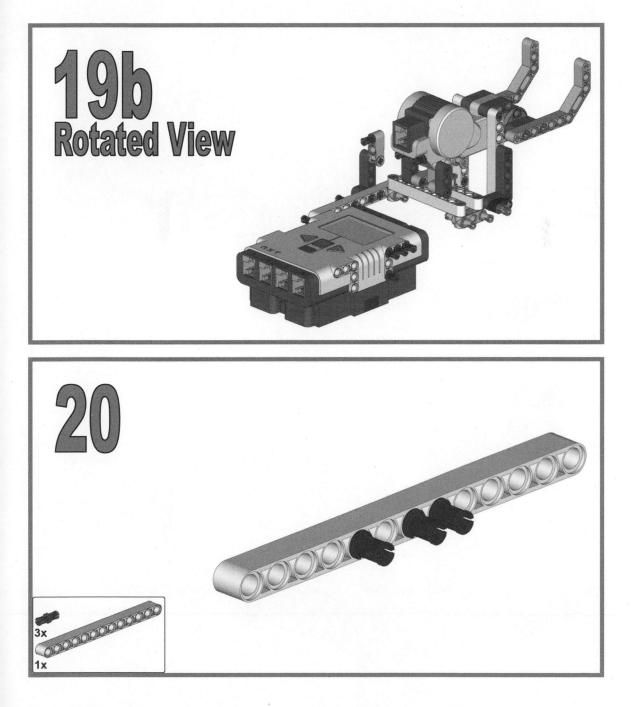

19b
Rotated View

20

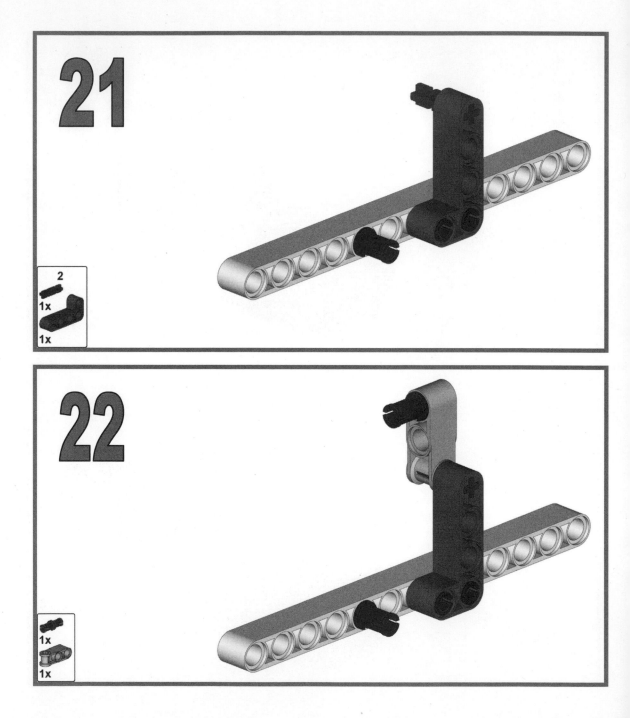

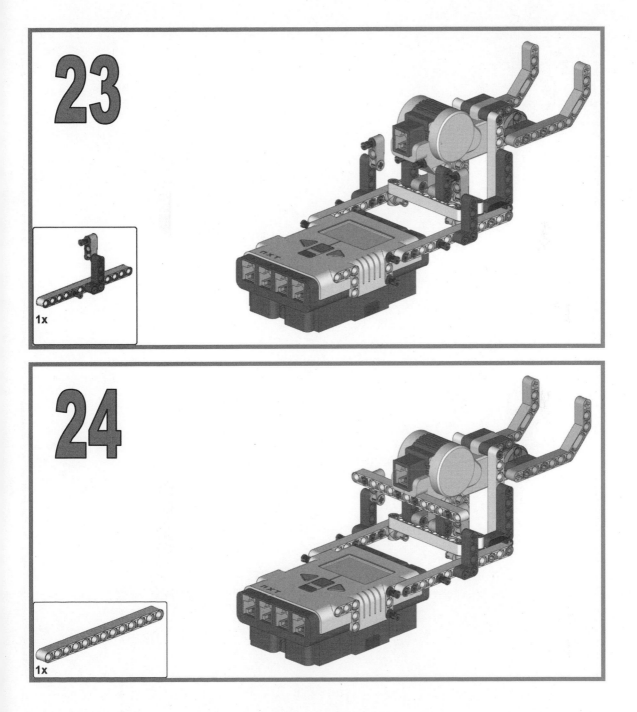

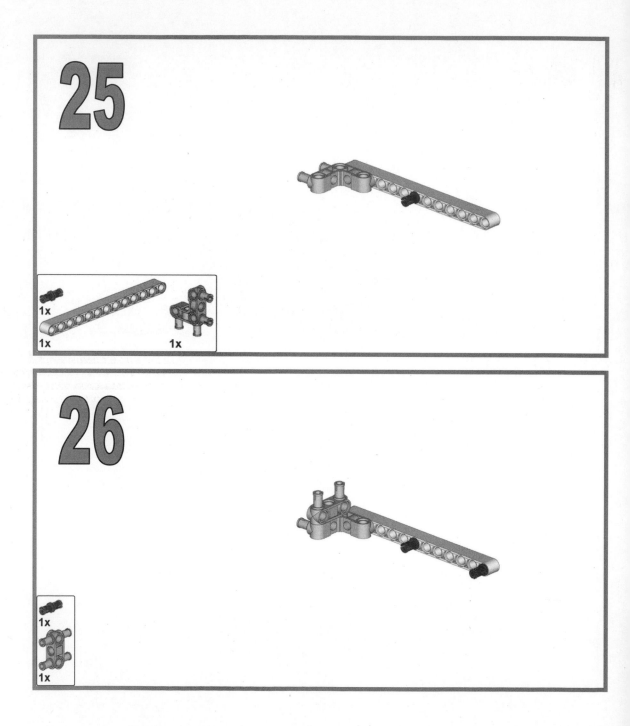

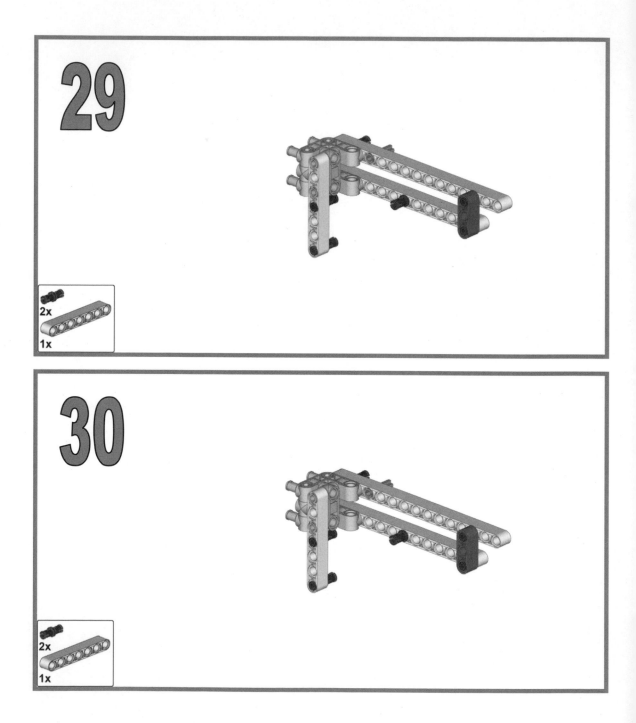

31a

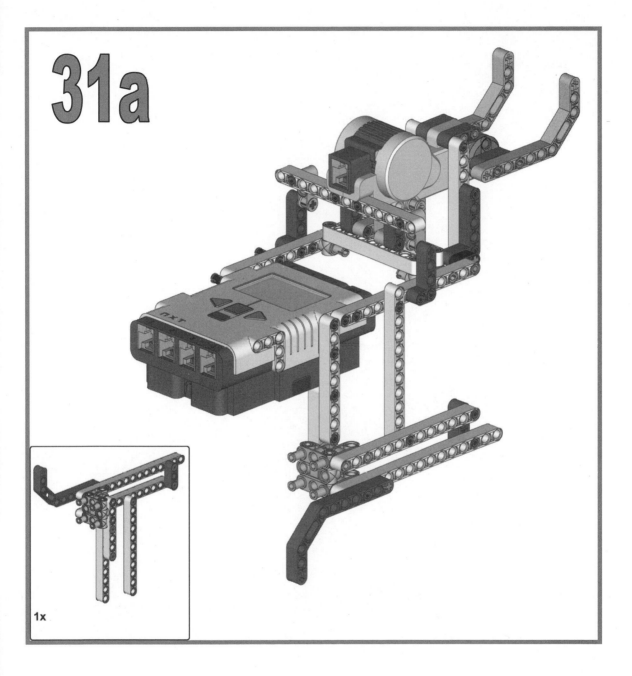

1x

31b
Rotated View

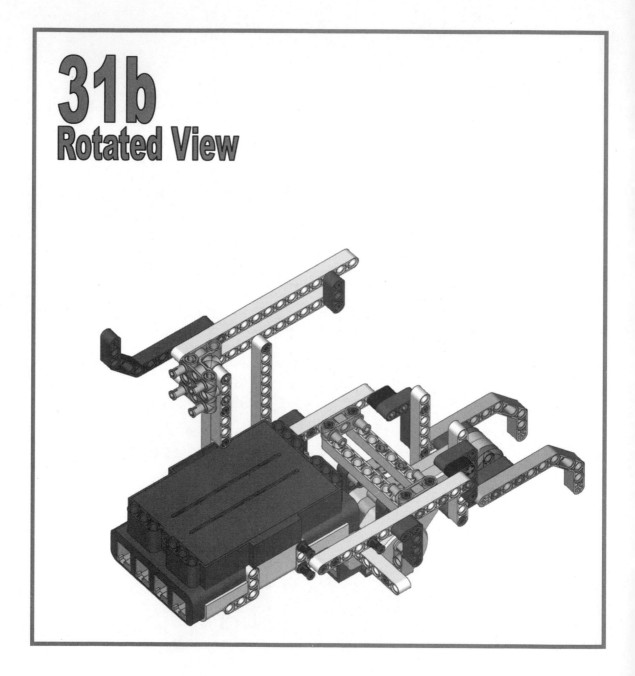

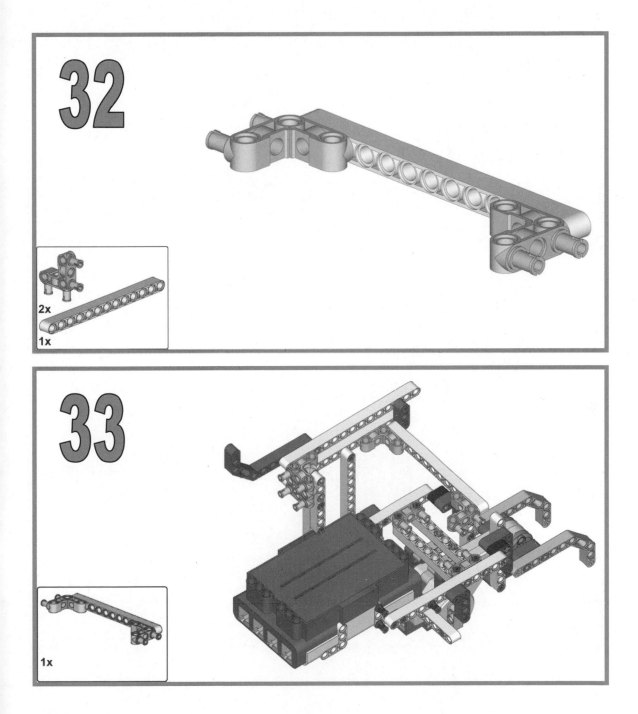

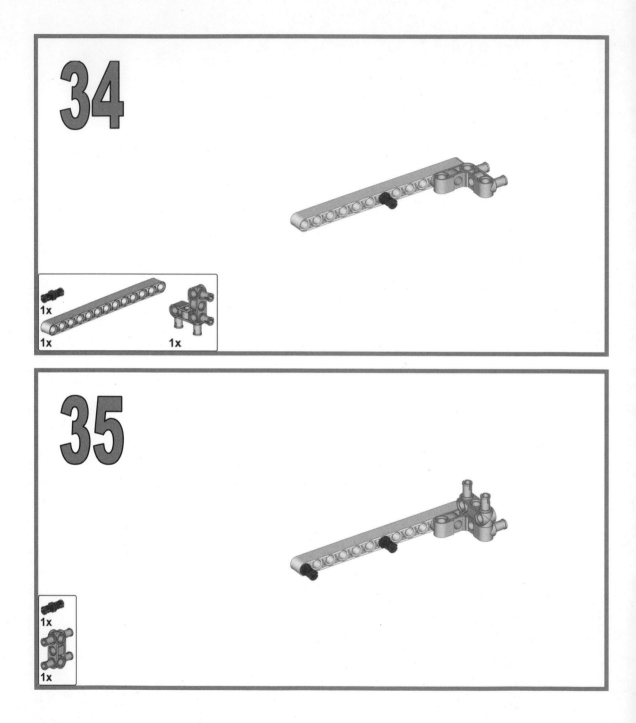

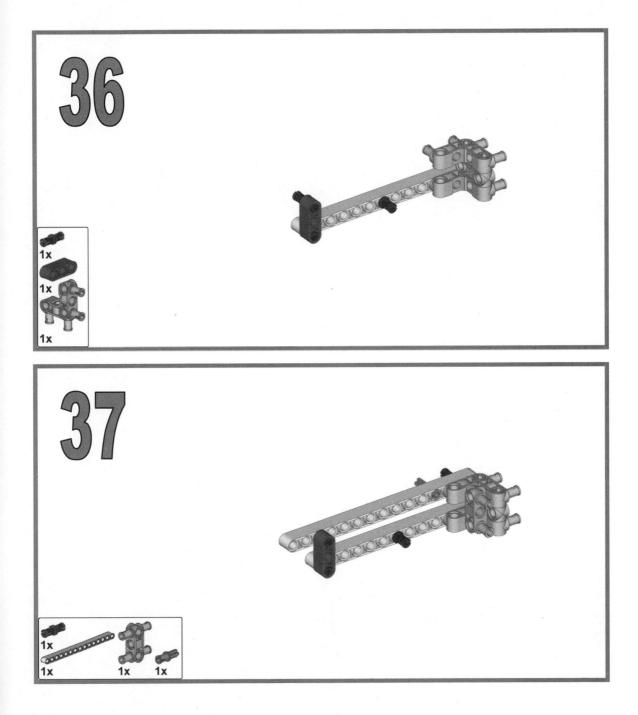

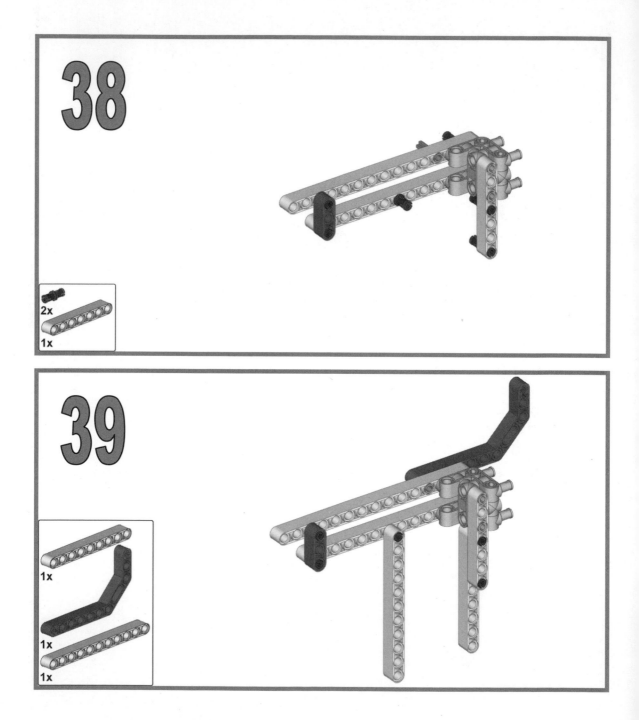

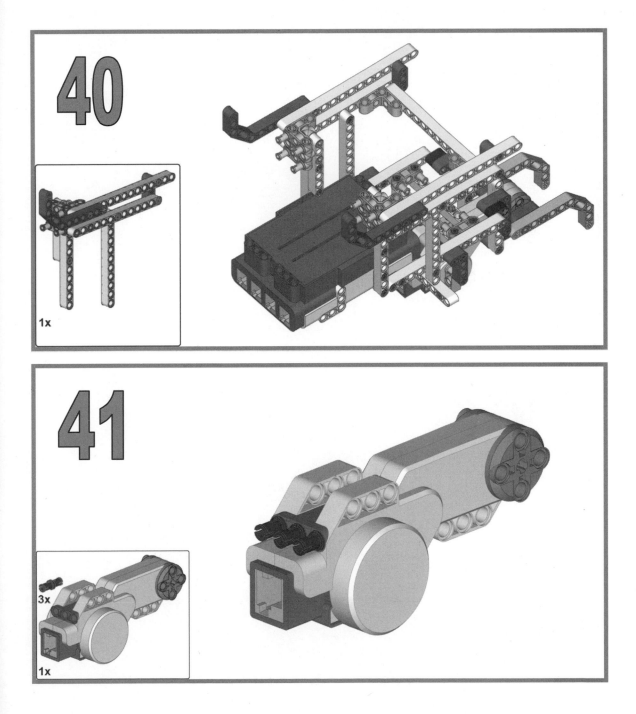

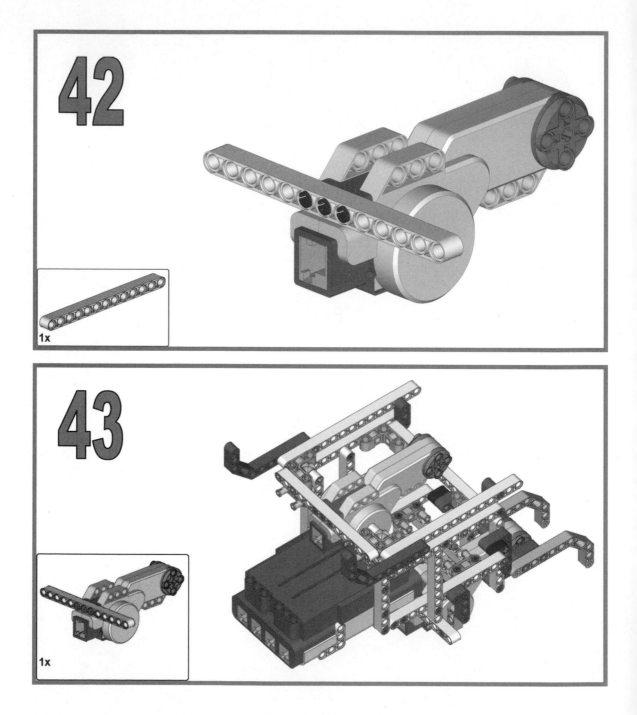

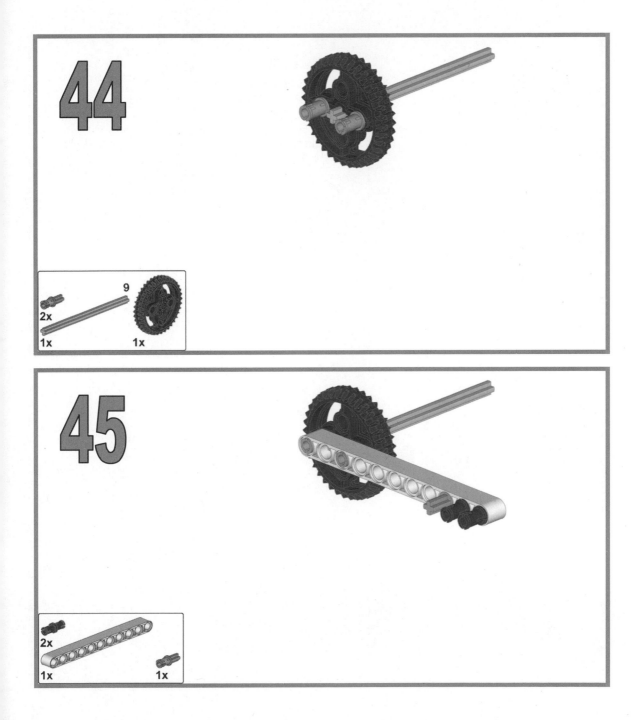

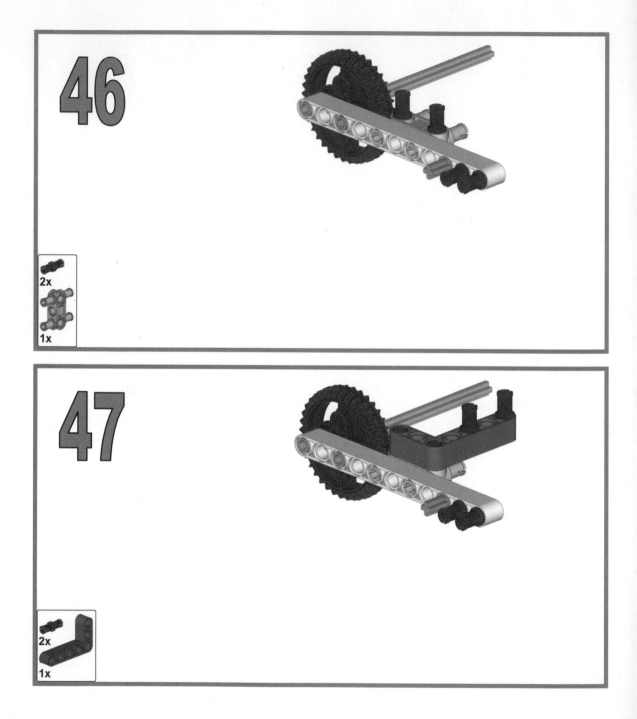

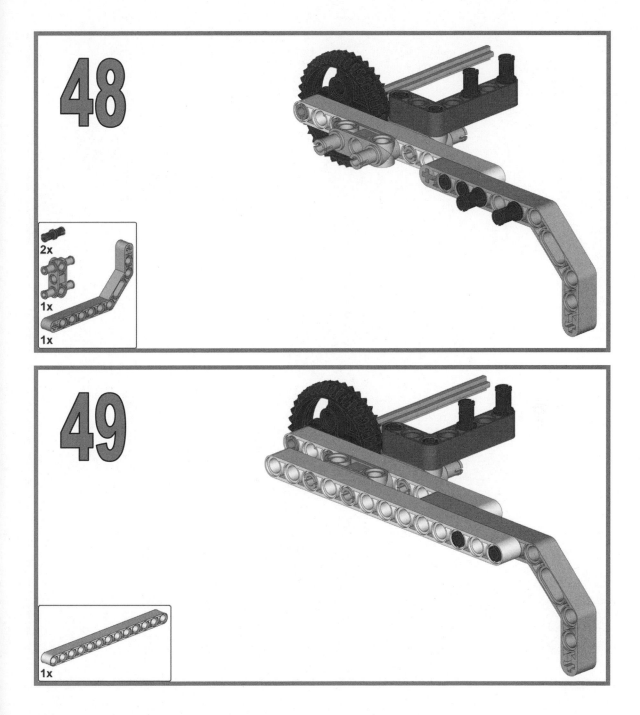

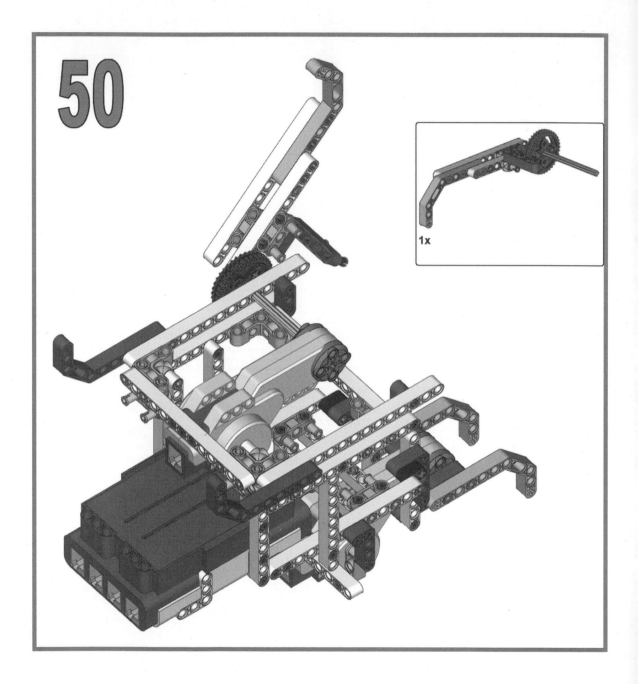

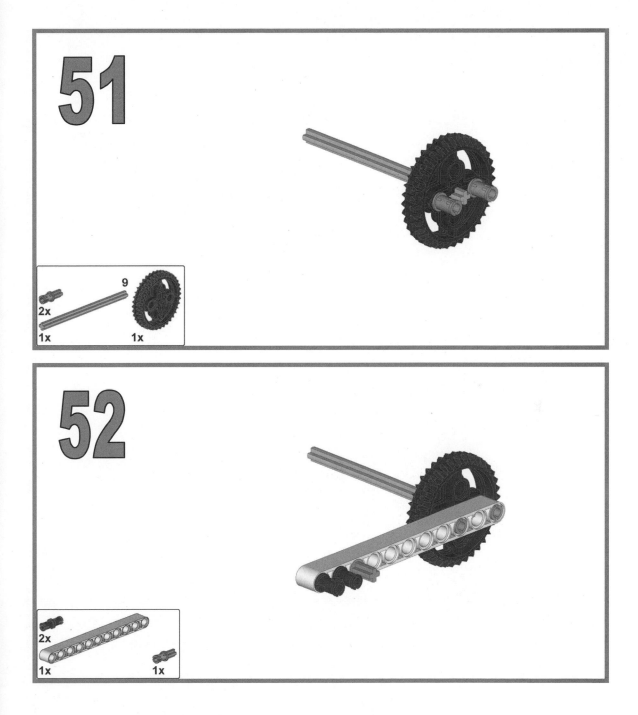

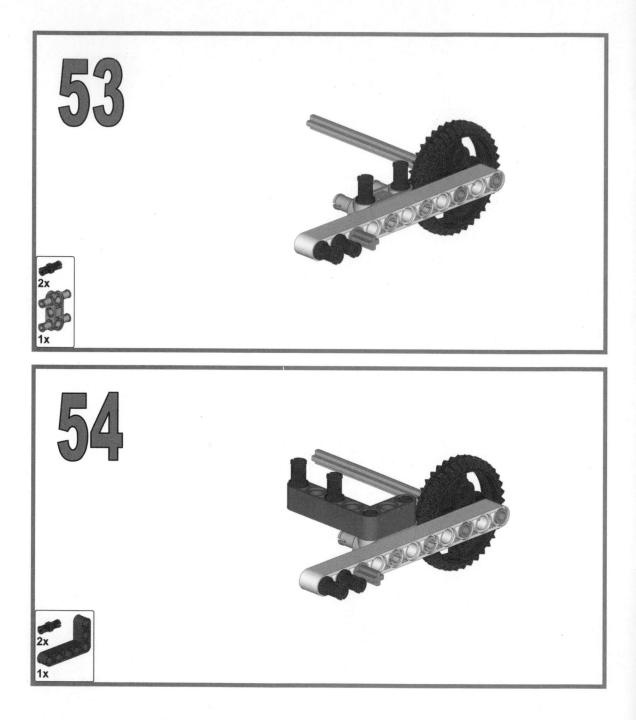

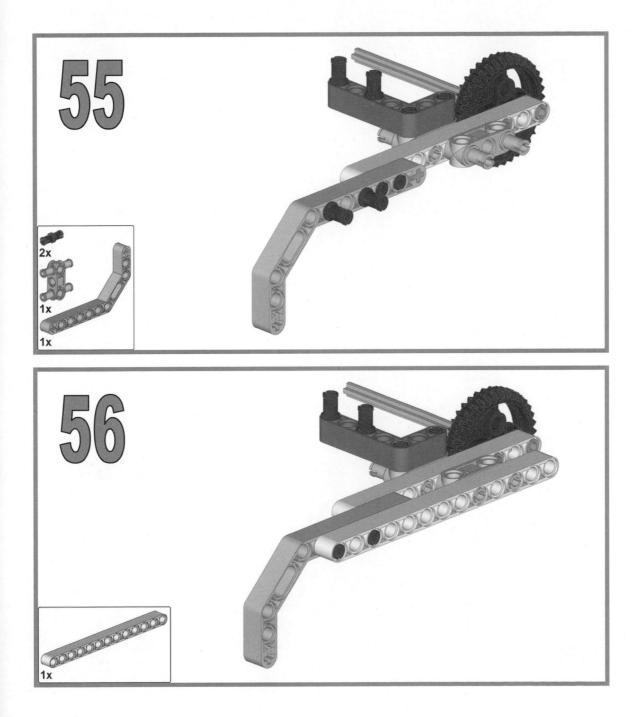

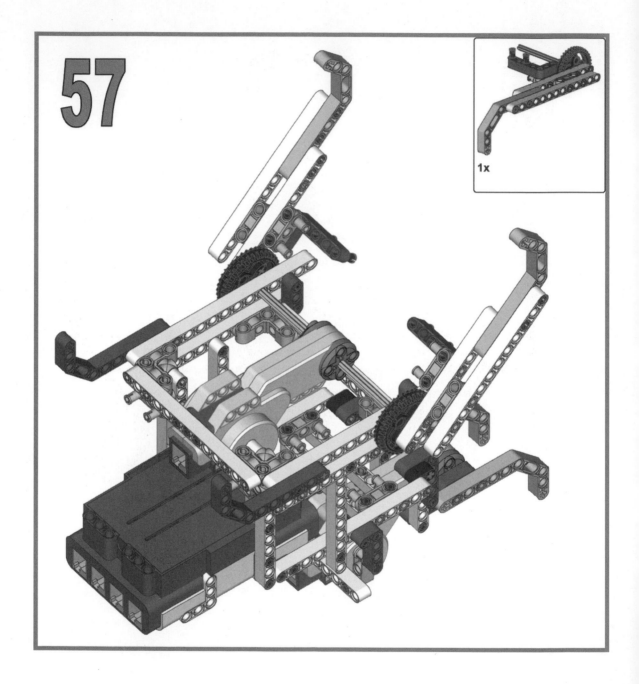

58

1x

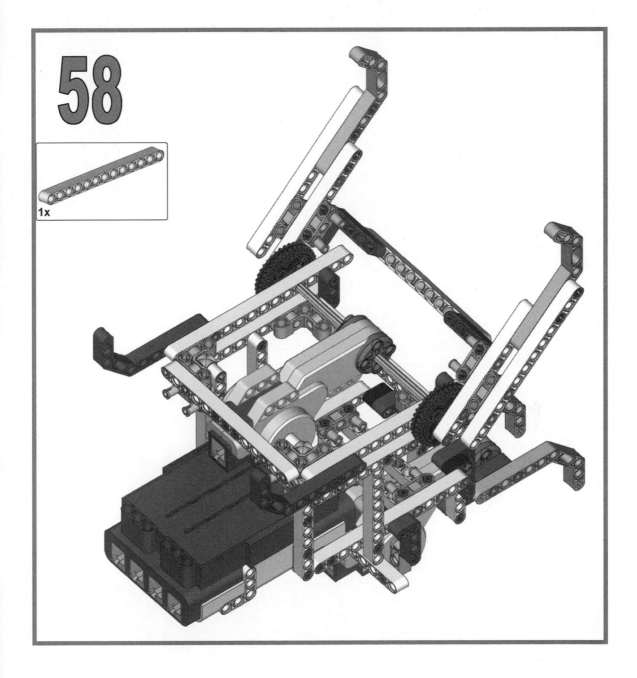

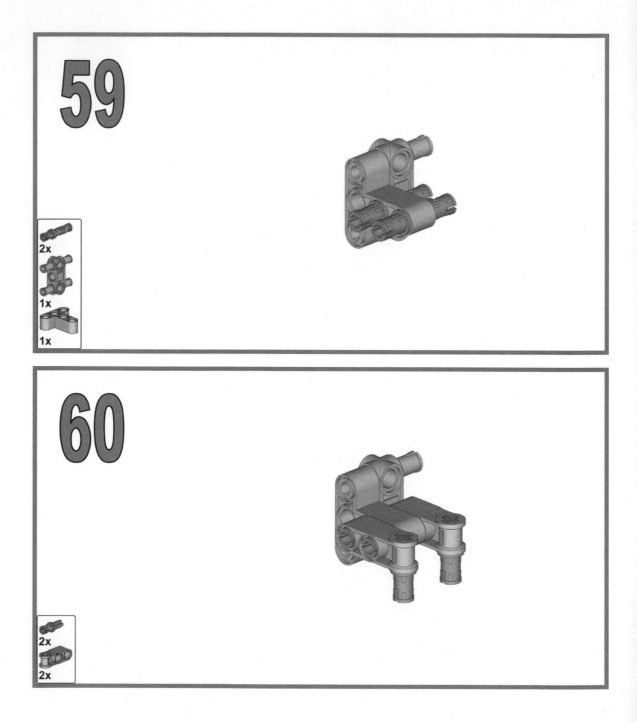

59

2x

1x

1x

60

2x

2x

61

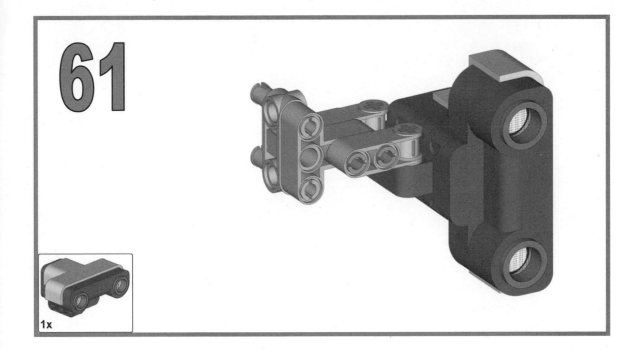

1x

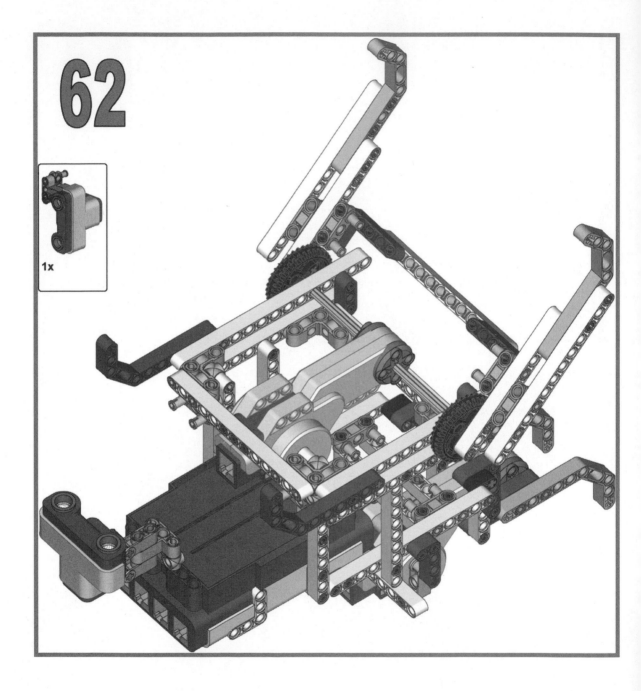

62

1x

63

Rotate

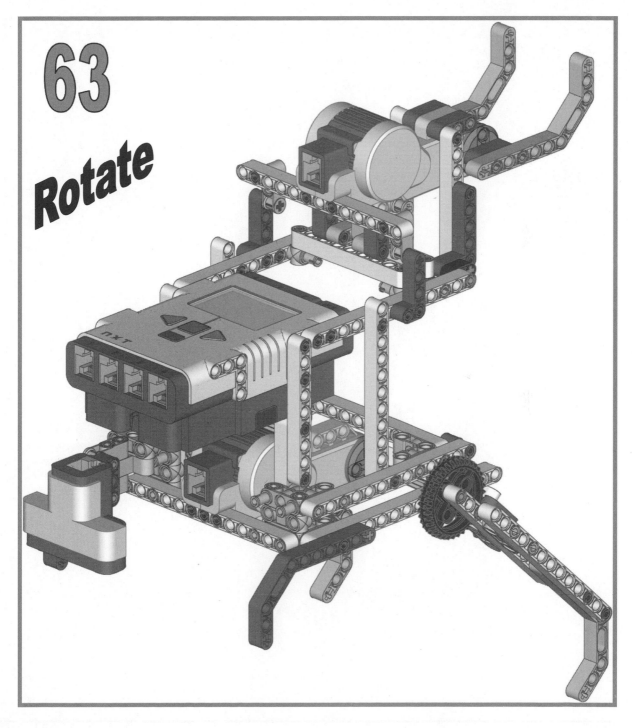

CHAPTER 8

RopeSwinger—Program It

Imagine that! A robot that crosses the room without using wheels or tracks. (If you've read The Mayan Adventure, you'll remember the StringBot crossed the room like a cable car.) You might think that the program used to get the RopeSwinger to find the lever and pull it will be complicated… but it's not. Think about it – the largest movement requires no action on the robot's part. It's simply hooked to a couple of pieces of string, pulled back, and let go! Only when it reaches the other side of the room does it really need to take action. And that's what this chapter is about; getting the RopeSwinger to find, grab, and pull that lever. Let's find out how to make that happen.

Swing Swing

I think it's a little humorous that there are really no blocks required for getting the robot to cross the room. It's all done with some string and faith in gravity. But once you pull that robot back and release it, the work starts.

What happens once you release the robot? Well, the robot needs to find the lever, and I've already decided that I'm going to use the Ultrasonic sensor instead of a Touch sensor to find it. My robot design (see Chapter 7) has the Ultrasonic sensor mounted at the bottom of the robot (when hanging from the two pieces of string I'll show you how to mount at the end of this chapter).

The Ultrasonic sensor needs to be scanning for the wall where the lever is mounted. When it detects the wall, it will then execute some programming blocks to grab the lever and release the strings. So the first thing I'll need to do is drop in a WAIT block that's configured to use the Ultrasonic sensor. You can see in Figure 8-1 that I've configured the WAIT block to break and run the next block once the Ultrasonic sensor detects something less than 20 inches in front of it.

■ **Note** How did I come up with the value of 20 inches? Testing, testing, and more testing. During the testing phase I talk about at the end of this chapter, I ran test after test to determine what the best setting was for the Ultrasonic sensor. I found that when the Ultrasonic sensor was set to 20 inches, the speed at which the "grabbers" closed down matched the swinging speed and allowed the robot to grab the lever. When the setting was 30 inches, the grabbers closed too early. When the setting was 15 inches, sometimes the grabbers closed too late. The value you set for the WAIT block will likely differ from my value.

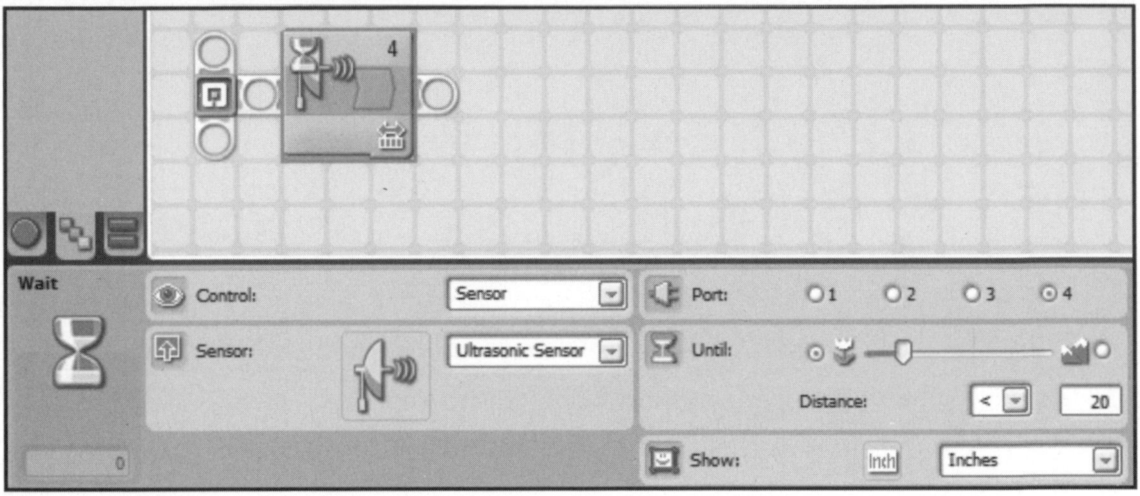

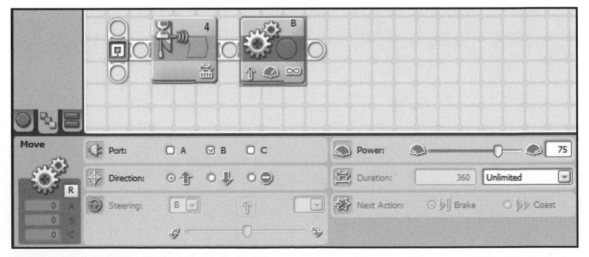

Figure 8-1. *The WAIT block will use the Ultrasonic sensor.*

Once the Ultrasonic sensor is triggered, there are two things that must occur next: grab the lever and release the strings. But we do not want these happening at exactly the same moment. So we will have to make certain to build in a small waiting period to give the robot time to grab and hold the lever and then release the strings.

First, drop in a MOVE block configured to rotate motor B with its Duration set to Unlimited, as shown in Figure 8-2. Motor B controls the grabbers that will grab and hold on to the lever.

Figure 8-2. *A MOVE block will control the grabbers.*

Because I configured the MOVE block for an Unlimited duration, the motor will continue to apply force – the robot will keep holding on to the lever until another MOVE block tells motor B to stop or the program ends.

Now that the robot has grabbed the lever, we'll need it to release the strings, but I'd like to give the robot time to grab the lever and then stop any swaying or rocking. This is easily done by dropping in a simple WAIT block and configuring it for a short amount of time as shown in Figure 8-3.

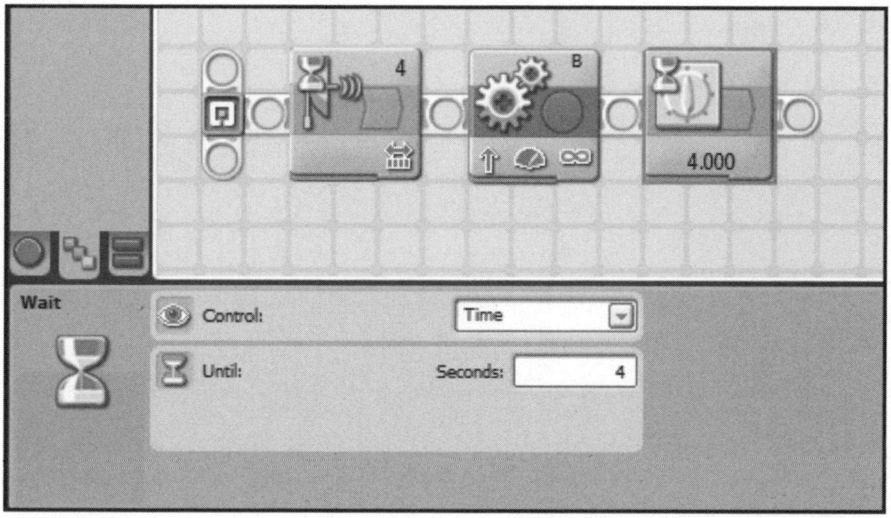

Figure 8-3. The WAIT block will allow the robot to pause before releasing the strings.

I've configured the WAIT block to pause for four seconds, but feel free to decrease or increase this during your testing phase.

And now it's time for the robot to release the strings. I need motor C to rotate just enough to allow the two eye-bolts to slip off the angled beams I used. (Figure 8-12 shows the image of the mechanism I created to hold the eye-bolts in place.)

Figure 8-4 shows the final MOVE block dropped into the program and configured.

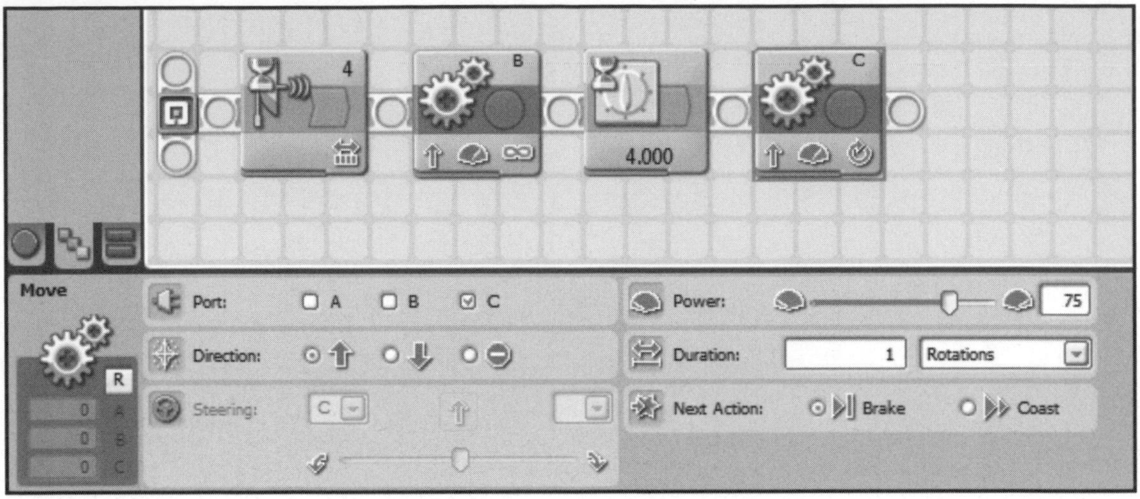

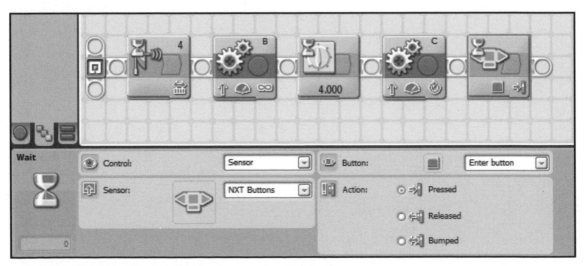

Figure 8-4. The last MOVE block will release the robot's hold on the strings.

After the strings are released, the robot's weight should be sufficient to pull the lever down. Once the lever is pulled, however, you do not want the robot to let go of the lever - a fall could cause some pieces to pop off the robot. Remember, when the program ends, power to the motors will stop – this will cause motor B to stop exerting force and the grabbers will release the lever.

To prevent this, drop in a simple WAIT block configured as shown in Figure 8-5. The WAIT block will keep running until you press the Enter button (orange button) on the NXT Brick.

Figure 8-5. This WAIT block will keep the program from ending.

And that's it! A very simple program, wouldn't you agree? You'll find as I have that sometimes the most complex robots have the simplest programs… and the easiest to build robots often require dozens and dozens of blocks to work. But that's part of the fun of programming a robot – you never know what's going to be involved until you start testing. And speaking of testing…

Pulling the Lever

This challenge was a fun one to create and setup. There are many ways you can simulate the lever, but I'm going to show you how I did it—feel free to modify it to suit your needs.

First, you need to create the lever. Take a look at Figure 8-6, which shows the final design of my lever. I'll tell you how I made it next.

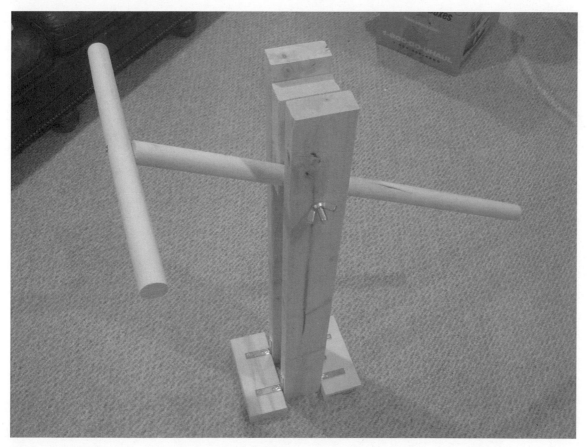

Figure 8-6. The lever used in testing my RopeSwinger

I built this device for less than $12.00. Here's the breakdown:

* One 2x4 (8' in length) cut into five pieces – two long pieces (3' in height), and three short pieces (each approximately 7" long).
* One 4' wooden dowel (1" diameter) cut into two pieces – 1-1/2' (the lever handle) and a 2-1/2' piece (the lever shaft)
* One 5" bolt (1/2" diameter)
* One ½" wing nut
* Four L-brackets.
* Two 2" wood screws
* Ten 1" wood screws

Figure 8-7 shows all the parts unassembled.

Figure 8-7. The pieces used to create the lever

First, bolt one of the 7" wood blocks to a longer block, as shown in Figure 8-8, using a single 1" wooden screw.

Use 1" wood screw to attach small block to long block

Figure 8-8. Insert the bolt that will allow the lever to swivel.

Next, clamp the second long piece to the first long piece (with short block bolted to it) and make sure ends are flush. Drill a single ½" hole through all three pieces approximately 7" from the end. You'll be inserting the 5" bolt through this hole later.

After you cut the wooden dowel, use two 2" wood screws to secure the handle to the end of the shaft. Drill a ½" hole approximately 11" from the end of the shaft, as shown in Figure 8-9.

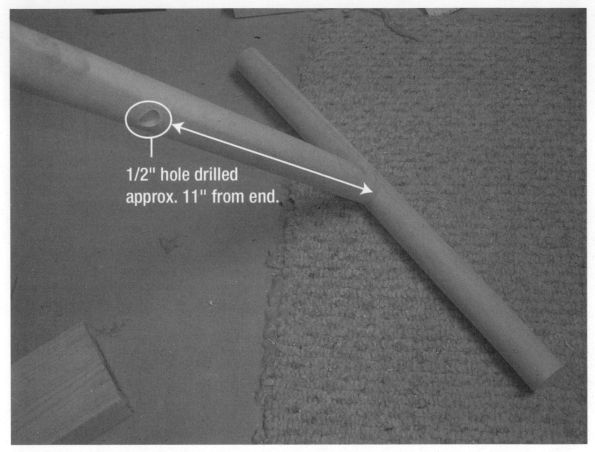

1/2" hole drilled
approx. 11" from end.

Figure 8-9. Drill a hole in the lever.

Place the lever's shaft between two long wood pieces (and the single small wood piece). Insert 5"
bolt and secure with wing nut as shown in Figure 8-10.

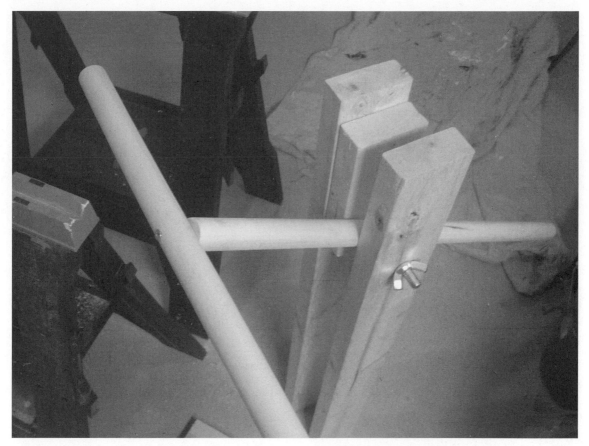

Figure 8-10. Secure the lever between two long wooden legs with bolt and wing nut.

Now attach the two remaining small wood blocks to the longer pieces using the L-brackets and eight 1" wood screws as shown in Figure 8-11.

Figure 8-11. Attach two small blocks for stability.

Place the lever device near an open doorway. I attached two pieces of string to the doorway (I used eyebolts screwed into the wood at the top of the door's frame, but you may need to improvise based on where you wish to run the challenge) as shown in Figure 8-12. You can also see that I've placed a sheet of peg board (poster board will also work) in front of the device to act as the wall. Two eye-bolts are then hot-glued to the ends of the string and I hook the eyebolts underneath motor C's "arms" – when motor C rotates, the arms will move up and release the eyebolts. If this is unclear, build the robot and I think you'll understand better how the hold-and-release mechanism works.

Figure 8-12. My testing area for the RopeSwinger.

Once you complete your testing area, you should proceed slowly and carefully by pulling your robot back to various distances to determine the best location for releasing it so it reaches the lever. Mark that spot with some tape to indicate where you need to stand when holding the robot.

■ **Note** You can perform this challenge with the robot being close or far away from the lever. Just keep in mind that the farther away you are from the lever device, the higher the ceilings you will need. A higher ceiling will allow for a longer swing time and a more challenging attempt to get the robot to accurately grab the lever.

Next, tweak the program by changing those settings (such as the Ultrasonic sensor value in the first WAIT block) that affect the grabbing of the lever and the release of the strings.

Have fun!

CHAPTER 9

Hook and Pull

Location: Southwest Guatemala

102 miles SW of Guatemala City

Coordinates: 14º 04' N / 90º 09' W

Weather Conditions: 82 degrees Fahrenheit, Humidity 60%

Day 5: King Ixtua's Treasure Repository, 8:39 a.m.

Evan's back and arms ached. He had spent hours helping his uncle's team place plywood sheets over the lowered bridge and nailing them into place. Although the wood used to make the bridge had held up well over the years, Evan's uncle was not willing to use it to cross the room. After the bridge had lowered successfully, Erin and Dr. Hicks negotiated with one of the expedition's guides to return to a nearby town and purchase the wood and other hardware.

During the three hour wait, Evan had helped Tag relocate the tripod lights into the second chamber, then he watched as Tag worked with some of the Gautemalan guides to attach a safety harness system to the ceiling of the room. Anyone crossing the bridge would also be wearing a harness; someone falling off the bridge would only fall a few feet before the safety harness system locked. Even with the safety features, however, Evan's heart still pounded at the thought of crossing that bridge.

Now, after the bridge had been reinforced, Evan watched as his uncle slowly crossed the bridge, the safety harness rope trailing behind him with only a few feet of slack.

"The bridge feels very solid," said Dr. Hicks. "There's no bounce at all."

Tag had insisted on crossing first, but Evan knew his uncle would never put one of his students in danger until he had first tested the bridge himself. Erin had her hand on Evan's shoulder; he winced as her grip hardened.

"Ow… ow…," Evan muttered. "Steel grip you've got there."

"Oops. Sorry," said Erin, letting go of his shoulder. "Years of rock climbing."

"Don't worry," replied Tag. "That harness sysem is top of the line. He could jump off there and it would catch him in a split second."

"I don't want any of you testing that theory," Dr. Hicks called back. He had reached the opposite side of the room and stepped off the bridge. He walked over to Evan's robot, which was still clinging to the lever. "Evan, your robot looks to be in one piece."

Evan smiled. He had been worried that the robot might fall or slide off the lever and break apart, but it hadn't. Instead, the robot's grippers had tightened around the handle and, after releasing the two pieces of rope, its weight had pulled the lever slowly towards the ground. A loud cracking sound was followed by the wooden bridge lowering slowly and then resting on the stone pedestals.

Dr. Hicks undid the safety harness. "Tag, go ahead and pull the harness back across. I'd like Erin next, then Evan."

"Got it," replied Tag. He pulled on a small nylon tether attached to the harness and Evan watched as it swung across the pit and into Tag's hands. "Okay, Erin. In you go."

"Erin, please bring over another flashlight and your camera," said Evan's uncle. "Evan, when you come over, bring your flashlight."

A few minutes, later Evan was breathing hard. Erin had crossed easily enough, but now Evan was only halfway across the bridge and he stopped.

"Evan, it's okay," said his uncle. "Tag's got you—you're not going to fall. Just look at me. Keep walking across."

Evan took a deep breath and blew it out. "I'm wearing a harness. I'm wearing a harness…" He began to walk across the bridge again.

"That's it, buddy," said Tag. "Ten more feet."

Evan wished for a moment that he was more like his robot, showing no fear as it swung across the deep chasm. Three more feet, he thought.

Uncle Phillip reached out a hand and grabbed Evan's forearm. "Got you," he said. "Good job."

Evan smiled weakly. "I mean it—I really *really* hate heights."

Uncle Phillip laughed. "Got it, nephew. Let's hope that's the last of Tupaxu's pit traps, okay?"

Evan nodded slowly.

Dr. Hicks turned back to Tag. "Tag, we're going to check out what's behind the door. Once the all-clear is called, we'll get one of the guides to come down and get you across, okay?"

"Sounds good, Dr. Hicks," replied Tag. "I'm not going anywhere. Just be careful."

Dr. Hicks nodded and turned to Evan and Erin.

"Okay, let's see what's behind this door."

Watch Your Step

Evan was disappointed. Expecting a large, cavernous room to be greeting the team, he instead shone his flashlight down a dusty, dark hallway (see Figure 9-1). The passageway was a little more than five feet tall; Uncle Hicks would have to walk hunched over, but Evan and Erin wouldn't have a problem. At the end of the thirty-foot hallway was a partially open wooden door. Whatever was beyond the door, however, the weak light from three flashlights was not enough to illuminate it.

"It looks like the door to the third chamber has already been opened," said Erin.

Uncle Phillip frowned. "Maybe… maybe not. There doesn't appear to be a handle or lock on the door."

"Maybe pulling the lever opened this door, too," said Evan.

"Let's take this slow," said Dr. Hicks. "Erin, you're behind me, then Evan. When we reach the door, I'll need all of your flashlights. Step where I step, please."

Evan walked slowly behind Erin. He watched as his uncle examined the stones set in the floor, possibly looking for traps. He focused on stepping exactly where Erin was stepping, hoping she was doing the same with his uncle's footsteps.

Halfway down the hall, Evan stopped. The dust was tickling his nose. He squeezed his eyes tight and clamped his teeth. But it didn't help.

"Ah… Ah…Achooooo!"

Evan's sneeze echoed in the tight hallway and he lost his balance for just a moment. His left foot lifted and then returned to the floor. He felt the stone below his foot sink and heard the sound of stone scraping on stone.

"Evan! Do not move that foot!" yelled Uncle Phillip.

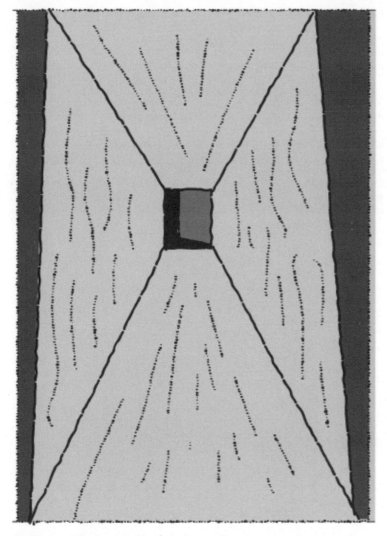

Figure 9-1. The long hallway isn't as safe as it appears.

Tricky Tupaxu

"It's a press-and-release trigger," said Dr. Hicks, after spending almost twenty minutes examining the stone and surrounding area. "I missed it myself, Evan."

Sweat was running into Evan's eyes, even though the temperature in the hallway was cool.

"My leg is starting to shake, Uncle," said Evan.

"That's okay," replied his uncle. "Just don't lift your foot. Lock your knee and put some of your weight on your other leg if you need to. Erin should be back any minute."

Evan shook his head. "I'm sorry, Uncle Phillip. I should have been more careful."

"Look at me, Evan. This is not a problem. We'll fix it and then we'll keep moving forward, okay? Here comes Erin now."

Evan heard a banging noise behind him but couldn't turn to look.

"How ya doing, Evan?" asked Erin. "Miss me?"

Evan gave a weak smile to his uncle. "What took you so long?" he asked.

Erin's hand appeared over Evan's shoulder, handing a saw to his uncle. "I've got a five foot piece of two-by-four and a few smaller pieces of plywood," Evan heard her say.

"Okay, Evan, here's what we're going to do. Whatever trap Tupaxu created here will only be triggered if that stone is released. Erin is going to wedge this two-by-four between the ceiling and the stone, okay? Try and scoot your foot just a few inches to the left or right without releasing the pressure."

As Evan moved his foot to the right, he watched as Erin place the wooden beam to the left of his foot.

"Can you move your body a little to the right, too?" asked Uncle Phillip.

"I think so," replied Evan. He winced as he moved slightly.

Erin had the wooden beam pointed almost directly up towards the hallway's ceiling. "It looks like about one inch of clearance at the top," said Erin.

Uncle Phillip crouched and began to saw a small piece of thin plywood. "It's going to take a few pieces, I think."

A few minutes later, Evan watched as his uncle wedged the small cut pieces between the top of the two-by-four beam and the ceiling.

"Erin, head back to the first chamber. Evan, I'm going to place my foot over yours, okay? I want you to pull your foot out and go back to the first chamber. Do it now. No arguments."

Evan nodded and pulled his foot away. The wooden beam appeared to be holding the stone, but Uncle Phillip slid his foot into the spot where Evan's foot had been.

"Go now," said Uncle Phillip. "I'm coming behind you in a few seconds."

Evan turned and walked quickly back to the first chamber. He joined Erin and they both watched as Evan's uncle slowly removed his foot. The wooden beam appeared to be holding down the stone.

Uncle Phillip quickly exited the hallway and rejoined the team. "Okay, that was a good lesson for all of us," he said. "Tupaxu knew a monkey's weight wouldn't trigger that stone. We're going to have to be more careful about examining everything as we move forward."

Evan nodded. "Everything."

Uncle Phillip smiled. "I'm going back in to examine the entire hallway. Erin, let me borrow your flashlight—mine's not bright enough. And Tag, I could use some of those small marker flags. Everybody stay here."

The Four Warriors

Thirty minutes later, Uncle Phillip called the team back into the long hallway. He had placed small flags over two more stones. "Those are all I've found," he yelled back to Evan and Erin. "Just step around them and come see this."

Tag had finally joined them and he handed Evan and Erin each a new flashlight. "I hope your uncle found all the traps," he said. Tag had a larger battery-powered tripod flashlight slung over his back.

Evan nodded. "Me, too. I've had enough traps for one day."

Evan, Tag, and Erin joined Dr. Hicks at the end of the hallway.

Dr. Hicks pushed the wooden door open and walked in. "It's safe," he said. "I've checked out the entire room. Just don't approach any of the four colored doors yet."

As Evan joined the team in the room, he watched as Tag set up his tripod flashlight in the far left corner. Tag flipped a switch; the brightness was a shock, and Evan quickly shut his eyes.

After his eyes adjusted to the intense white light, Evan walked to the center of the room where his uncle and Erin were standing.

"Wow," he said. "That is awesome."

"Unbelievable," said Erin.

Evan's uncle just nodded.

The first thing Evan noticed was the four large statues of Mayan warriors along the back wall. Each statue stood approximately seven feet in height, and it looked like they were carved from the actual stone that formed the walls; each warrior appeared to be jumping out of the wall to block a door to their left.

Tag pointed. "Look at the necklaces," he said.

Evan looked closer. Each warrior was adorned with a feathered headdress and a few tattered bits of clothing, but the twinkling of gold and jewels around each statue's neck was unmistakeable.

"Hey! Come look at this," said Erin. She had moved towards the left wall and was standing on her toes, shining her flashlight into a square hole cut into the wall.

Evan followed his uncle to the wall. An opening in the wall, maybe one foot square in size, was cut into the wall at about eye-level for Dr. Hicks.

Evan watched as his uncle shone his flashlight into the hole, twisting his head and neck left and right to get a better look at whatever was in there. Twice he watched his uncle turn around, look at the statues, and then return to the hole.

Finally, Uncle Phillip backed away from the hole and turned around.

"Well, team," he said, "it looks like we're going to have to play a game of 'Let's Make a Deal' and pick a door."

Hooks and Doors

A few hours later, Evan sat down in the center of the room with Tag and his uncle. Erin had been sent back to the campsite to do some special research.

"Okay, Tag, lead us through your sketch here," said Uncle Phillip.

Tag pointed down at one of his drawings. "There are four doors on the back wall here, each one guarded by a warrior – Yulaxa, Tilamasi, Munala, and Ranopa. Their names are engraved at the base of each statue."

Uncle Phillip nodded. "Yes, these were four of King Ixtua's most honored warrior priests assigned to Tupaxu as bodyguards. He wrote about them in some of his scrolls."

Tag pointed to his second drawing (Figure 9-2). "Here, inside the one-foot square cut into the wall, are four small hooks. Each hook has a colored band painted on the floor in front of it and is approximately twelve inches above the floor. Above the hooks is a small box. I have no idea what's in the box or how to open it," replied Tag. "The dimensions of this small area are three feet deep, four feet wide, and three feet tall."

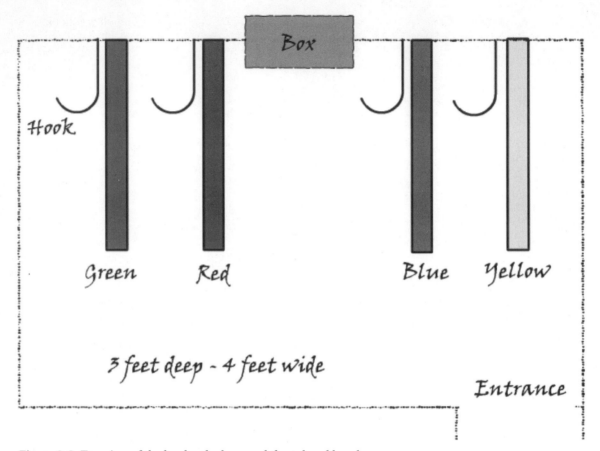

Figure 9-2. Top view of the hooks, the box, and the colored bands

"My best guess," said Dr. Hicks, "is that each of these hooks will open one of those doors. Three of the doors are traps, and one is the real thing. But which one?"

"I think I know."

Erin walked through the entry door. She was carrying a small scroll and took a seat on the ground. "Let me show you."

Unrolling the scroll, Erin pointed to some fading Mayan glyphs. "None of the scrolls we recovered from King Ixtua's library mention this room. But I did find this scroll, written by Tupaxu. This is his seal here."

Evan could see a small symbol in the lower left corner of the scroll.

"The scroll talks about how Tupaxu planned to have the four warrior priests protect the king's treasure. Here are the two symbols I want you to pay attention to. This one is the symbol for royalty. It's a variation, and it's King Ixtua's symbol. And the one next to it here," Erin indicated with her finger, "represents the royal color. Red."

"But could it really be that easy?" asked Dr. Hicks.

Tag shrugged. "Well, choosing a door at random only gives us a twenty-five percent chance of success. I agree with Erin… red sounds like the best choice. I could easily rig up a small bit of wood with a ring on the end to pull the red hook."

"I agree," said Evan's uncle. "But it's still too risky for anybody to stay in here and pull that hook. What if the red hook is the wrong one? We don't know what pulling the wrong hook will do."

Evan glanced again at Tag's sketch. *A few feet into the room, turn left, pull the ring. How hard could that be*, he wondered.

"I think I have an idea…"

Evan's Solution

"I like it," said Uncle Phillip, inspecting the small robot. "None of us are in danger, and we can easily retrieve the robot before pulling the hook."

Evan smiled. "All I need is a metal ring of some sort with some twine or string tied to it. The robot is ready to go."

Tag rummaged in his backpack. "I'll have to go back for the ring, but here's the twine. That's over fifty feet, I think. It should be more than enough for us to stand outside the room and pull it."

Uncle Phillip patted Evan on the back. "Nice work, Evan. Now, let's see if we can get that red hook pulled and open the right door."

The story continues in Chapter 13…

■ ■ ■

CHAPTER 10

RingTosser—Design and Planning

Once again, you're faced with building a robot that must be able to do multiple jobs to accomplish a challenge. Finding a wall, locating a specific color, and placing a ring in a specific location—it's a lot for one robot to do! But don't stress—the Design Journal worksheet will help you to get a grasp on all the challenges and what they'll require in terms of building and programming.

The RingTosser

Write **RingTosser** in the Robot Name box on a blank Design Journal worksheet, or create your own name for the robot. The name can be very descriptive, or not—the real information on what this robot is all about will be contained in the Robot Description.

■ **Note** There are blank Design Journal worksheets in the back of this book. If you need more pages, feel free to make photocopies of the Design Journal worksheet or visit the Apress Web site to download the page in PDF format.

The Robot Description

When writing my Robot Description, I try to keep it simple. I imagine myself hitching a ride on my robot and observing everything that needs to be done. I don't want to get too detailed here—I'll save that for the Task List section. Instead, I want to just try and get two to four sentences that give the simplest explanation for what the robot will be doing.

You don't have to know which sensors you'll be using, how many motors, or even how the robot will move around. Keep asking yourself the question, "What is this robot supposed to do?" and use the Robot Description box to write in your response. You can see what I put down for my Robot Description in Figure 10-1.

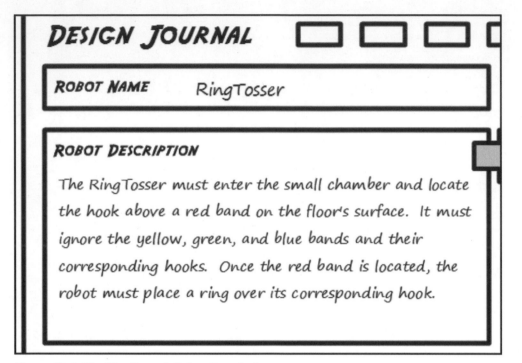

Figure 10-1. The RingTosser's Robot Description.

I have yet to find anyone who has written a robot description identical to mine; no two are ever the same. But you should find a few similarities between your description and mine. Did you make note that the robot is supposed to be looking for the red band? Did you also figure out that it simply needs to ignore any other colors it finds? All that matters is finding the red band; once the robot finds it, it can complete the second part of its job—hooking a ring on to the hook. Notice that my description is not extremely complicated or detailed at this point. I'm just getting a basic understanding of what the robot will be trying to accomplish.

My Robot Description is specific about two items, however—detecting color and placing a ring. Everything else at this point—how the robot will move and how it will find the color and the hook—is just details that we'll begin to address now, starting with the Task List.

The Task List

The Task List, for me, is sometimes easy to complete and sometimes difficult. It all depends on how much thought I put into the Robot Description. As I picture myself riding along with the robot, I start to think about things such as obstacles it might encounter, objects it may need to move, pull, or try to find. Usually the first task is very easy—something like "Enter the chamber." It doesn't get simpler than that, right?

The Task List continues to be the most important section on the Design Journal worksheet; the tasks you list here will help you later in the programming stages of your robot design. You can see my tasks listed in Figure 10-2. Don't worry if your list doesn't match mine exactly—you may very well have a different method for finding the red band and hooking the ring. But let's walk through my list quickly and see what's in store for the RingTosser.

TASK LIST

1. Enter the chamber
2. Move forward until wall detected
3. Turn left
4 Move forward
5. Scan for red band
6. Stop when red band located
7. Turn right
8. Move forward until wall detected
9. Reverse short distance
10. Place ring on hook

Figure 10-2. The RingTosser's Task List identifies key movements or actions.

After I start the program and release the robot, ideally I want it to be able to line up as perfectly as possible to the hook above and in front of the red band. To do this, I'd like my robot to make as many 90 degree turns (left or right) as possible. So, I've decided to let my robot roll forward along the right wall until it bumps the back wall. Once that wall is detected, I want the robot to stop and turn left. At this point, the robot will be ready to start scanning the colors on the floor.

As it moves forward, it will either find a red band or one of a different color. I want my robot to ignore anything other than red… but once it finds red, it needs to stop and turn right. Now it should be facing the hook.

Right now, I'm not certain how I'm going to get my robot to place the ring on the hook, but I do want to make certain that the robot is close enough to the wall to perform this action. So, I'll have the robot roll forward until the wall is detected. Once it bumps the wall, I'll have it stop, roll back a small distance, and get ready to place the ring.

Once the ring is placed, the robot can either stay where it is or find its way out of the room. I didn't add those steps because at this point, if the ring is hooked, the robot's job is really done. (Feel free, however, to add some tasks to have it exit the area and get back to you safely.)

Limitations and Constraints

As you build and program the RingTosser, you need to always keep in mind any limitations or constraints placed on the robot. That's easy enough! First, the entrance to the small challenge area is a square that's one foot tall by one foot wide. This is important because if your robot is too big, it won't fit through the opening. (This doesn't prevent you from inserting the robot sideways or at an angle… but if the robot is too wide or tall, no amount of twisting and turning will get it in there. Of course, you could always build the robot inside the challenge area… not a good idea, though.)

Figure 10-3 shows what I wrote down in the Limitations/Constraints box. While I don't expect my robot to be taller than three feet, it's still a good piece of information to keep in mind while building some sort of mechanism to carry and place the ring.

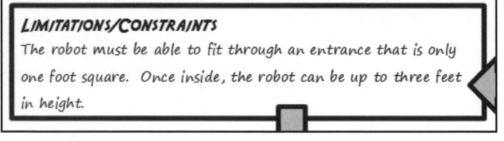

Figure 10-3. *The RingTosser has only a few limitations.*

Mindstorm

Finally… a chance to write down some of my thoughts on how I might build and program the robot to solve this challenge!

Don't hold back here! As with all mindstorming sessions, the rule is that there are no bad ideas. So write down anything and everything you can think of that might help this robot solve this challenge. As you can see in Figure 10-4, I've got a short list of ideas that I feel will be important for me to include with my robot design if I'm to successfully get that ring on the hook.

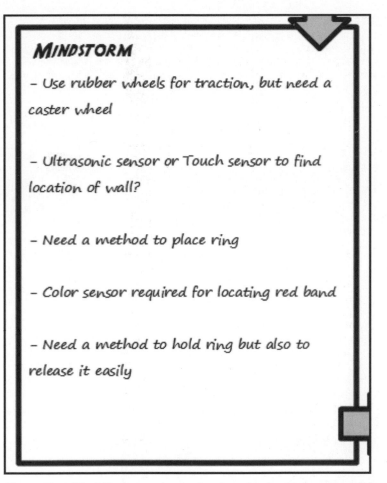

Figure 10-4. The Mindstorm section is where I write down my possible solution ideas.

One of the first things I always try to do when thinking about my robot is to decide on its main method for movement. In Chapter 6, the robot was designed to swing using two pieces of string, but that's not the case here. With a flat, hard surface, I try to go with the rubber wheels. You might want to try to use the treads that come with the kit, but for me, I prefer wheels. (Don't worry, though—I'll get to those treads soon!)

One thing I've learned about robots that use rubber wheels is that they don't always turn so well. I know I'm going to need two motors, one per wheel, for left/right movement. Another motor is going to have to be allocated to the ring placement mechanism (whatever that turns out to be). I could make my design little more complicated and use one motor for rotating the wheels and another motor for controlling direction, but the easier solution (for me) is to use a simple caster. The caster will rotate in place and allow my robot to make left and right turns with ease.

For the RopeSwinger, I chose to use the Ultrasonic sensor to detect the wall and trigger the robot's grabbers, but for this robot I think using a Touch sensor will work just fine. I'll have the robot moving forward slowly enough that when the Touch sensor triggers (touches the wall), the robot should be able to stop quickly.

137

For me, the most complicated part of this robot (or at least the trickiest) is going to be devising a method for consistently placing the ring on the hook. I can perform some tests using the Challenge Area setup (see Chapter 12) and come up with a method that works, but I know it's going to involve some sort of movement that drops or slides the ring on to the hook. Because the distance from the floor to the hook is constant, I'll be able to design a mechanism that holds the ring at the best height for accurately getting it on the hook. That's the fun part, testing and testing various solutions until you find one that works—and works well.

The Color sensor is a no-brainer. (A Light sensor can also easily substitute since the four colors used in the challenge can be selected based on the value they return to the Light sensor.) One of the factors I'll need to test is the best placement for the Color sensor—front, left, or right? Wherever it's placed on the robot, it should not interfere with the movement of the robot or the ring placement mechanism.

Returning to the ring mechanism for a moment, one of the last Mindstorm items that occurred to me was that I need to design a way for the robot to release the ring and not hold on to it. Tricky! With a single motor, I guess I could design some sort of claw or hand, but somehow that seems complicated. The best solutions are typically also the simplest and least technical. Keep that in mind as you design your robot (or jump ahead to Chapter 11 to see my final solution).

Now that I have my `Robot Description`, `Task List`, `Limitations/Constraints`, and `Mindstorm` information, I can sketch out a rough design for my robot; I'll use placeholders for sensors, motors, and other items (such as the ring placement mechanism) but I can at least get a basic idea for the shape and design of my robot.

Sketches

Let me recap what I know about my robot:

- It will use two wheels and a caster for movement
- The Color sensor will be mounted to detect the color bands on the floor
- The Touch sensor will be placed in front to detect the wall
- Two motors will be used for the wheels and left/right turning
- One motor will be allocated for the ring placement mechanism
- I need the ring placement mechanism to easily release the ring

Based on these ideas, I've drawn a rough sketch of what my RingTosser should look like (and the final design comes very close). I've included my rough sketch in Figure 10-5.

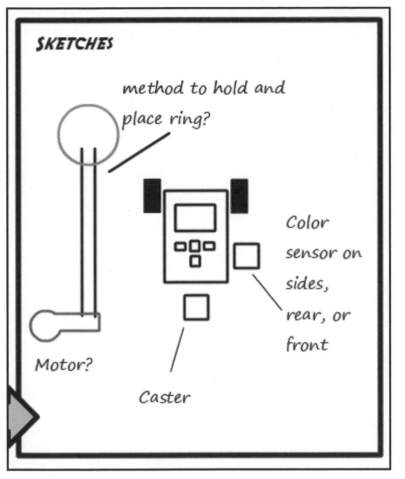

Figure 10-5. The RingTosser is going to be a modified Tribot of sorts.

I'm able to do a very decent job of placing the wheels, sensor, and caster. It's that crazy ring placement mechanism that has me stumped. That said, I still want to include it in the drawing. So, rather than leave it out, I've included it to keep me thinking about possible solutions. One thing that may or may not have occurred to you is this: when the robot is approaching the hook, the best way to place the ring will be if the ring is being held parallel to the wall (if the ring were a solid disc, the disc surface would be parallel to the wall, not perpendicular).

The best thing I can come up with is some sort of ladder-like mechanism that will sit above the robot and maybe rotate forward/backward. If the "ladder" rotates forward far enough, maybe the ring can slide or fall off and snag the hook. We'll see.

Okay, enough "thinking" about the robot—it's time to get building. Chapter 11 will provide you with my final robot design for my RingTosser, and Chapter 12 will provide the program. But don't accept this design as the final word—by all means, if you haven't been coming up with your own potential robot designs at this point in the book, I encourage you to give it a try! Your design may ultimately be one of the best solutions for getting the ring on that hook! Good luck!

■ ■ ■

CHAPTER 11

RingTosser—Build It

You can see my version of the RingTosser in Figure 11-1. It's very possible that your robot may share a similar design with mine... or it may be 100% unique.

This robot is 80% symmetrical. Most of left side (what you see in the figure) is a mirror image of what you'll see on the right side. As you're building, just keep in mind that when you see the instructions showing some pieces inserted on the left side, sometimes you won't see the matching part(s) inserted on the right side.

Figure 11-1. Evan's version of the RingTosser

■ **Note** If you modify or try to create your own version of the RingTosser (or any other bot in this book), please take a picture and e-mail it to me. I would enjoy seeing your final bot in action. I've included my e-mail address in the Introduction.

And now, on to the construction of the RingTosser!

Step by Step CAD Instructions – RingTosser

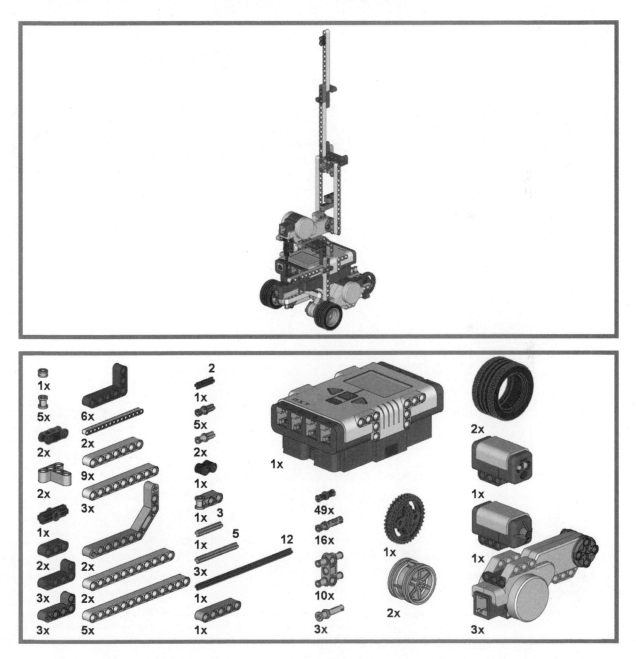

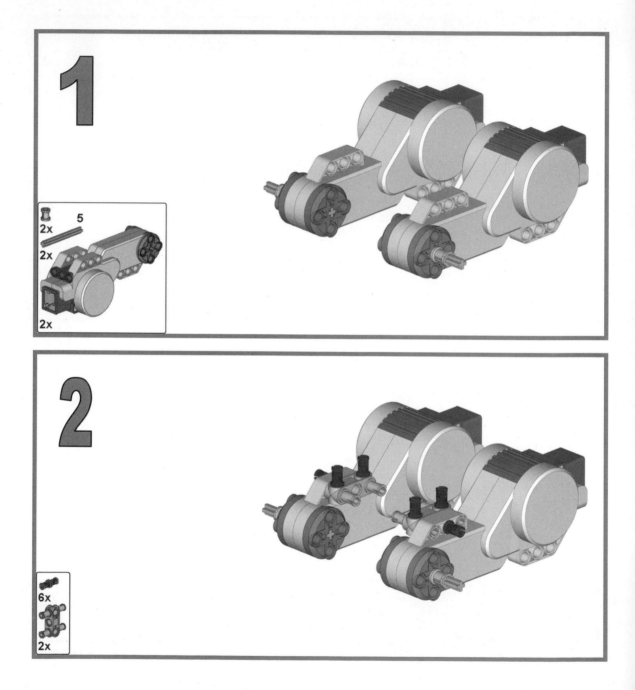

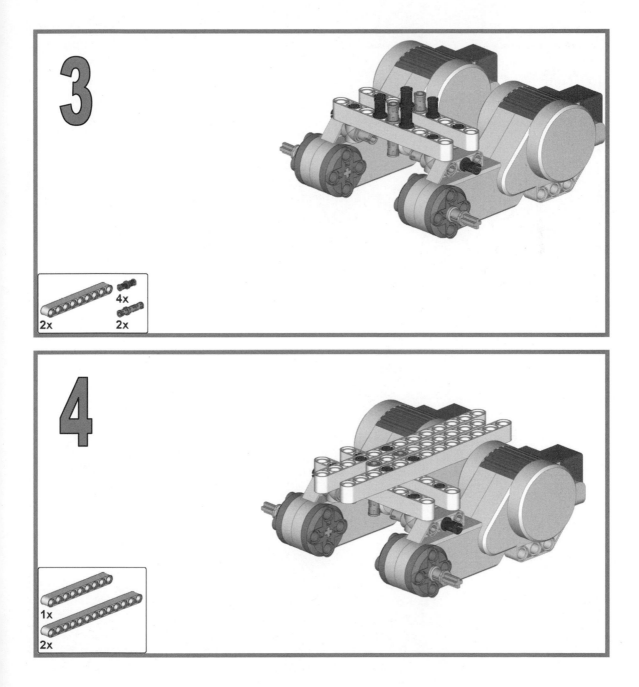

5

Rotate

6

4x

2x

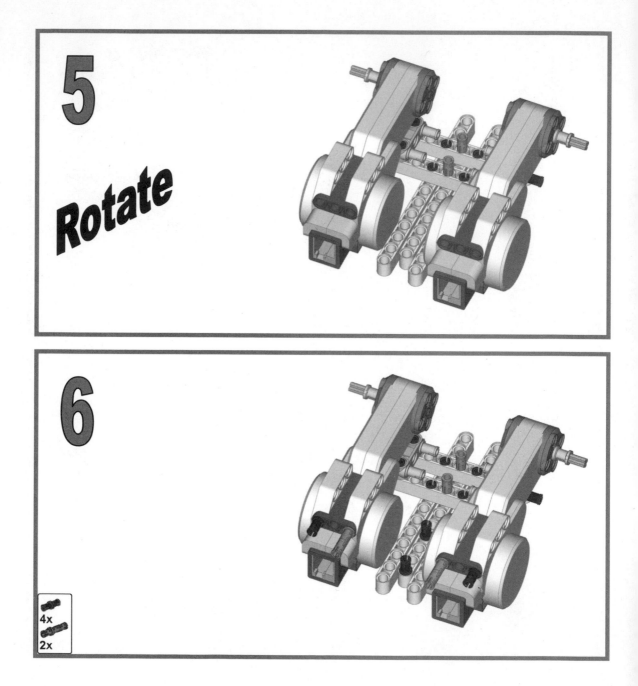

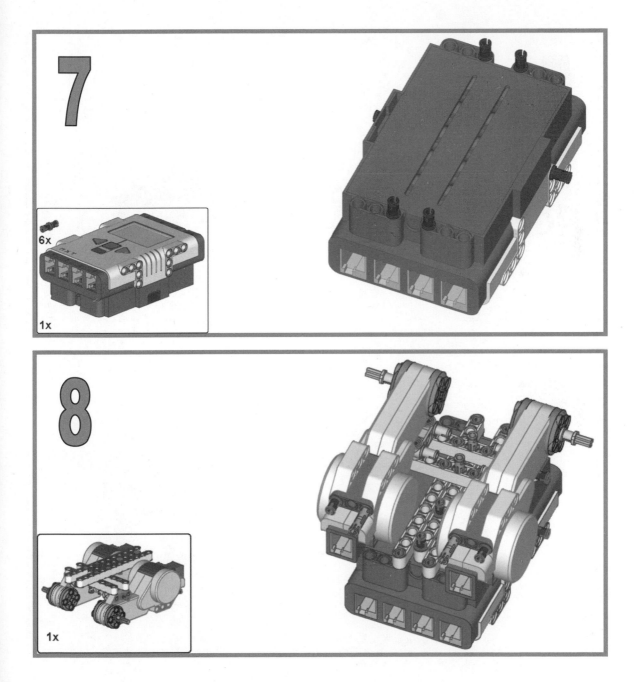

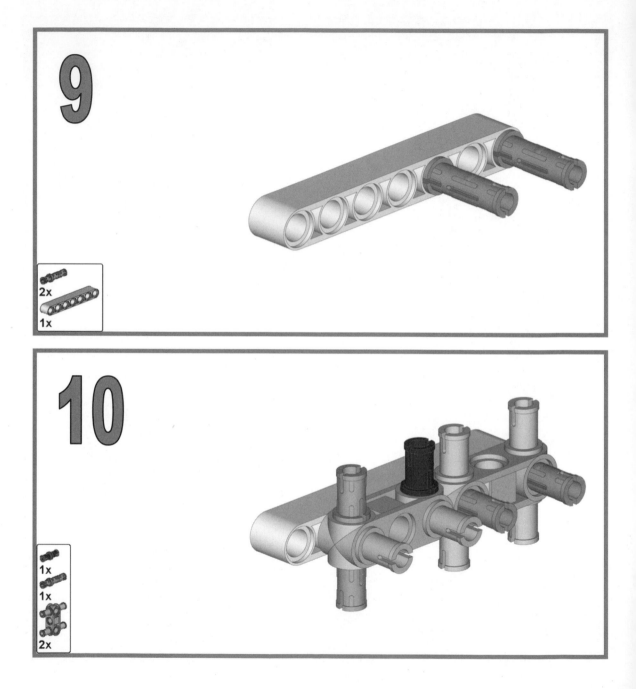

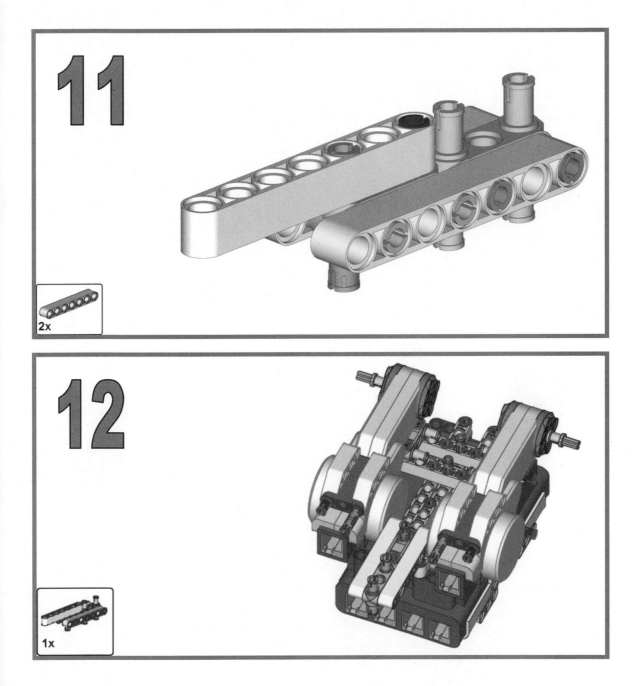

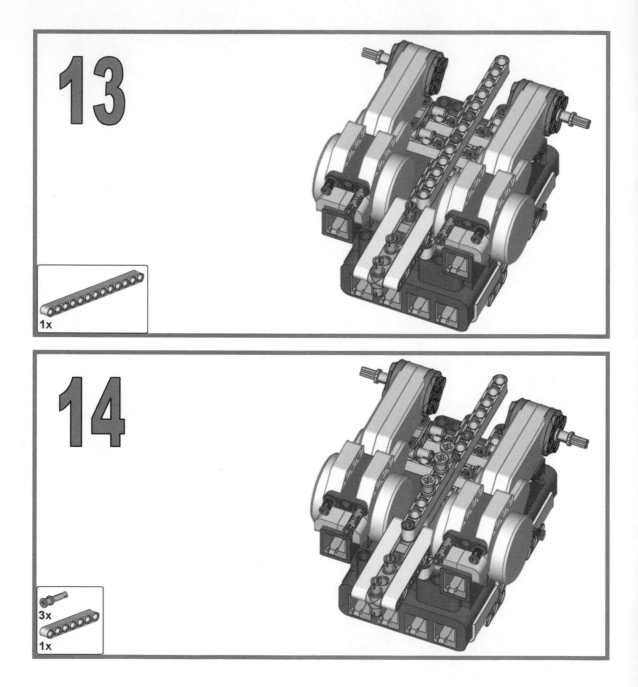

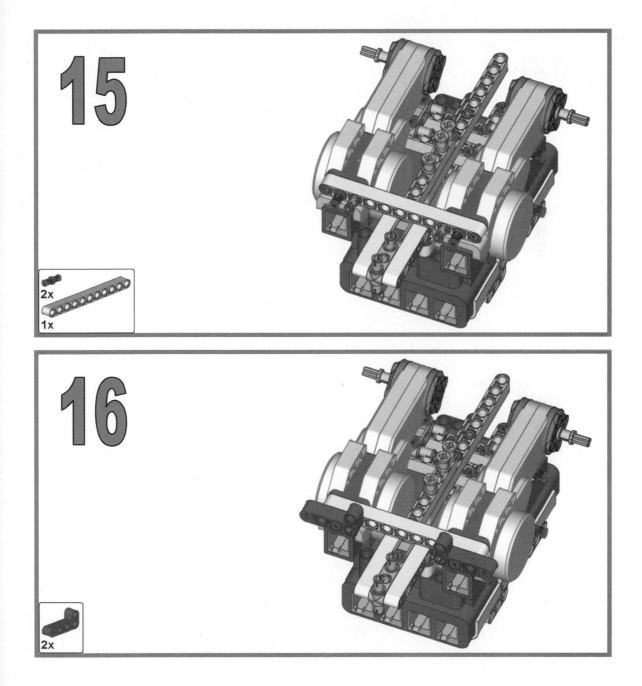

17

Rotate

18

2x

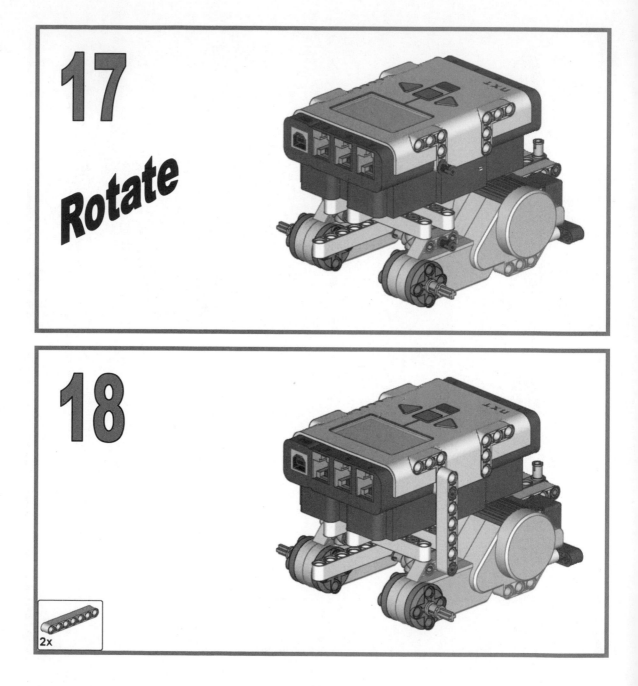

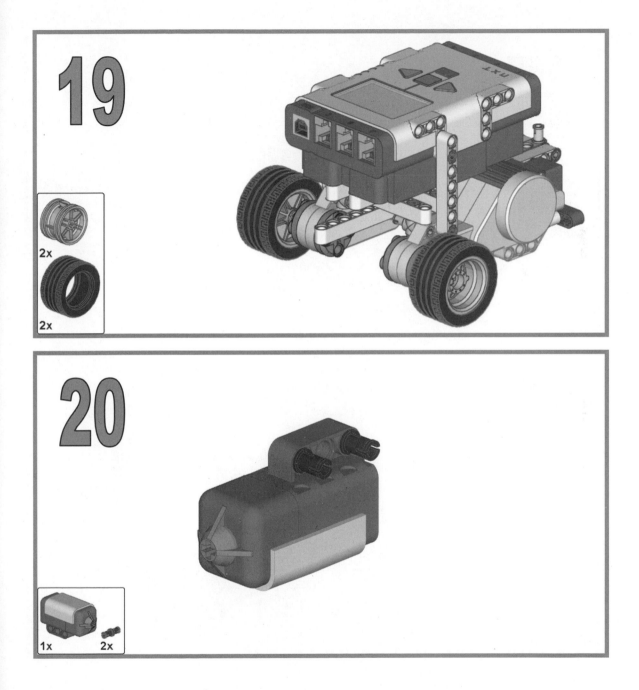

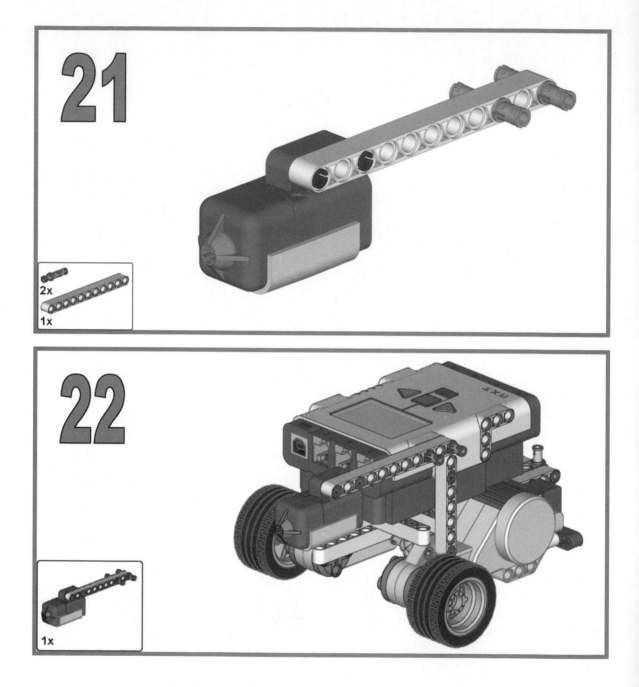

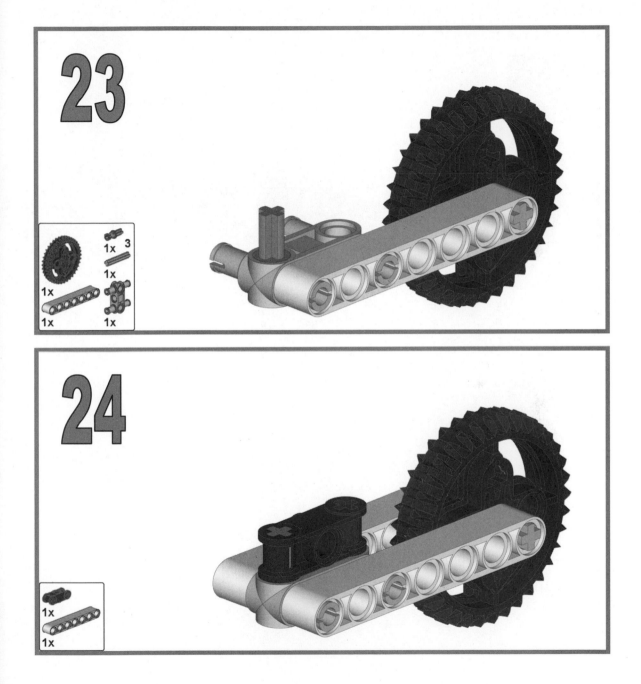

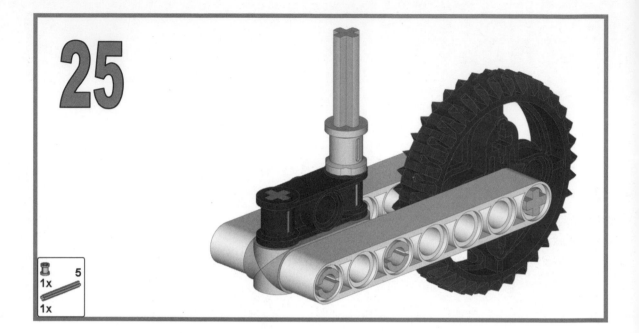

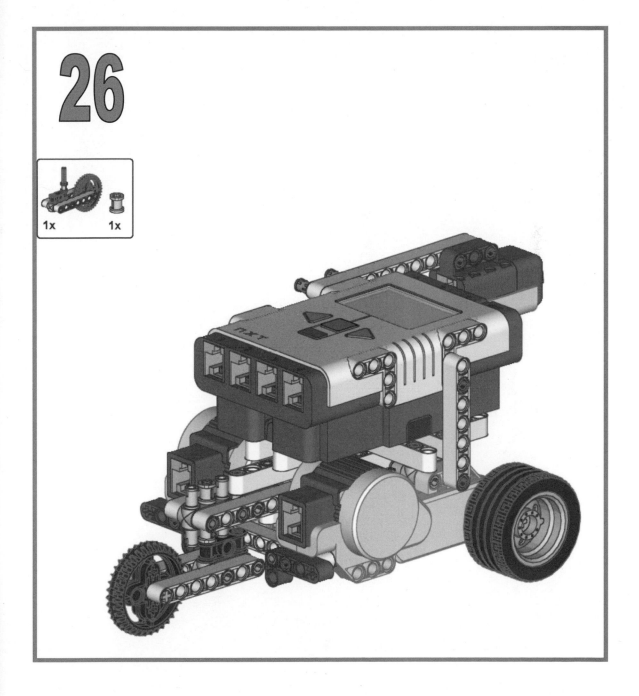

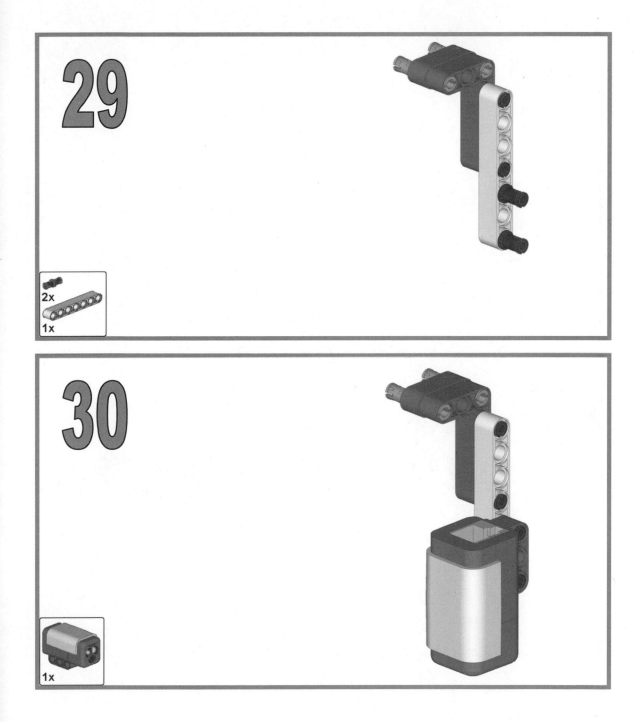

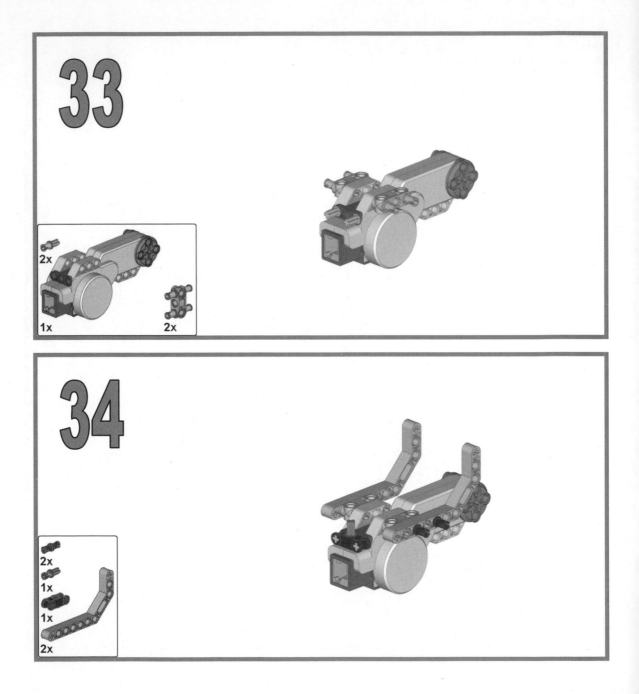

33

2x
1x
2x

34

2x
1x
1x
2x

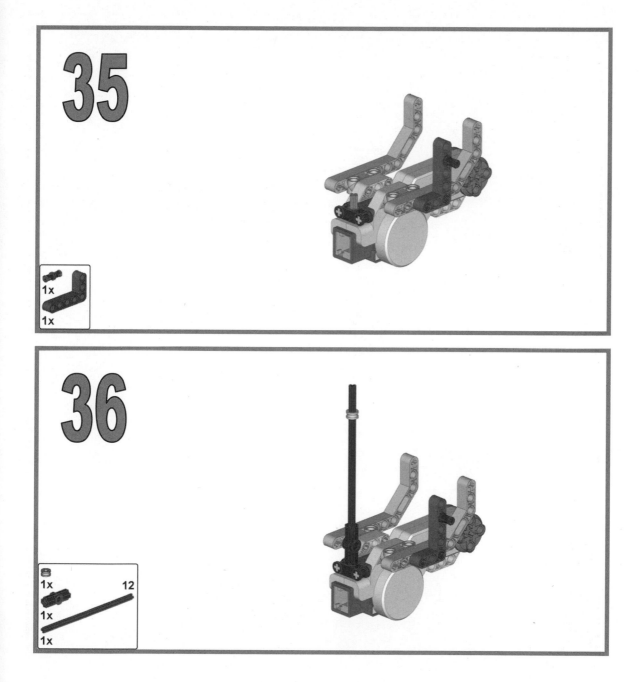

37

Rotate

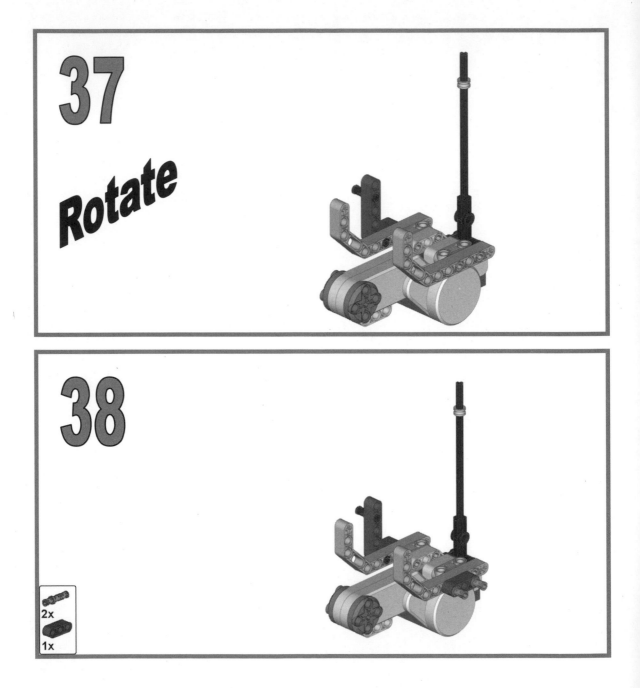

38

39

1x
1x

40

Rotate

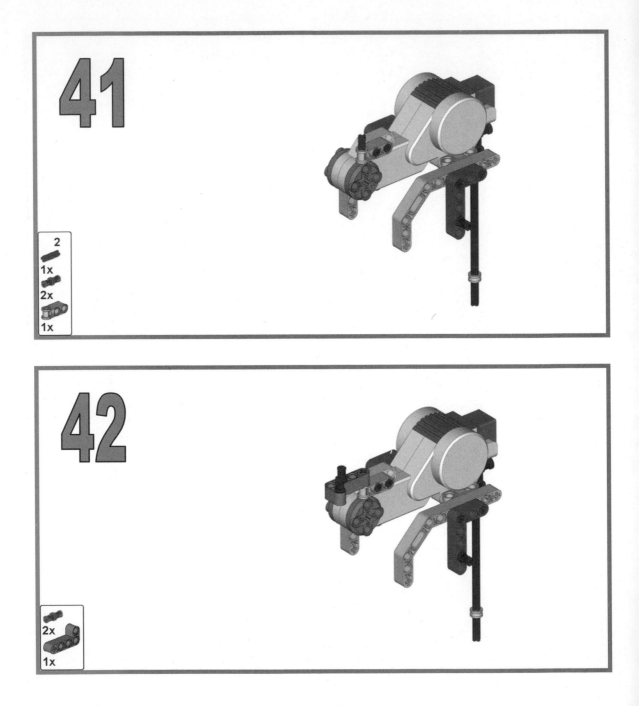

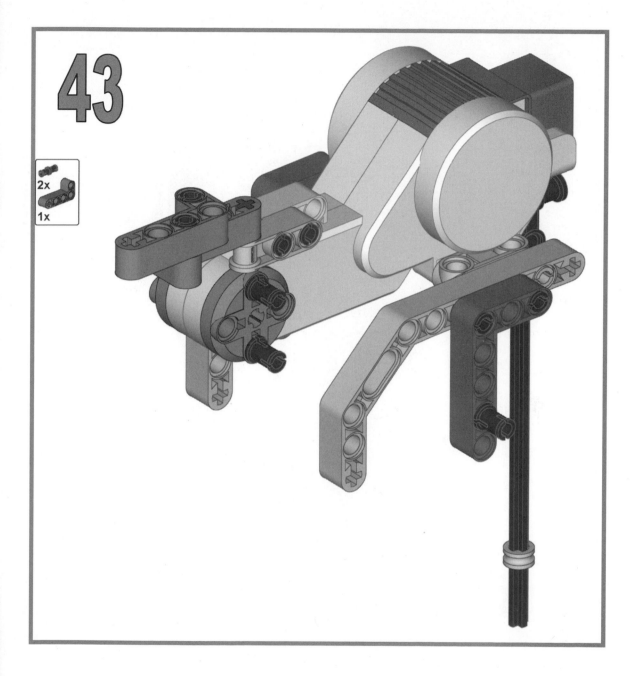

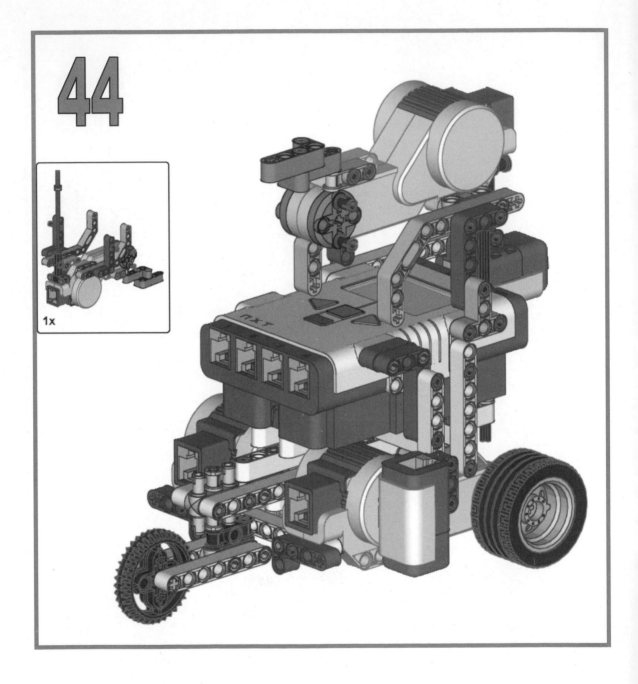

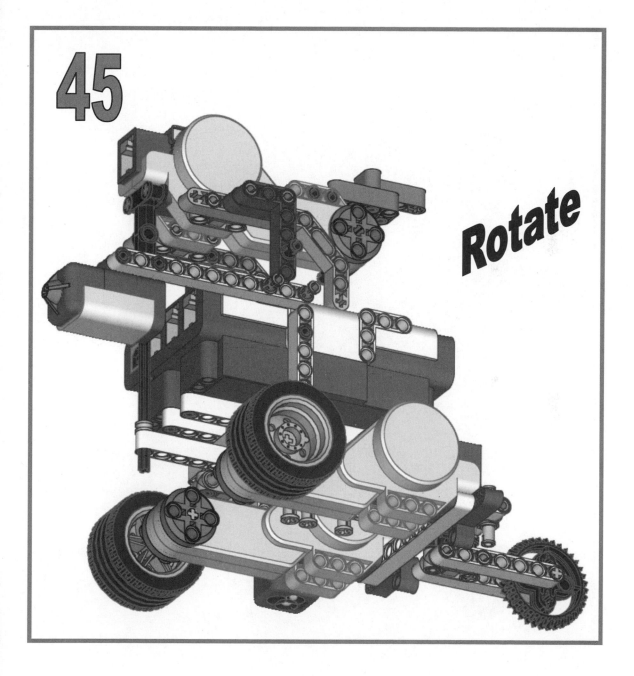

45

Rotate

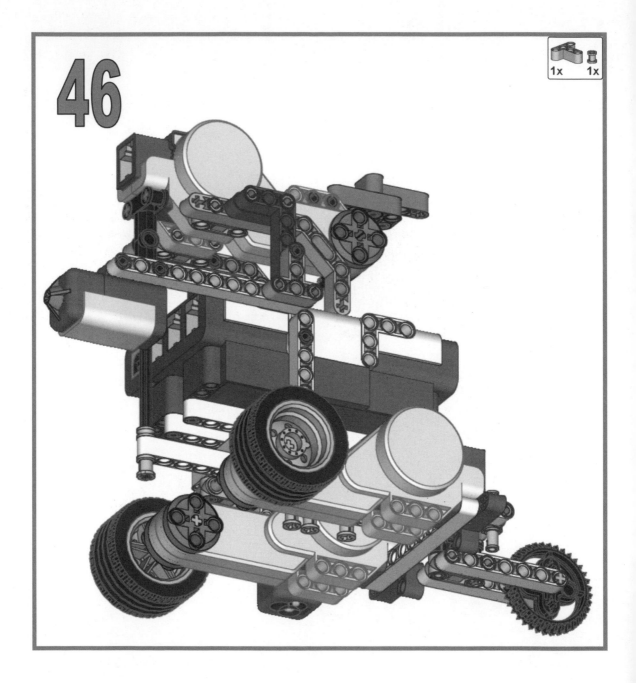

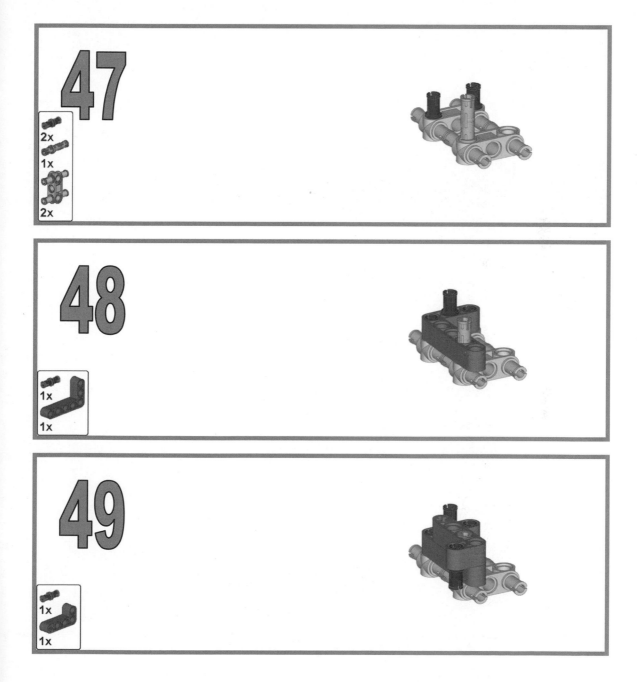

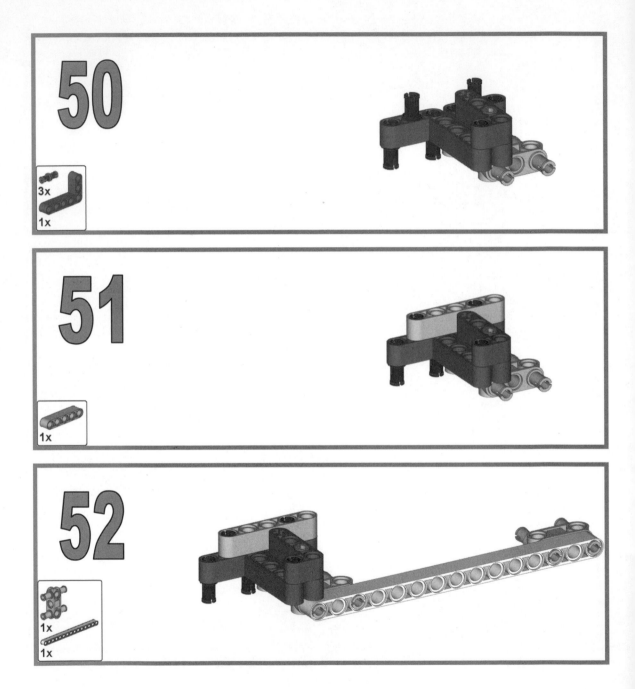

53

1x

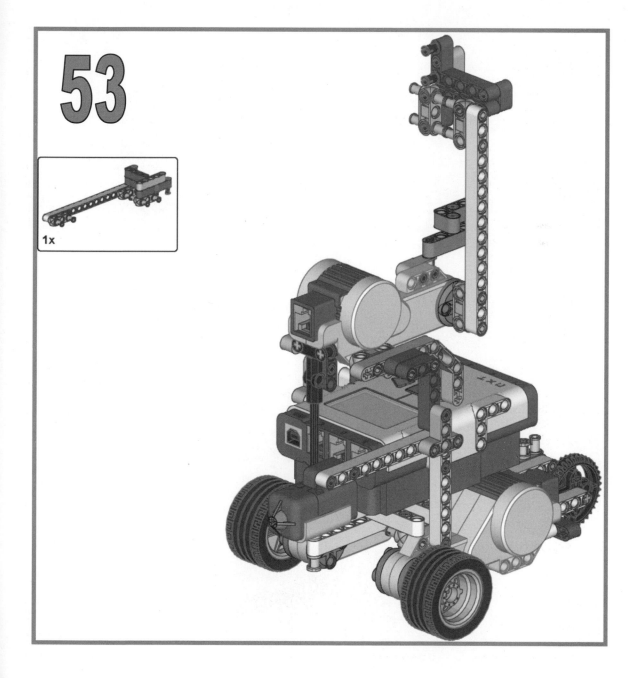

54

Rotate

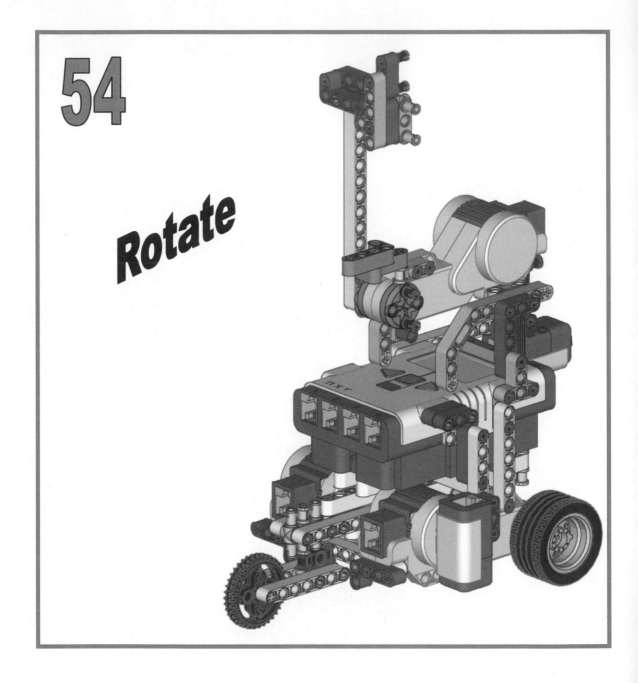

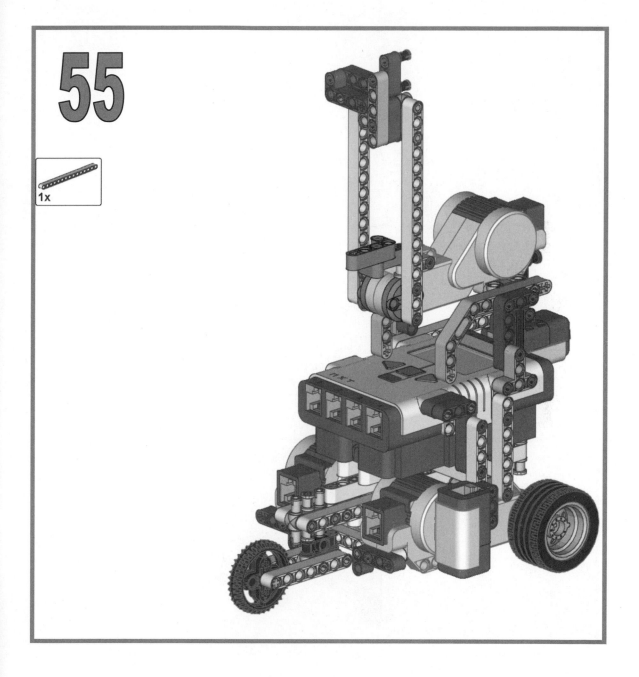

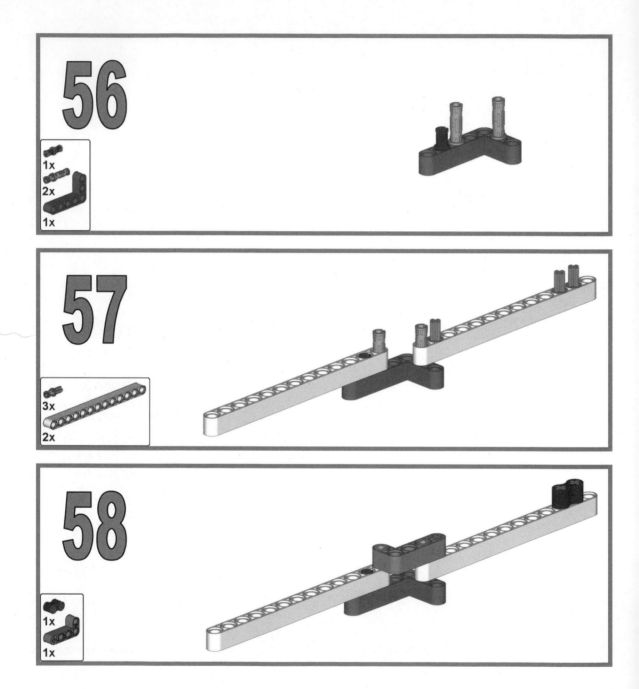

59

1x

■ ■ ■

RingTosser—Program It

If you think about the actions this robot will be performing, you may find that the program for this challenge isn't all that complicated. You'll need some programming blocks for the robot to move around forward, left, and right—things you've already done in earlier chapters. You're also going to need to configure the Color sensor (or Light sensor) to differentiate the red band, but you got some experience with this sensor with the MazeRunner, so programming the RingTosser to find a particular color won't be too difficult.

But what about placing that ring on the hook? Well, as you'll soon see, it involves nothing more complicated than a few simple MOVE blocks. But I'm getting ahead of myself—let's open up a blank NXT-G program and start putting blocks in place.

It Starts with Rolling

The RingTosser moves around on wheels, so I think you won't have any difficulty in figuring out which block to drop into the program first. If you're running the challenge that I describe at the end of this chapter, you will most likely start your robot rolling along the right wall towards the back wall. So, drop in a single MOVE block and configure it as shown in Figure 12-1.

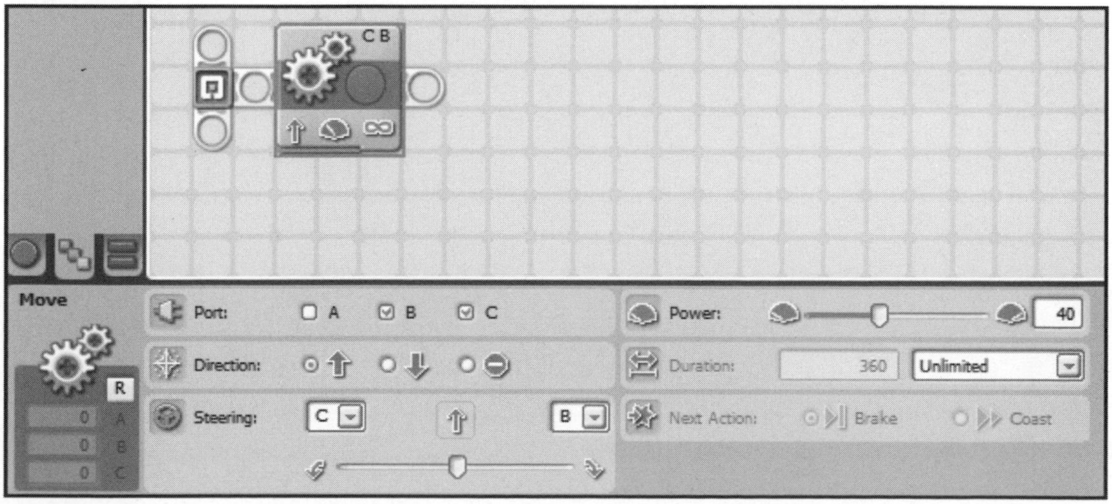

Figure 12-1. The MOVE block gets the RingTosser rolling towards the back wall.

Once the robot starts rolling, however, we'll need it to stop when the Touch sensor detects the rear wall. Figure 12-2 shows a WAIT block configured to use a Touch sensor. The robot will keep moving because this block will keep the rest of the program from executing until the Touch sensor is pressed.

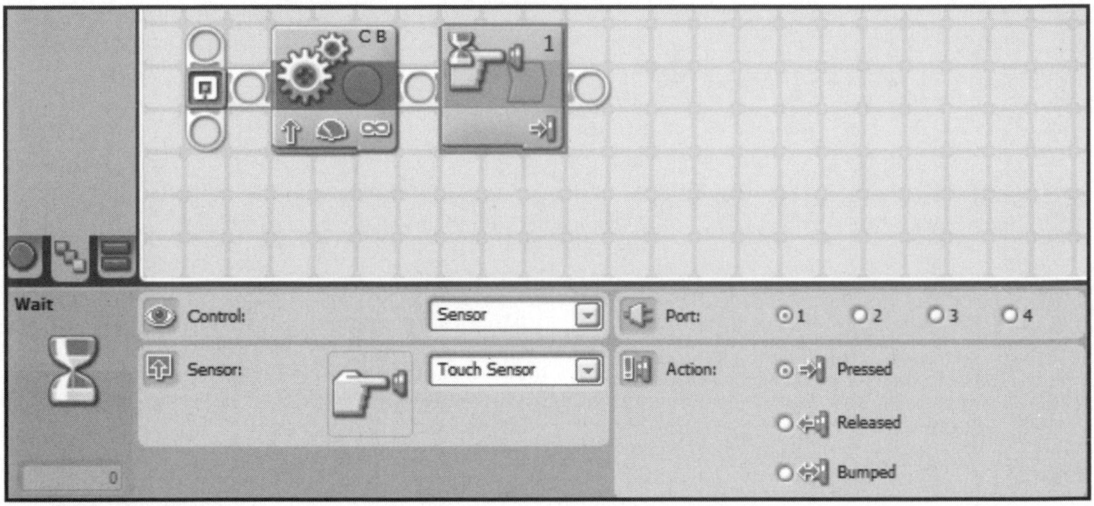

Figure 12-2. A WAIT *block will keep the robot rolling until the Touch sensor is pressed.*

Once the Touch sensor is pressed, the robot should immediately stop. This is an easy one—I've dropped in a MOVE block configured to stop motors B and C, as shown in Figure 12-3.

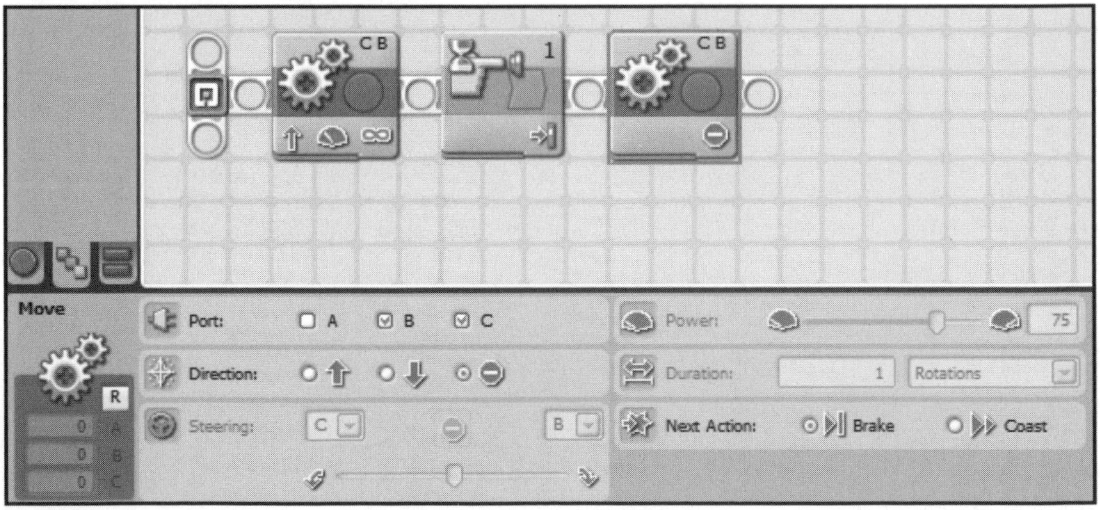

Figure 12-3. This MOVE *block will stop the robot's motors.*

At this point in the challenge, the robot is right up against the rear wall. I'm going to have it back up a short distance (about four inches) so it can prepare to turn left. To do this, I've dropped in another MOVE block and configured it as shown in Figure 12-4. It will roll back half a rotation of each motor.

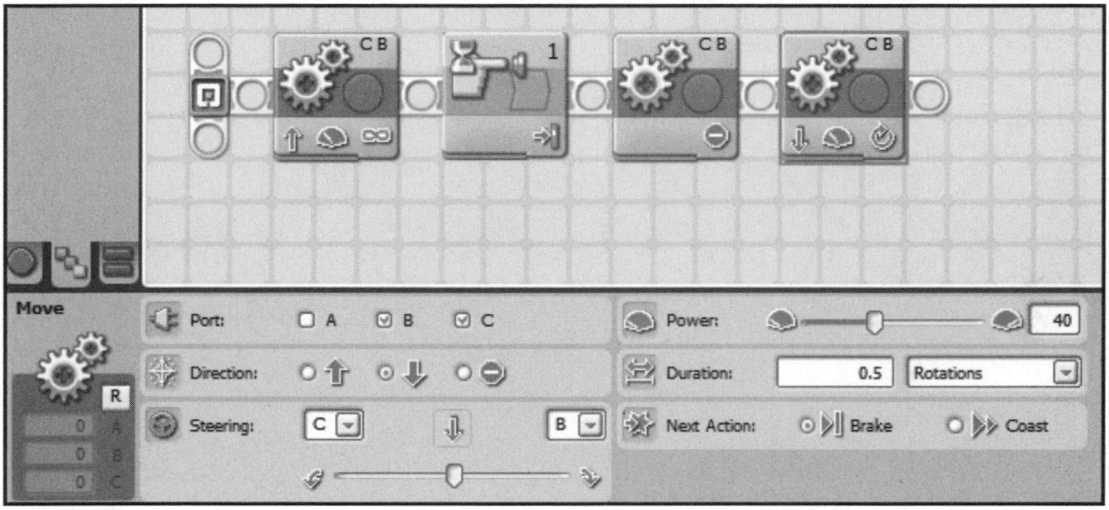

Figure 12-4. The next MOVE block will have the robot roll backwards a short distance.

■ **Note** For all the MOVE blocks, I'm using a Power value of 40. If this is too slow for you, feel free to increase the speed. During my testing, however, I found that using too high of a value for the Power (speed) would cause odd behavior when making turns. Be sure to test various speeds to determine the best value for your robot.

Now it's time to make that left turn. You guessed it – another MOVE block! Figure 12-5 shows the MOVE block I configured to allow the robot to turn left. I used a value of 230 for the Duration, but this value may be different for you depending on the types of wheels you use, the type of surface the robot is rolling on, and the speed. Play around with different values until you can get your robot to make consistent 90 degree turns.

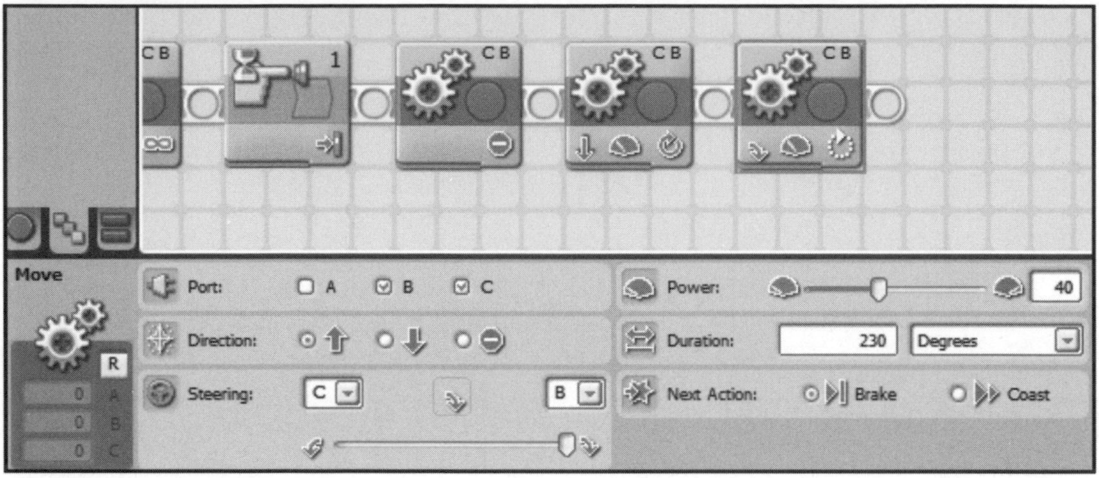

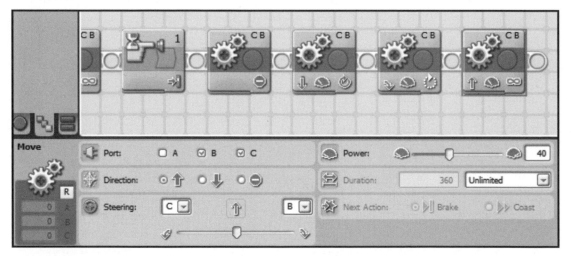

Figure 12-5. This MOVE *block will force the robot to make a 90 degree turn to the left.*

After it makes the left turn, it will then need to begin moving forward so the Color sensor can scan the floor for the red band. Figure 12-6 shows yet another MOVE block configured for forward movement.

Figure 12-6. *The robot will begin to move forward again after turning.*

Once it begins to move forward, the robot will need to keep moving forward until the Color sensor detects red (or any other color or shade of gray you choose to use as your "trigger" color for the challenge). Figure 12-7 shows how I've configured my WAIT block to keep the program from moving forward until the Color sensor detects red.

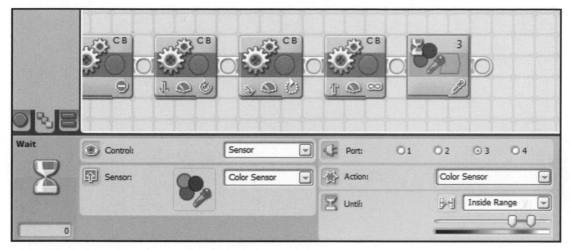

Figure 12-7. *The Color sensor will look for the color red.*

And, of course, once the color red is detected, the WAIT block will let the program continue so that the next block can stop the robot. Figure 12-8 shows the MOVE block that stops the robot at the red band.

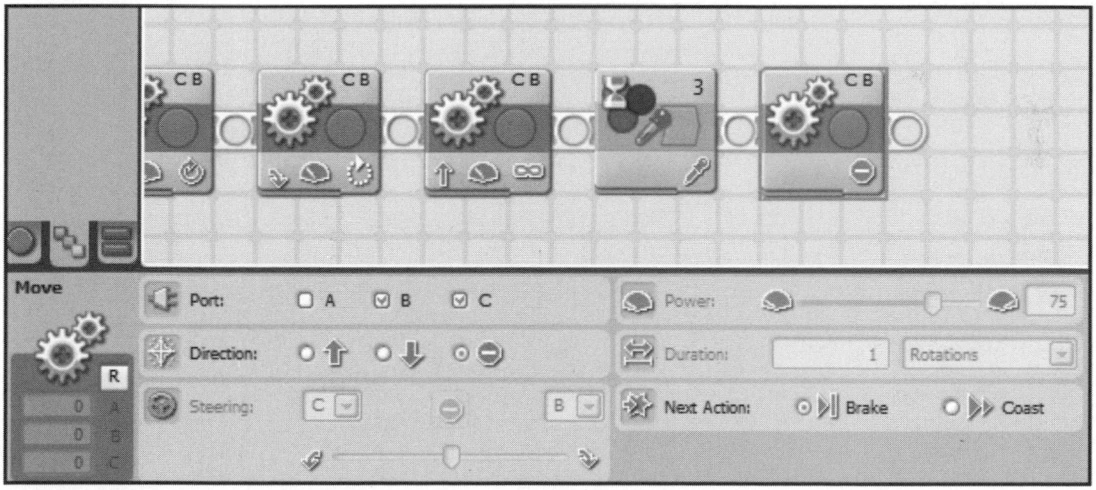

Figure 12-8. *This* MOVE *block will stop the robot at the red band.*

Now, instead of turning left, we need the robot to make a right turn. This block is almost identical to the one for a left turn; I've configured it as shown in Figure 12-9.

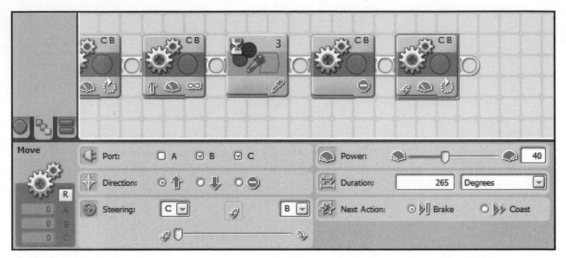

Figure 12-9. This MOVE *block will turn the robot 90 degrees to the right so it faces the hook.*

Why does this MOVE block have a value of 265 for Duration and not 230? The only reason I could come up with is that the robot is not 100% symmetrical from left to right. One side has the Color sensor and the other side does not. Also, my ring placement mechanism is not symmetrical either. There may be a slight weight difference from one side of the robot to the other—the only way I could get my robot to make a 90 degree turn to the right was to increase the value to 265. Your value will very likely be different, so plan on testing this value numerous times to get your robot to make that perfect right turn.

Okay, so after the robot has turned, I want it to move forward until it bumps the wall. You already know how to configure the WAIT block to stop the motors when it detects the wall, so Figure 12-10 shows the next batch of three blocks (MOVE, WAIT, MOVE) that allows the robot to approach the wall, bump it with the Touch sensor, and stop.

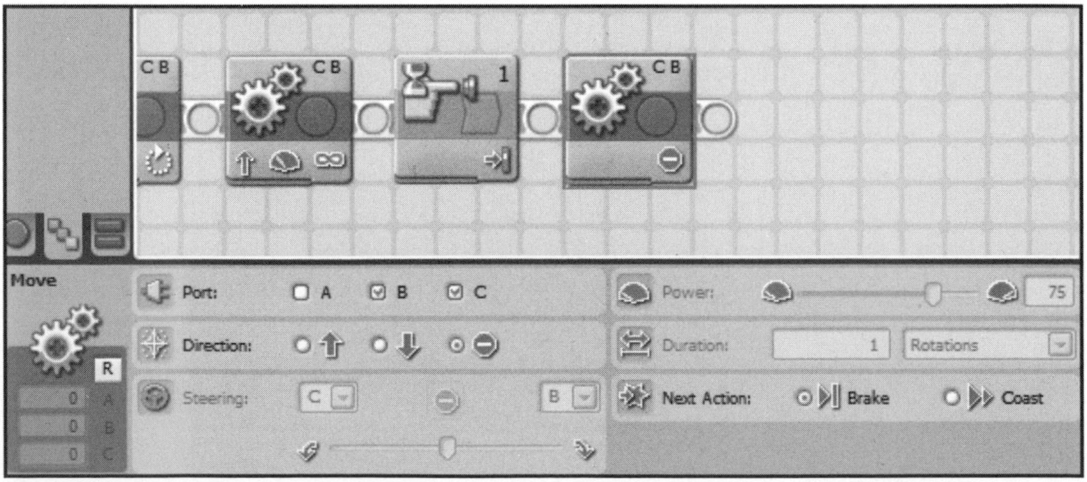

Figure 12-10. *Add this sequence of three blocks for the robot to bump the wall and stop.*

Now I'll have the robot back up once again about half a rotation. Figure 12-11 shows the MOVE block and its configuration panel for this step.

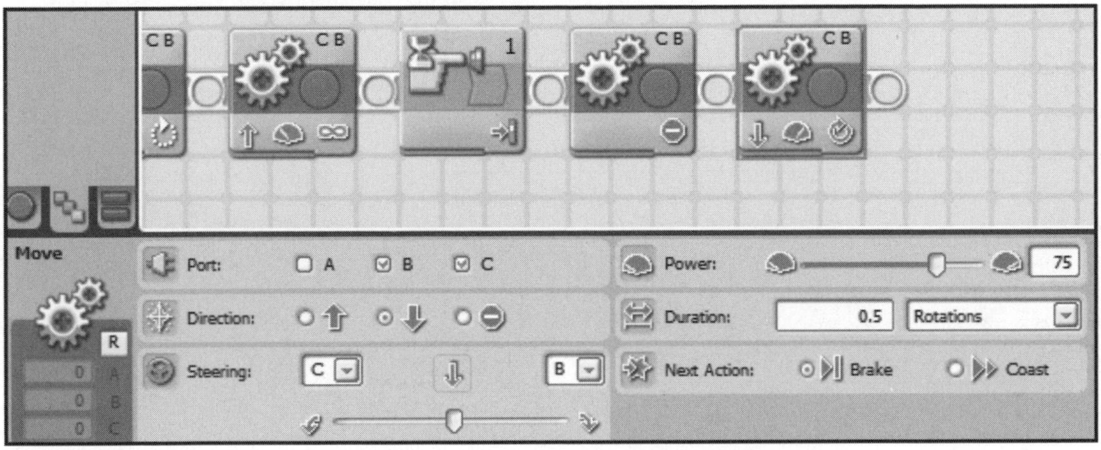

Figure 12-11. The robot will need to back away from the wall a short distance.

■ **Note** If the robot backed up half a rotation earlier before turning left, then wouldn't it be half a rotation back from the wall when it finds the red band? Not necessarily. If the robot doesn't make a perfect 90 degree turn, it could find the red band and be a little closer or a little farther from the wall. By having the robot once again find the wall and then back up half a rotation, I know that the height of my ring placement mechanism will get the ring right on the hook!

Now it's time to get that ring on the hook. For my robot, motor A will simply rotate the ring placement mechanism forward 50 degrees. This will allow the ring that is slightly resting on the small rubber Technic piece to fall off and (hopefully) on to the hook! Figure 12-12 shows the MOVE block I've configured for this action.

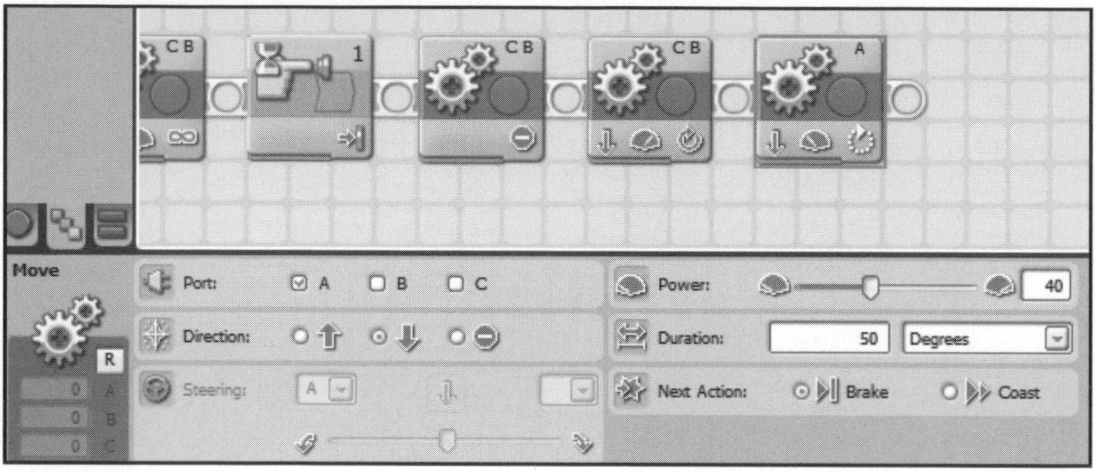

Figure 12-12. *Motor A will rotate forward and the ring should fall on to the hook.*

Figure 12-13 shows a WAIT block that I've added that will pause for three seconds before the robot rolls away from the hook. This should give the ring time to slide off the rubber piece at the end of the ring placement mechanism.

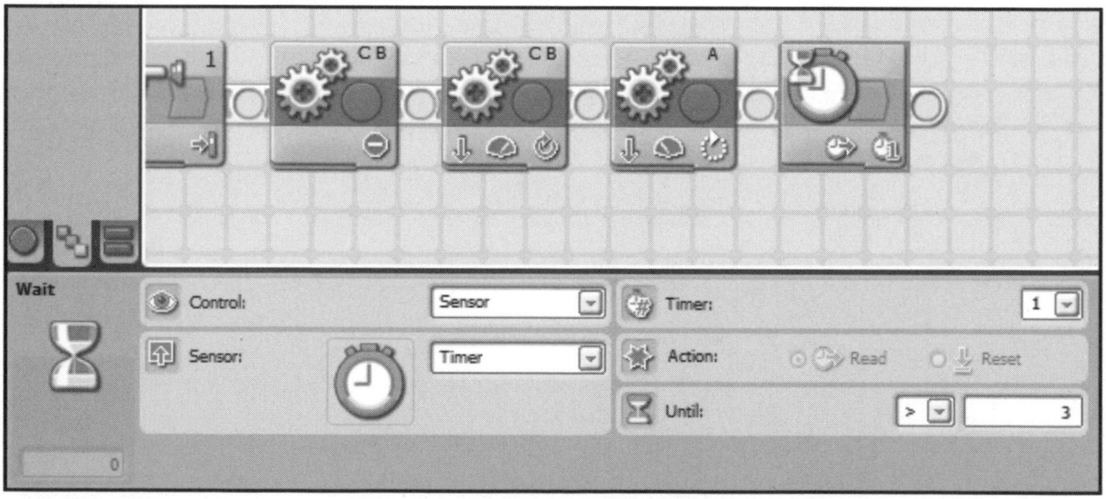

Figure 12-13. *The robot will wait three seconds before moving away from the hook.*

And, for the last block, I'll have the robot move away from the hook a short distance. Figure 12-14 shows the final MOVE block and its configuration panel.

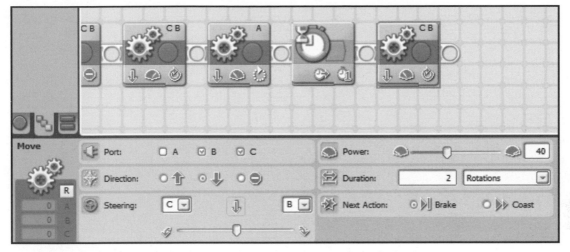

Figure 12-14. *The robot will reverse direction and move away from the hook.*

Building the Challenge Area

One of the many requests I received for *The Mayan Adventure* book was for more help with setting up the challenges, and I'm happy to oblige. In this section, you'll find some instructions for building the challenge area for the RingTosser robot. I'll walk you through creating the challenge area that I used, starting with the device that will allow the hooks to unlatch the small box containing the name of the warrior and the door to open the way to the next challenge.

Don't feel bound by my instructions here. I always encourage students, teachers, and parents to modify the challenge however they see fit.

For this challenge setup, I purchased all the required wood and hardware for approximately $12.00.

First, start by making four hooks. I used a single 3' long 3/8" dowel and cut it into four equal parts (9" each). From each of those pieces, I cut a 1-1/2" end; these ends were hot glued to the 6-1/2" pieces as shown in Figure 12-15.

Figure 12-15. *The hooks are made from a single 3' piece of 3/8" dowel.*

Next, I took a piece of 3' 2 × 4 and used wood screws to attach two 7" pieces as shown in Figure 12-16.

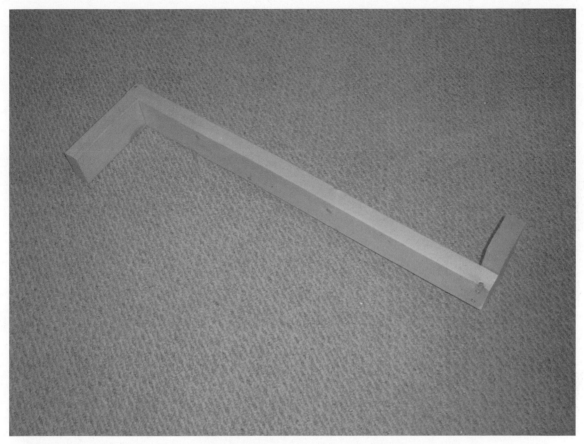

Figure 12-16. *Use wood screws to attach the small pieces to the large piece.*

Attach a small box with a hinged lid using wood screws to one of the smaller pieces as shown in Figure 12-17. The box is mounted upside down so the hinged lid will fall open (towards the ground) when the clasp is unlatched. (I obtained the small wooden chest for $3.00 at a local craft store but any box with a lid will work.)

Figure 12-17. *Use wood screws to attach the chest.*

Next, attach a 3' length of thin wood (1/4" thick and 3" wide is suitable) to the long 2 × 4 piece as shown in Figure 12-18. This piece will support a piece of foam board that will serve as the rear wall. I attached it approximately 15" up from the floor.

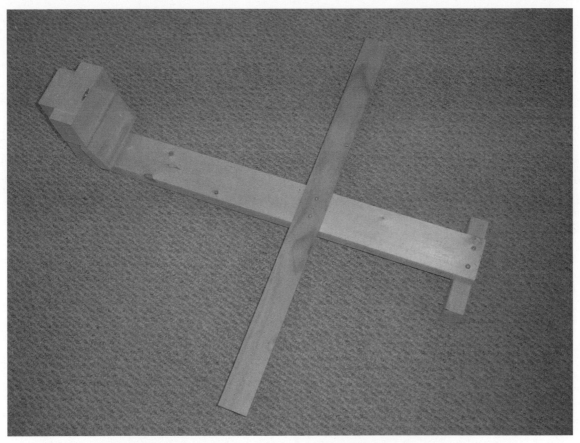

Figure 12-18. *A length of thin wood will provide support for the foam board wall.*

Stand the wooden base up and glue a piece of foam board (or poster board) as shown in Figure 12-19. The foam board should be touching the floor.

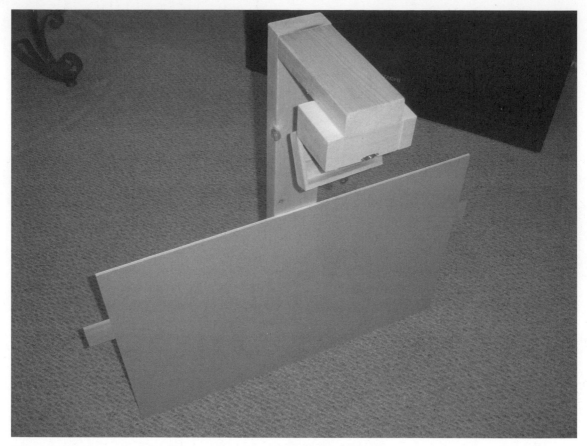

Figure 12-19. *Foam board will act as the rear wall and hold the hooks.*

Use a ½" drill bit and drill four holes (from the back) through the thin piece of wood and through the foam board. Use a ruler to place the holes at equal distances from each other. (The hooks will go through these holes, so you want to make sure the holes are not too close together.) Figure 12-20 shows a few of the drilled holes.

Figure 12-20. *Drill holes to hold the four hooks—two per side.*

Figure 12-21 shows the four hooks inserted into the foam board. (The hooks should easily slide in and out—if they do not, drill the holes in the thin wood slightly larger.)

Figure 12-21. *The four hooks are inserted into the foam board.*

Next, cut strands of string, twine, or leather (I used leather cord) and super-glue them to the ends of the hooks (from the rear) and then super-glue eye-hooks to the ends of the short strands. Figure 12-22 shows a few of the hooks with the leather strands and eye-hooks.

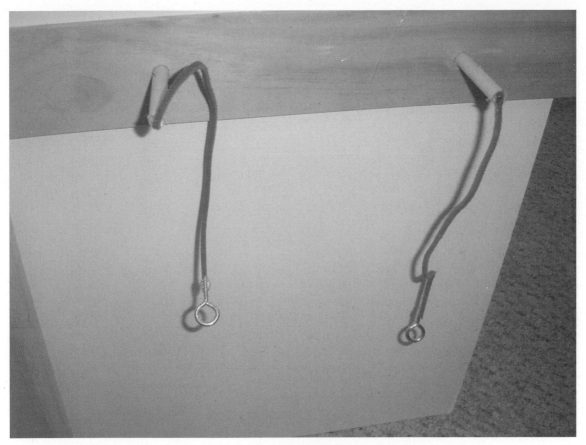

Figure 12-22. *Super-glue eye-hooks and leather cords to the rear of the hooks.*

Next, super-glue a strand of leather or cord to the latch on the chest; this cord will unlatch the chest when it's pulled, as shown in Figure 12-23. Route this cord through a couple of eye hooks so that the other end of the cord is hidden from view and behind the foam board. (You may wish to change the color and hook for different challenges, as this will keep a challenger from knowing which hook will open the chest.)

Figure 12-23. *Super-glue eye-hooks and leather cords to the rear of the hooks.*

Glue a small metal hook (I used a picture-hanging hook) to the end of the cord and attach it to the eye-hook on the red band's hook cord, as shown in Figure 12-24.

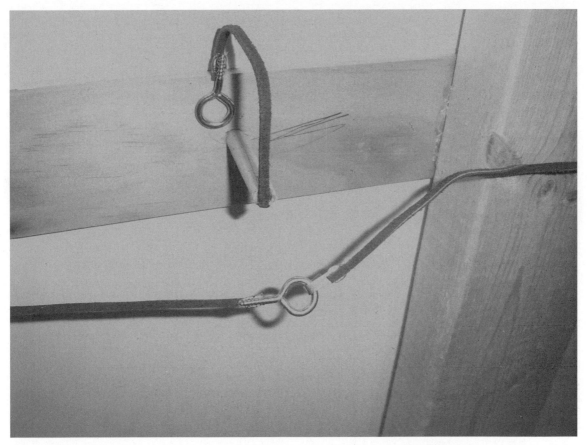

Figure 12-24. *Hook the cord that goes to the chest to the red band hook's eye-hook.*

Place colored bands in front of the hooks as shown in Figure 12-25. Also, place a card in the chest with the name of the Warrior who is guarding the correct door to open—let the person setting up the challenge decide which one it will be.

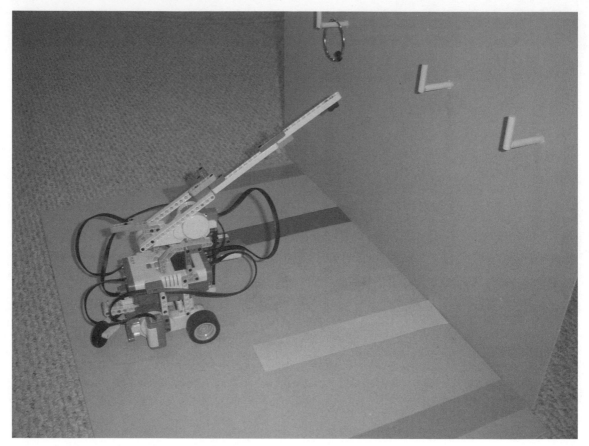

Figure 12-25. Colored bands are placed in front of each of the hooks.

Finally, place a ring on the robot as shown in Figure 12-26 and run the challenge!

■ **Note** I used a second small rubber Technic piece as shown in Figure 12-25 to keep the ring from moving side-to-side. The rubber gives it just enough of a "grab" on the beam behind it to keep it in place. You may also find that some of the cables on the robot get in the way—don't be afraid to use some extra parts to hold the cables in a certain spot. Finally, if you find that a color isn't working well as a trigger, change it! My Color sensor didn't always easily detect yellow, but red worked fine. There are no rules to be broken here—change the challenge and improvise if necessary.

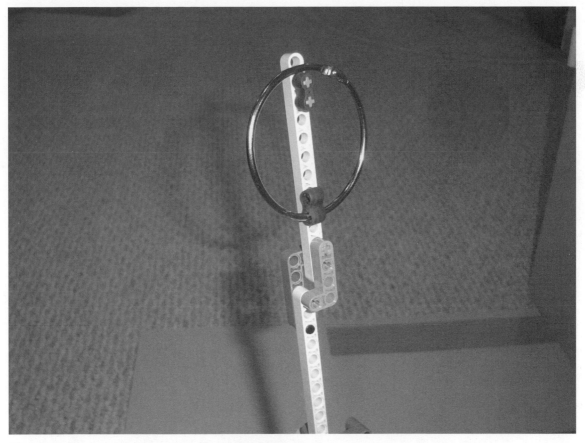

Figure 12-26. A small rubber Technic piece holds the ring.

You'll have to do some tweaking on your robot's program; factors such as the floor surface (I used foam board), height of the hooks, and other differences in your robot and your challenge area setup as seen in Figure 12-27 will all affect the program.

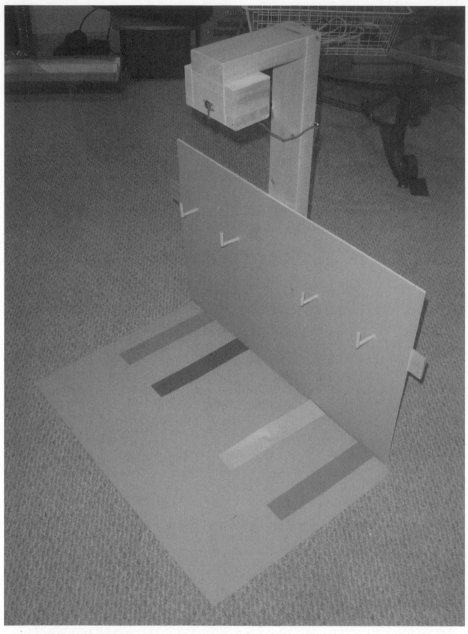

Figure 12-27. The Challenge Area ready for action.

Now, get that ring on that hook and pull! When the chest door falls open, you should find the name of the warrior who is guarding the door you must open to continue toward King Ixtua's treasure repository.

■ ■ ■

CHAPTER 13

Rock and Roll

Location: Southwest Guatemala

102 miles SW of Guatemala City

Coordinates: 14º 04' N / 90º 09' W

Weather Conditions: 91 degrees Fahrenheit, Humidity 64%

Day 6: King Ixtua Treasure Repository, 9:27 a.m.

Uncle Phillip had given Tag the honor of pulling the twine; the small hook pulled from the wall and they heard a loud grinding noise coming from the room. When the team re-entered the chamber, they found a pleasant surprise. Not only had the door for Munala opened, but Munala's statue had moved as well. Underneath the statue was a hollowed out space containing a small scroll.

Uncle Phillip carefully handed the scroll to Erin. "For my translation expert," he said. "I have a feeling that scroll contains some information we're going to need."

"I'm going to head back to the surface," Erin said. "Be careful, all of you."

Evan stood in the center of the room, breaking down his robot and putting the parts back into the case.

"That was good work, Evan," said Tag. "Your little robots have really been the key to our getting this far." Tag turned and continued taking photographs of every inch of the room, including the statue and down the newly exposed hallway.

"Thanks," replied Evan.

Uncle Phillip turned from his examination of the statue and smiled at Evan. "I agree with Tag. I don't think we would have made it past the first chamber without your robots. I think there's a future for you in robot design, Evan."

Evan smiled. "I don't know. I'm really enjoying history now; my grades have improved, too. Maybe I could do both?"

"Archaeology and robotics, huh?" said Uncle Phillip. "I think that may very well be the future, Evan."

"Dr. Hicks! Look at this," yelled Tag, pointing down the hallway that was hidden earlier by the closed door to the right of Munala's statue.

Evan followed his uncle over to the doorway and looked inside. The hallway ran about twenty feet before turning left. But that wasn't what surprised Tag. A flickering light was barely noticeable from around the corner.

"Candle or torch light," said Uncle Phillip. "Could opening the door have triggered that?"

"Seems possible," replied Tag. "If the scrolls are correct, the next chamber should contain the final challenge for entering the treasure room. Maybe we won't need to bring the tripod lamps with us."

Uncle Phillip turned to Tag and Evan. "I'm going to proceed down the hallway and look for traps. You two stay here."

Evan nodded. "Watch your step," he said with a grin.

The Story Wall

Evan watched his uncle move slowly down the hallway, only inches at a time. He would examine the floor, then the walls, and then the ceiling. It was a slow process, but Evan understood the caution. Tupaxu had proven his resolve to protect his king's treasure by including many lethal traps. After an hour had passed, Uncle Phillip had gone around the corner. A few minutes later he came back and requested large sheets of paper and some charcoal sticks from Tag and then disappeared again around the corner.

Thirty minutes later, Uncle Phillip emerged from the hallway with the papers folded under his arm. "No traps," he said.

"Tag, take your camera down the hallway. I need you to photograph all the etchings on the wall just around the corner. You'll also see an open doorway, but do not go in the room. Photograph as much as you can of the room without stepping inside," said Uncle Phillip.

Tag nodded. "Sure. I'll try to be quick."

Evan pointed at the folded papers that his uncle was carrying. "Anything interesting?"

"Let's take a look," Uncle Phillip replied. "Help me lay these out, side by side, please. There were etchings on the wall for about ten feet and I used the charcoal to make rubbings."

Evan finished placing four pieces of paper on the floor. Mayan glyphs, each the size of his fist, were easily visible on all the sheets.

"It's a story wall," said Uncle Phillip. "I'll have to verify some of these with Erin, but if I'm translating this correctly, it's the story of the King's burial day."

"Does it say anything about the next chamber?" asked Evan.

"It does have some unusual glyphs that I'm not completely familiar with—it's possible. See this one here," said Uncle Phillip, pointing at one of the symbols. "At first I thought that was the glyph for court or judge, but it's got a variation on top that I've never seen."

"Look at that one," said Evan. "I like its shape."

"That's the symbol for 'mountain,'" replied Evan's uncle. "Its usage in that collection of glyphs indicates an obstacle to overcome. That sounds about right given that we're talking about Tupaxu's challenges."

Evan heard footsteps and turned. Tag emerged from the hallway smiling.

"What a great room!" he yelled. "I took some good photos with the zoom lens. From what I saw, it appears that Evan's next robot better have some climbing power."

Uncle Phillip nodded. "I had the same thought," he said. "Let's head back to the surface, take a look at your pictures, and show these glyphs to Erin. But first, is anyone else hungry?"

An Uphill Battle

Over a sandwich lunch with lemonade, the team sat in chairs facing Tag's laptop. Tag cycled through over forty pictures numerous times. Some were pictures of the wall that Uncle Phillip had described. Glyphs had been chiseled into the stone, forming the story wall. Other pictures showed the interior of a room lit by numerous torches. Somehow Tupaxu had designed a method to light the torches when Munala's door opened. A nice trick, thought Evan.

After finished looking at the photos, Erin continued her examination of the charcoal rubbings sitting on a nearby tabletop, while Tag printed the photos on a small printer in the corner of the tent. Then, an hour after lunch started, Erin called the team together.

"Story walls are nothing new to Mayan ruins. These glyphs, fortunately, are well preserved—we don't find them in this great of shape often. It took some digging, but I think I've got the correct translation figured out."

Erin pointed at the first piece of paper. "This one," she said, "tells the story of how Tupaxu's four warrior-priest bodyguards were given the duty to protect the king's treasure. The king elected to have his treasure buried in a mountain. The one outside, I'm guessing."

Uncle Phillip pointed at a glyph on the second sheet. "That glyph doesn't translate exactly into mountain, though," he said.

"That's right. It translates more into obstacle. After the king's death, Tupaxu knew there would be attempts by neighboring villages to steal the king's treasure. The hiding place for the treasure was not a well-guarded secret. Workers for miles around had been used to construct the chambers below us. Tupaxu knew that attempts would be made to steal the treasure."

Evan frowned. "There are always thieves, aren't there?"

Erin nodded. "Yes, but Tupaxu had a plan. He had his four warrior priests stand watch every day at four different locations on the mountain. Anyone trying to enter the tomb would have an uphill fight against four skilled defenders. Over time, he let the rumor spread that these warrior priests were protected by strong magic. If one of the priests was killed or left his station, a large boulder would seal the entrance forever and trap any intruders inside."

"But what about when the priests got older and couldn't defend the entrance?" Tag asked.

Uncle Phillip pointed at the third sheet. "Now these glyphs makes sense," he said. "A good ghost story always lives on."

"Yep," said Erin. "The story continues that the four warrior priests were so diligent in their duties that the gods rewarded them by sending four warrior spirits to take their places. They never needed sleep, held a sword in one hand and a spear in the other, and were as tall as two men! I think that would probably keep me from straying too close to the mountain."

"And that brings us to the fourth and final sheet," said Uncle Phillip. "It appears to be a set of instructions."

"For the fourth challenge?" asked Tag. "The ramp?"

Evan remembered seeing a few of Tag's pictures with a stone ramp in the center of the room.

Erin picked up one of Tag's photos. "I don't think Evan's going to like this one."

The Ramp of the Warriors

"Rolling boulders?" asked Evan. "You're kidding! This isn't an action movie!"

Tag laughed. "I really would have liked to have met this Tupaxu," he said. "The guy sure didn't believe in making anything easy."

Uncle Phillip placed a hand-drawn sketch in front of Evan. "Okay, based on Erin's translation and some rough measurements from Tag's photos, I think this is the setup," he said.

Evan glanced at his uncle's drawing (Figure 13-1).

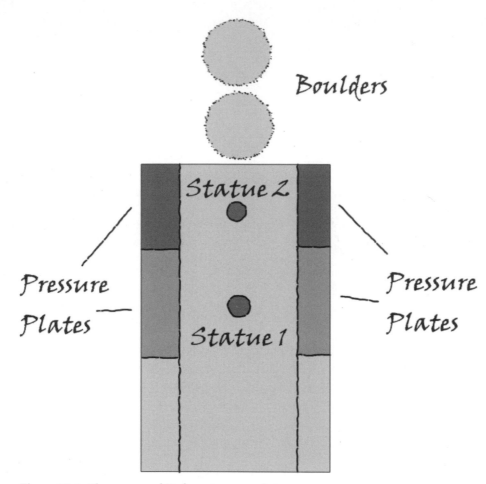

Figure 13-1. *The ramp and its four pressure plates.*

"According to the instructions, a monkey would move up the ramp and push a statue to the right and onto one of the pressure plates. After the pressure plate was triggered, the monkey had to cross to the other side of the ramp and stand on the opposing pressure plate," said Erin.

"And the boulders?" asked Evan.

"If the monkey didn't trigger the other pressure plate quickly enough, one of the boulders would roll down the ramp. You'll notice there are two boulders, one for each statue. If both boulders are triggered, we'll be locked out of the king's treasure room forever. The columns in the room are designed to collapse and bring the ceiling down."

"Great," said Evan. "Any idea on how much time my robot will have to trigger the pressure plate?"

"It's a rough calculation, but around ten seconds," replied Uncle Phillip. "And your robot should sit on the pressure plate for a few seconds before moving. Just to be safe."

"So my robot has to push the statue on to its pressure plate and then cross the ramp and trigger the pressure plate on the other side."

"Twice," replied Tag. "Two statues."

"Right. Two statues," said Evan.

Erin sighed. "As far as I can tell, after triggering all four pressure plates, and avoiding releasing both boulders, one of the three doors in this room will be unlocked when a wooden plaque mounted over the door is released. That door is supposed to lead to the final challenge."

Uncle Phillip looked at Evan. "What do you think?"

Evan patted the robot's case sitting on his lap. "Well, I've only got one robot kit, and I don't think it will survive a boulder rolling over it. Can I take a look at the room?"

"Sure," said Uncle Phillip. "Let's all go and take another look."

The Ramp Room

Evan stood in the doorway and looked into the room (see Figure 13-2). Most of the torches were almost burned out, and Tag was forced to bring down more tripod lighting.

About ten feet beyond the doorway was the beginning of a large ramp in the center of the room. At the top of the ramp, Evan could see a stone boulder, about a foot in diameter; a second boulder could be seen sitting behind it. Sitting on the surface of the ramp were two small wooden statues of Mayan warriors. Large stone columns stood behind the ramp. Three doors were visible, as well – one on the left wall, one on the right wall, and one on the rear wall.

Figure 13-2. The ramp challenge will unlock a door that leads to the final challenge.

Uncle Phillip pointed to the floor between the team and the start of the ramp. "That's definitely a mix of pressure plates. Probably nothing heavier than a small monkey can cross to the ramp without triggering some sort of trap."

Evan pointed at the ramp's left side. "Are those the pressure plates that my robot must trigger?"

"Yes," said Erin. "The dark colored stones are the plates."

Evan nodded. "And the angle of that ramp looks to be less than 45 degrees," he said.

"Closer to 30 degrees," replied Tag. "Do you think your robot can make it up a ramp like that?"

"Not sure," said Evan. "I'll have to do some testing first."

Evan's Solution

Later in the evening, Evan called Tag, Erin, and his uncle over to his worktable.

"I think this will work," Evan said. The small robot didn't look anything like a monkey, but it would hopefully do the job.

"Nice design," said Tag. "Is it heavy enough to push those small wooden statues?"

"I think so," replied Evan. "During my tests it was able to push wooden blocks around that are about the same size as the statues. The real trick is finding the statues on the ramp."

Uncle Phillip smiled. "It's getting late and I know we're all tired. Let's get some rest and we'll tackle the ramp first thing in the morning."

Evan nodded. "I'm sure I'm going to dream about boulders chasing me down a ramp," he said. He carefully placed his robot in a nearby trunk and closed the lid.

Erin yawned. "See you in the morning, team."

The story continues in Chapter 17…

■ ■ ■

CHAPTER 14

RampRider—Design and Planning

Not all robots move around on a flat surface; you built one robot that swings across a large pit, so building and programming a robot to ascend and descend a ramp shouldn't be any problem, right? Well, if the robot only needed to go up the ramp and then back down, this might not be too difficult, but this challenge has a few interesting twists to it that are going to require a little more planning. Let's once again walk through the design process and use the Design Journal worksheet to help us focus on giving this robot the best chance to successfully complete its mission.

The RampRider

For the Robot Name box, give your robot a name that's descriptive of its job; for me, RampRider seems appropriate. I also liked RockandRoller, BoulderDodger, and Wiley E. Robot. But in the end, the robot name is just a name—we need to think more about what this robot will actually be doing on that ramp.

■ **Note** There are blank Design Journal worksheets in the back of this book. If you need more pages, feel free to make photocopies of the Design Journal worksheet or visit the Apress Web site to download the page in PDF format.

The Robot Description

For the Robot Description, I envision myself riding on the robot as it goes about its work. I take notes on what it's doing—turns, lifts, pushes, scans, and more. These are the actions that will help you create a detailed description that will, in turn, help later when it comes to building and programming the robot.

I know my robot will have motors and sensors, but I don't yet know how many motors or what kinds of sensors. But I know what the robot must do as it moves up the ramp, so I'll use that to help write out the Robot Description as seen in Figure 14-1.

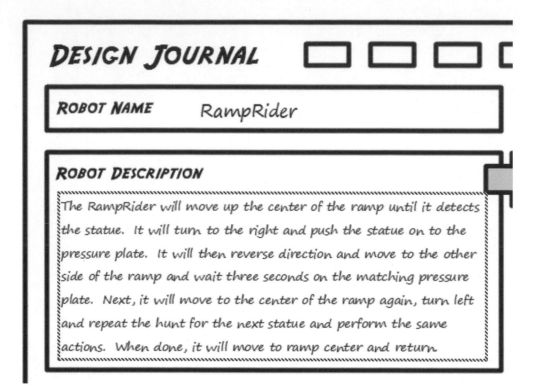

Figure 14-1. *The RampRider's Robot Description*

You may notice in this description that I've used words to indicate a repeating behavior. The robot will be searching for another statue (or more, if you wish to make the ramp longer and the challenge more complicated) and performing the same actions as with the first statue—push it on to a pressure plate, reverse direction, and roll onto the matching pressure plate on the other side of the ramp. Immediately I can see that when I begin programming, there will be an opportunity to use a LOOP block to make my program a little less complicated. The repeat behavior can be put inside a LOOP block to save me some time.

After the robot has triggered the last pressure plate (and avoided any rolling boulders), it just needs to return to the starting point on the ramp. To keep the robot from accidentally taking a tumble, I've added a bit of text to indicate it should return to the center of the ramp before coming home. I could probably save some programming steps by eliminating having it move to the ramp's center, but another goal of the challenge is to get your robot home safely!

Your Robot Description doesn't have to match mine exactly, but you need to make sure that you specify the movements required by the robot (pushing the statue, rolling back to the pressure plate, turning, and so on). Notice that my description doesn't say anything about using sensors, though; some descriptions can include this while others won't. It all depends on your understanding of the challenge. Right now, I'm not certain how I'll keep the robot from pushing the statue too far forward or from rolling off the ramp's edge when it backs up... but I'm sure it will involve sensors. Because the ramp in the story has different colored stone for the pressure plates, I'm sure the Light/Color sensor will come into play, but avoiding the edge is going to take some thinking. Fortunately, I don't need a solution for these obstacles yet, but I do need to break down the process in the Task List.

The Task List

With this Task List, there are still a few unknowns—how many motors will I need and which sensors will I use? But those are building and programming issues, not related to the tasks the robot must perform. I've broken down the Robot Description I wrote in the previous section into smaller tasks and written them on my Design Journal worksheet as shown in Figure 14-2.

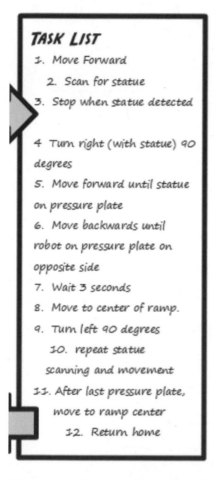

TASK LIST

1. Move Forward
    2. Scan for statue
3. Stop when statue detected

4 Turn right (with statue) 90 degrees
5. Move forward until statue on pressure plate
6. Move backwards until robot on pressure plate on opposite side
7. Wait 3 seconds
8. Move to center of ramp.
9. Turn left 90 degrees
    10. repeat statue scanning and movement
11. After last pressure plate, move to ramp center
        12. Return home

Figure 14-2. The RampRider's Task List identifies the tasks that must be performed.

The Task List is always useful to me because it gets me thinking about the upcoming build. For example, step 2 says it will scan for the statue. Will I use a Touch sensor to find it? What about the Ultrasonic sensor? There are pros and cons to using each of them, but I know that whatever method I use must be able to accurately find the statue sitting on the ramp's surface and not interfere with the robot "grabbing" and moving it to the pressure plate. (Grabbing may not be the right word, though— I'm not sure yet how I'll accomplish this movement.)

Once the robot finds a statue, it must be able to move it on to a pressure plate. In the story, the pressure plates are made out of a different colored stone, but my challenge setup (described in Chapter 16) will use tape to indicate the locations of all the pressure plates. I can use the Color sensor (or Light sensor) to detect the change in color between the ramp and pressure plates. When that change is found, I'll need the robot to stop or maybe move forward a little bit to make certain the statue is on the pressure plate.

Once the statue is placed, though, the robot's work isn't done. It has a short time (ten seconds, according to Tupaxu's scroll) to move away from the statue and trigger the opposing pressure plate. Turning around will waste precious time, so I'll just have the robot move in reverse... but how will I get it to stop before it goes over the ramp's edge? Once again, I can use a sensor for this problem, but which one—Color or Ultrasonic? Good questions to ponder.

After three seconds, the robot must move to the center of the ramp and turn left to go back up the ramp to find the second statue. It will be performing the same actions here, so no additional sensors will be needed—it's just another statue. But keep this in mind: the robot will be closer to the top of the ramp, meaning that it must move slightly faster since it will be closer to a rolling boulder should it fail to trigger the final pressure plate in time! Of course, the best solution for avoiding rolling boulders is to not trigger them in the first place, so our final robot chassis and program must get the robot to the pressure plate as quickly and accurately as possible.

Once the final pressure plate is triggered and the robot waits the required three seconds, it must then return to the center of the ramp and then turn properly so it can return to the start of the ramp for me to recover it.

Limitations and Constraints

There's one huge constraint that comes to mind when I look at the challenge: I don't want my robot falling off the edges of the ramp!

I'll add that to Figure 14-3 that shows my Limitations/Constraints box.

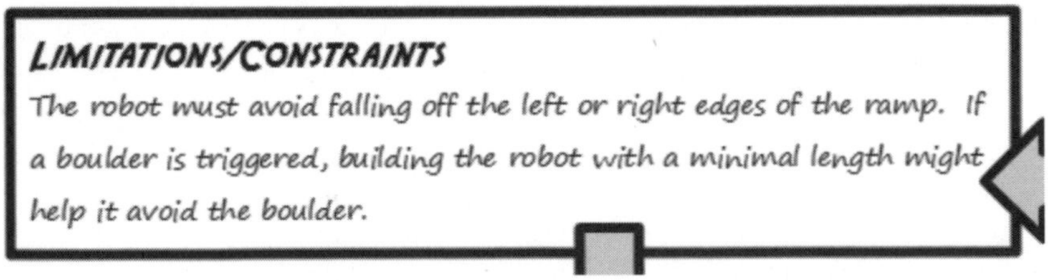

LIMITATIONS/CONSTRAINTS

The robot must avoid falling off the left or right edges of the ramp. If a boulder is triggered, building the robot with a minimal length might help it avoid the boulder.

Figure 14-3. The RampRider has two dangers that can affect its final design.

Obviously, I'll need to build the robot in such a way that it can detect those edges and avoid falling off. And since I'm starting to brainstorm (mindstorm!) about my robots design, it occurs to me that if my robot isn't too long it might just avoid a rolling boulder if it doesn't make it to the pressure plate in time.

Mindstorm

While I was writing my tasks and limitations, I began to get a better idea for what this robot would look like and how it might operate.

The first thing I want to do is write down these thoughts so I don't lose them. Figure 14-4 shows my initial ideas for the design of this robot.

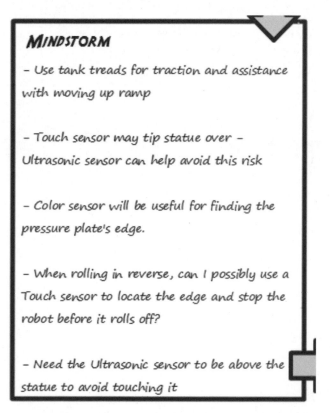

MINDSTORM

- Use tank treads for traction and assistance with moving up ramp

- Touch sensor may tip statue over – Ultrasonic sensor can help avoid this risk

- Color sensor will be useful for finding the pressure plate's edge.

- When rolling in reverse, can I possibly use a Touch sensor to locate the edge and stop the robot before it rolls off?

- Need the Ultrasonic sensor to be above the statue to avoid touching it

Figure 14-4. The Mindstorm section has some of my ideas to test during the building phase.

Most of my robot designs tend to use the rubber wheels for movement, but the NXT 2.0 kit comes with a set of tank treads that seem perfectly suited for helping my robot climb up that ramp. Making turns with the treads will require two motors, so that's one design decision made for me.

While thinking about the robot approaching a statue I realized that if I used a Touch sensor, with its small surface area., my robot might accidentally tip over one of the statues. It would work better to avoid touching the statues; this seemed to point me in the direction of the Ultrasonic sensor. But using the Ultrasonic sensor for detecting the statues meant I wouldn't be able to use it for detecting the edges of the ramp. I began to wonder if I could use the Touch sensor to detect the edge of the ramp and stop my robot. I'll investigate that during the building phase.

Finally, the little statues are approximately three inches tall, so I'm wondering if there's a way for me to detect them from above instead of mounting the Ultrasonic sensor on the front of the robot; again, I'll test that possibility during the building phase.

At this point, I can use my Robot Description, Task List, Limitations/Constraints, and Mindstorm information to create a sketch or two of the RampRider's potential design.

Sketches

What do we know about the robot that we need to build? Let's recap:

- The Color or Light sensor will detect the change in color from ramp to pressure plate
- The Touch sensor might be useful for locating the ramp's edge
- Two motors and treads will be used for movement and turning
- The Ultrasonic sensor will be used to try and detect the statues (from above)

My rough sketch of the RampRider can be seen in Figure 14-5.

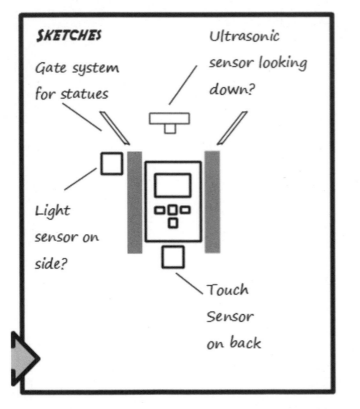

Figure 14-5. The RampRider has a lot of sensors and a different method for movement.

While my sketch gives me an overall idea on the design I'll be trying to build, it still raises a few questions. To "capture" the statue, I could create an elaborate mechanism to grab and hold the statue, but I'm thinking some sort of enclosure to the left and right of the robot might be all that's needed to push the statue around. This will act as a fence with a wall to the left and right of the statue. When the robot turns, the walls will push the statue in the direction of the turn.

I've placed the Ultrasonic sensor near the front of the robot, but I'm going to try to build the robot in such a way that I can point the Ultrasonic sensor towards the surface; when a statue approaches the robot's body, the Ultrasonic sensor should be able to detect it and stop the robot from continuing to roll up the ramp.

I placed the Color (or Light) sensor on the left, but it could easily be on the right side. As the robot approaches the pressure plate (blue painter's tape on my ramp; see the Challenge setup in Chapter 16) the Color sensor should detect that change. Testing may show that placing it on the right side will work better (or worse), but I won't know until I get the robot built and test it a few times.

Finally, the Touch sensor on the rear of the robot makes sense, but will it work? If I build the robot in such a way that the Touch sensor is pressing down on the table, then I can program the robot to stop when the button is released. If built properly, the Touch sensor button should release when it moves off of the ramp's surface and over empty space. Again, it sounds good on paper, but only testing will be able to verify if it will actually work.

Chapter 15 will give you the plans for building my final RampRider design. Build it or design your own robot to complete this challenge. Whichever option you choose, just remember that the Design Journal worksheet will help you focus on the important parts of the robot's design that you need to unlock the door and face Tupaxu's final challenge!

CHAPTER 15

■ ■ ■

RampRider—Build It

You can see my version of the RampRider in Figure 15-1. It's very possible that your robot shares a similar design with mine... or it may be 100% unique.

   This robot is 95% symmetrical, with the left side differing only with the addition of the Color sensor. Most of left side is a mirror image of what you'll see on the right side. As you're building, just keep in mind that when you see the instructions showing some pieces inserted on the left side, sometimes you won't see the matching part(s) inserted on the right side.

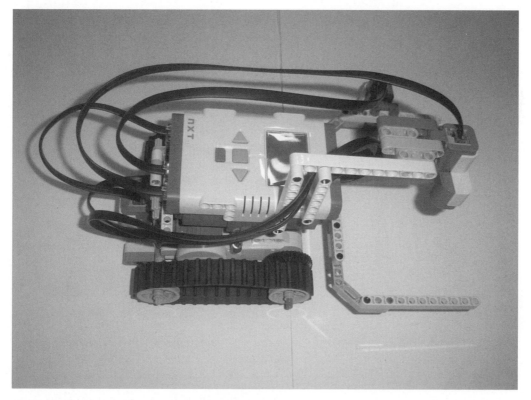

Figure 15-1. Evan's version of the RampRider.

■ **Note** If you modify or try to create your own version of the RampRider (or any other bot in this book), please take a picture and e-mail it to me. I would enjoy seeing your final bot in action. I've included my e-mail address in the Introduction.

And now, on to the construction of the RampRider!

Step by Step CAD Instructions – RampRider

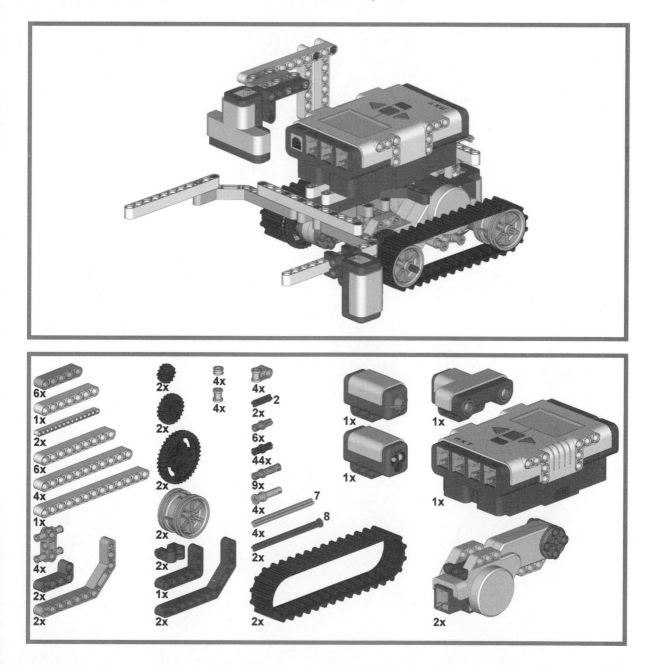

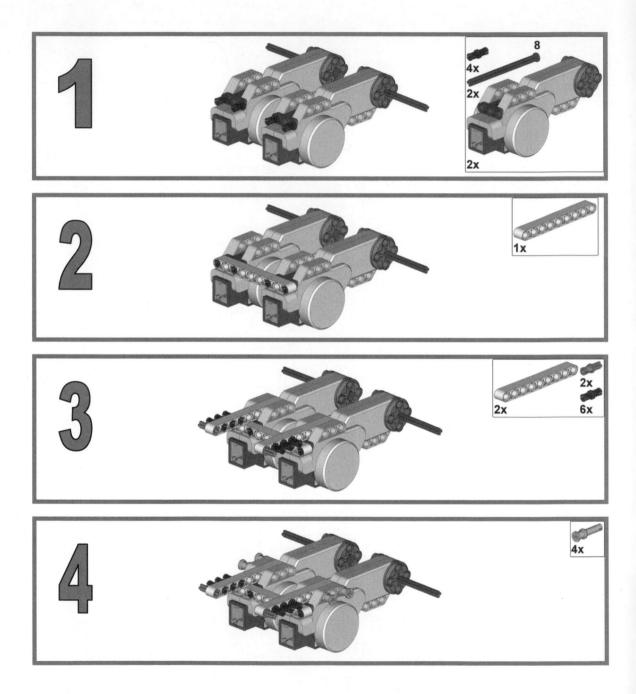

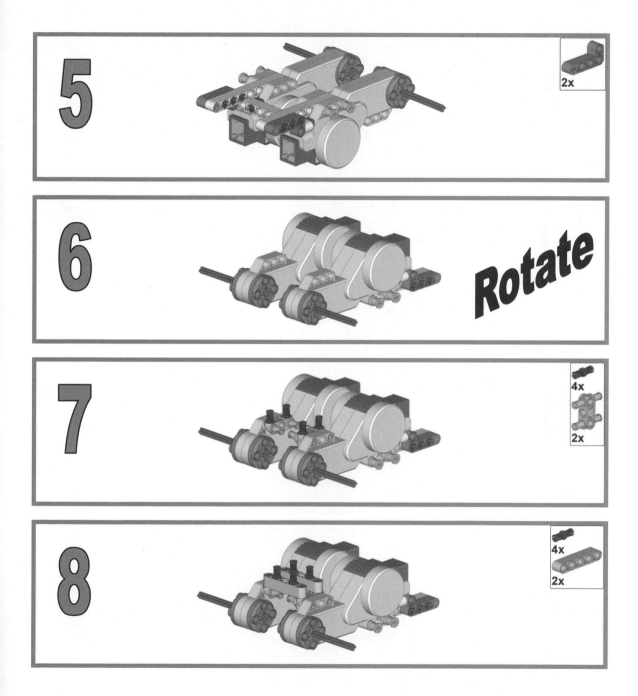

5 2x

6 *Rotate*

7 4x 2x

8 4x 2x

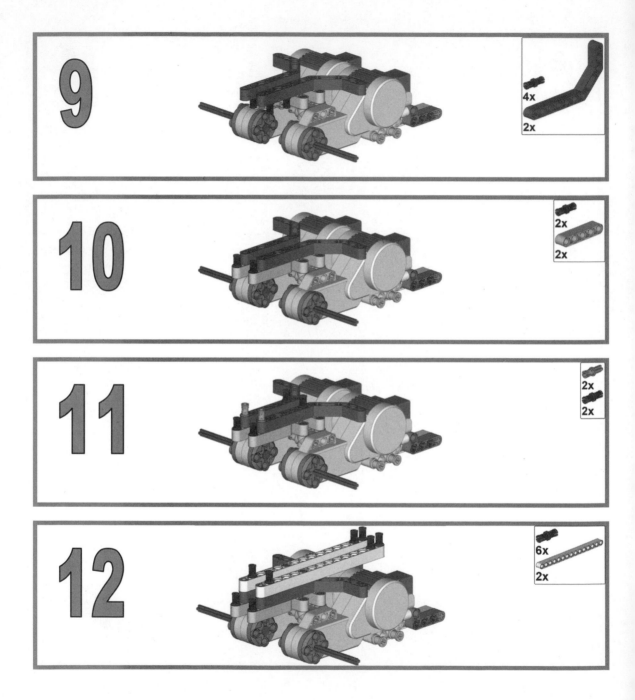

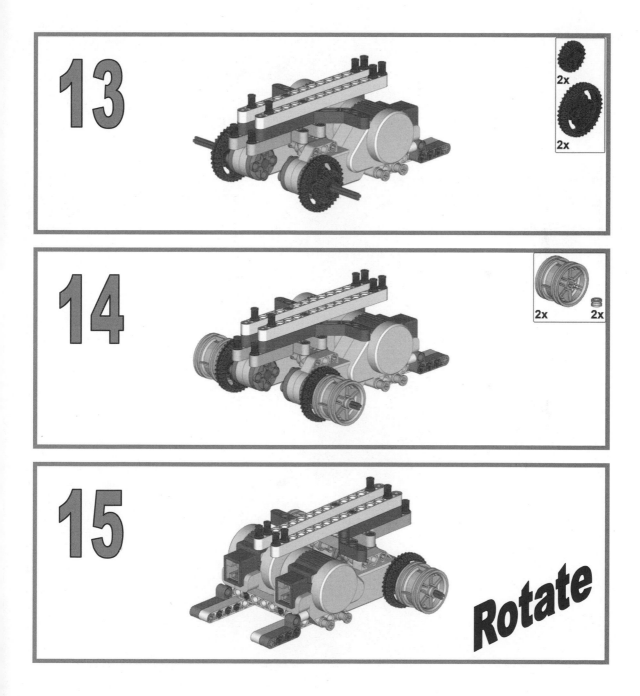

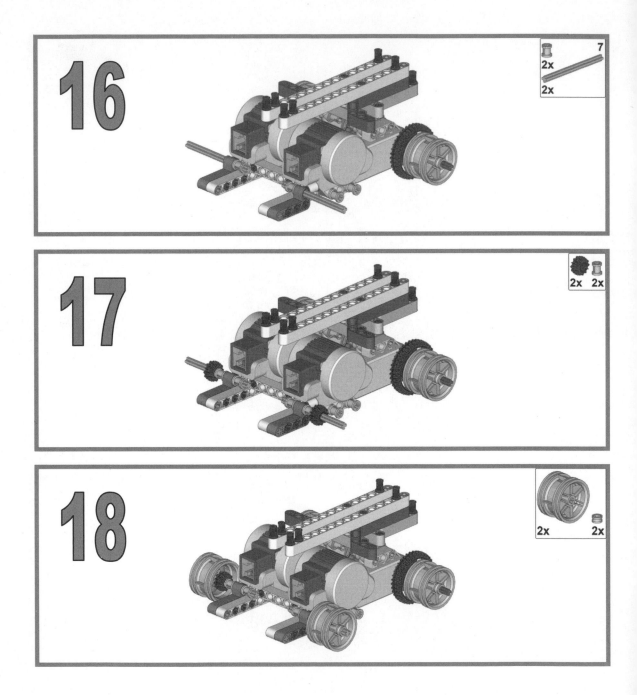

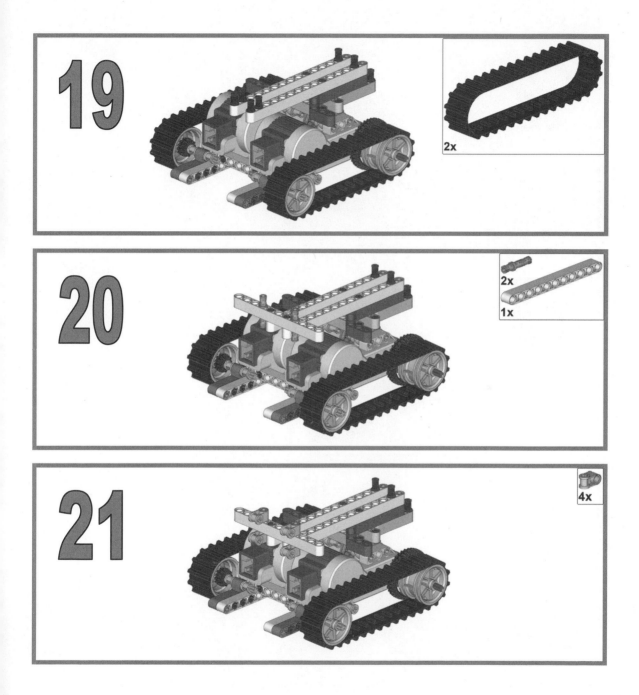

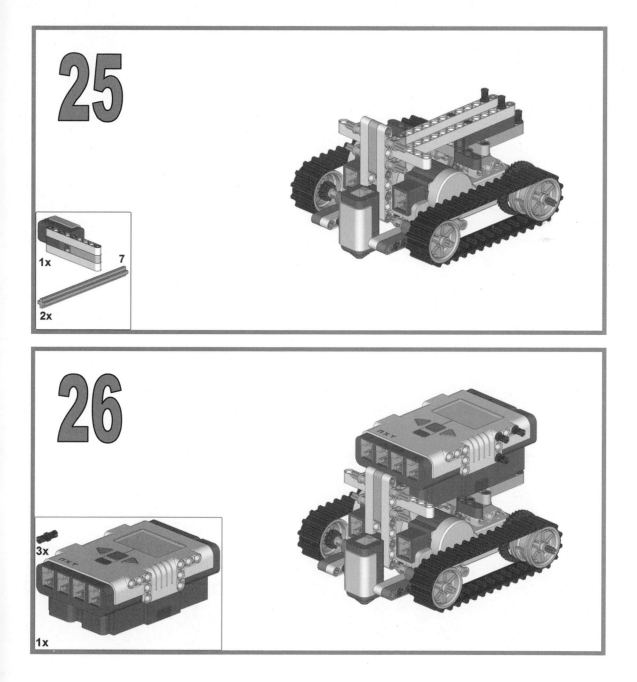

27

1x
1x

28

Rotate

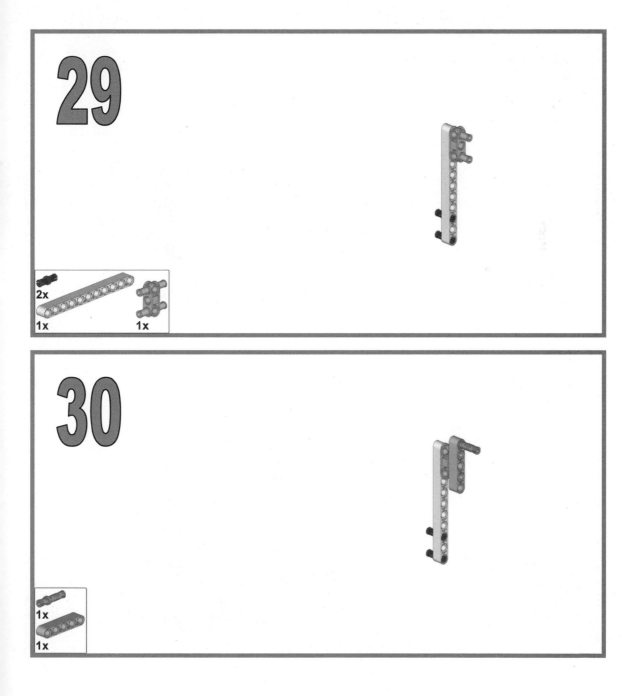

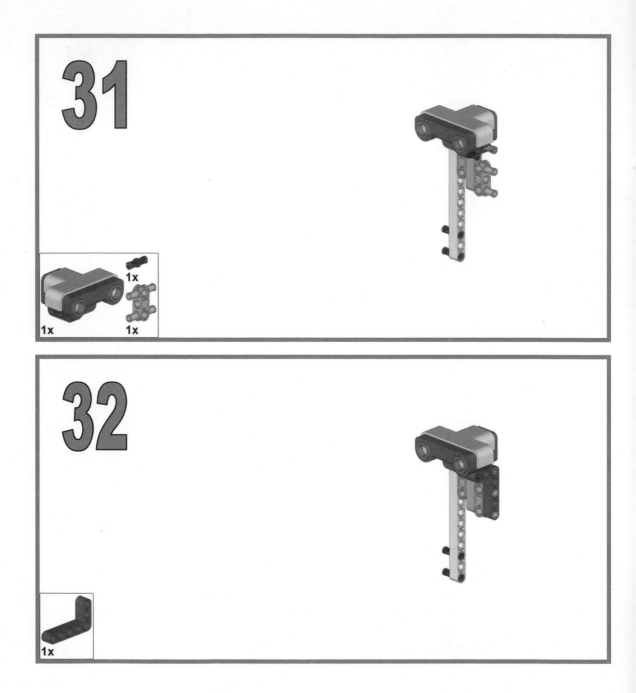

31

32

33

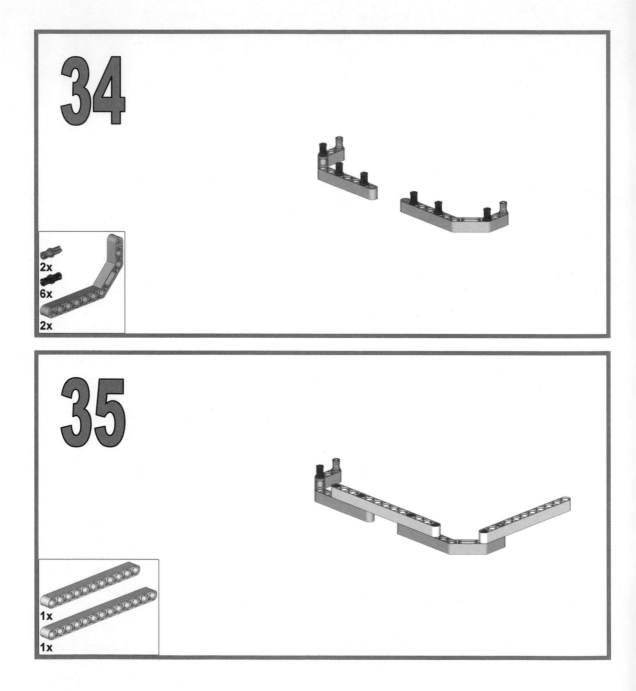

36

1x

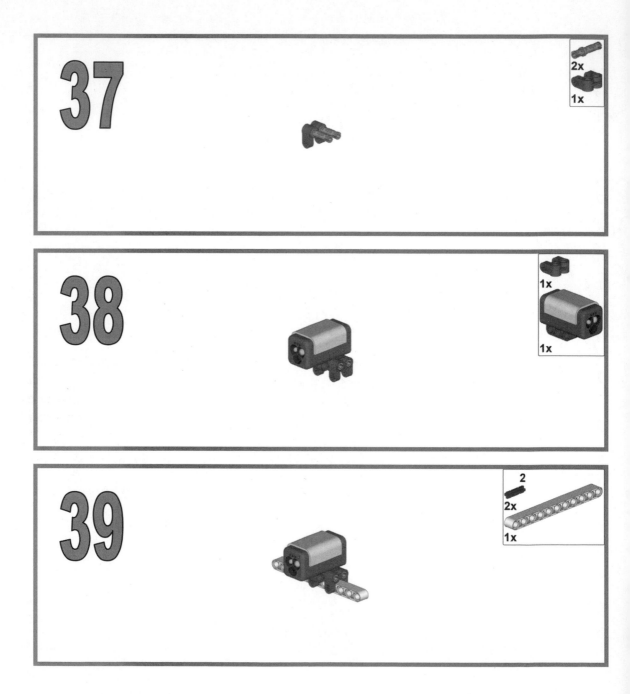

40

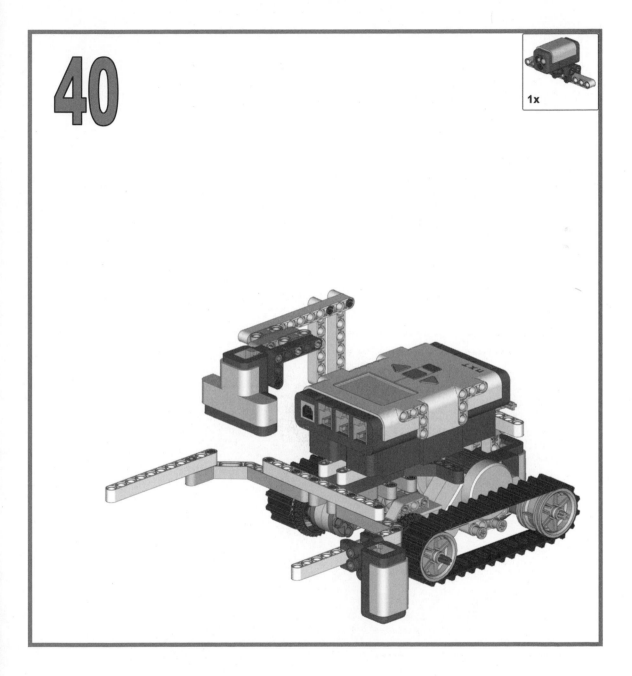

■ ■ ■

CHAPTER 16

RampRider—Program It

This robot has three goals: move the statues to their proper locations, find and trigger the ramp's pressure plates, and avoid rolling boulders. Most of its work will be repetitive: the robot will perform the same movements for each statue, so we can take advantage of this while programming the RampRider.

Let's get started by opening the NXT software and putting the proper blocks in place to get those statues placed properly and get the RampRider back in one piece.

Multiple Statues

This challenge requires the RampRider to perform a collection of tasks that we'll call the "Statue Movements":

1. Find the statue

2. Push the statue onto pressure plate

3. Move in reverse onto an opposing pressure plate for three seconds

The robot will perform the Statue Movements twice, for the two statues on the ramp (possibly more, if you wish to increase the ramp length and add more statues). Our program will then contain Statue 1 Movement blocks and Statue 2 Movement blocks. But won't the blocks for Statue 1 Movement and Statue 2 Movement be identical?

We could easily copy and paste all the blocks required for the Statue 1 Movements to create the Statue 2 Movements, but there's a much simpler solution that I'm sure you've already considered—the LOOP block. We'll use a LOOP block that will loop twice (executing any blocks inside it twice) and contain the blocks required to satisfy the Statue Movements.

Figure 16-1 shows the LOOP block and its configuration panel. The Control option has a drop-down menu that's been configured to Count, and the Count value has been set to 2.

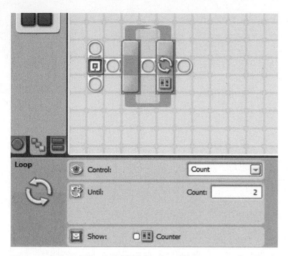

Figure 16-1. The LOOP block will execute the Statue Movements twice.

Now, we'll start placing blocks inside the LOOP block that will control the robot's movements as it locates and places the statues. The first one, obviously, will be a MOVE block that gets the robot moving up the center of the ramp. Figure 16-2 shows the MOVE block configured for Unlimited duration. Set the Power to 30 so the robot will move slowly up the ramp; this will make it easier for the Ultrasonic sensor to locate a statue.

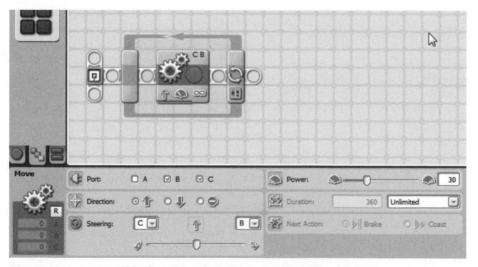

Figure 16-2. A MOVE block will get the robot moving up the ramp.

Speaking of the Ultrasonic sensor, the robot should now start scanning for a statue. Figure 16-3 shows the WAIT block that's been added and configured to use the Ultrasonic sensor. You may need to experiment with the Distance value; for my tests, a value of 3 (inches) was used but this will depend on how tall your statues are or how far above the robot the Ultrasonic sensor is mounted. By adding this WAIT block, the motors will continue to spin until the Ultrasonic sensor detects a statue.

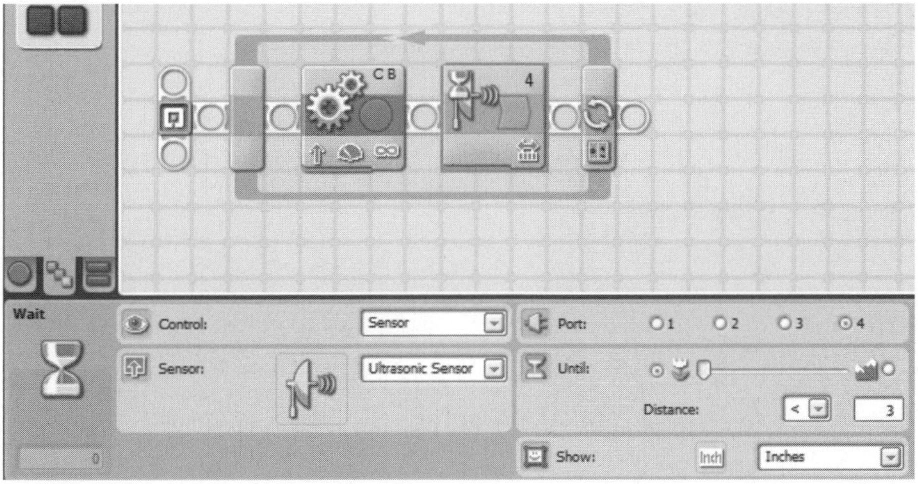

Figure 16-3. The WAIT block will keep the motors spinning until the Ultrasonic sensor is triggered.

Once the Ultrasonic sensor is triggered, the statue has been detected. During my own testing, I found that once the Ultrasonic sensor detected the statue, it was still a few inches away from the statue; moving a little closer would make it easier for the robot to grab, rotate, and push the statue. Figure 16-4 shows another MOVE block I added that moves the robot forward a short distance. You'll need to experiment and determine this distance using trial-and-error.

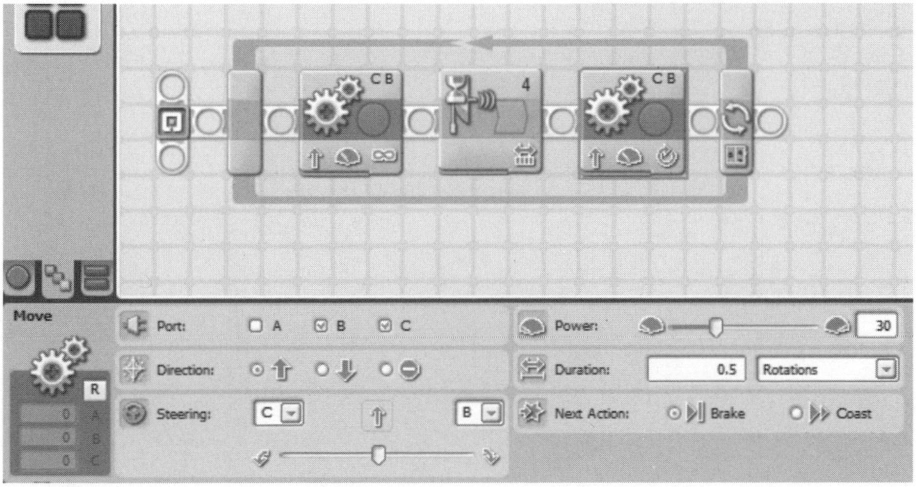

Figure 16-4. The next MOVE block will have the robot roll forward a short distance.

■ **Note** For all the MOVE blocks, I used a Power (speed) value of 30. If this is too slow for you, feel free to increase it. During my testing, however, I found that using too high of a value for the Power would cause odd behavior when making turns. Be sure to test various speeds to determine the best value for your robot.

At this point the robot should be close enough to move the statue with its gate (or whatever method you've built) by rotating to the right. Figure 16-5 shows the MOVE block that causes the robot to make a 90 degree turn to the right. You'll need to experiment with the Duration value—the angle and material of the ramp you are using will affect how the robot turns with the tank treads.

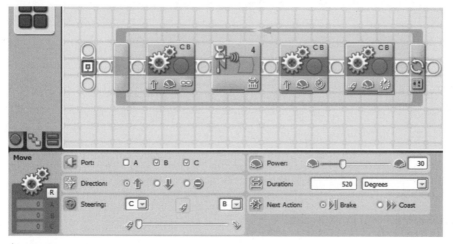

Figure 16-5. The MOVE block will rotate the robot to the right.

After the robot makes the right turn, it should begin moving forward slowly. Add another MOVE block as shown in Figure 16-6.

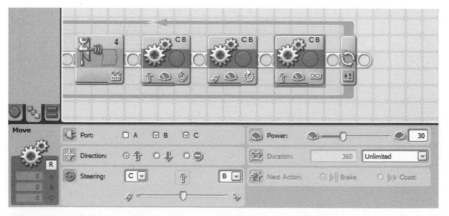

Figure 16-6. After turning, the robot will begin to move forward again.

The robot will need to use the Color sensor to detect the pressure plate. For my challenge area, I used blue painter's tape to create rectangles indicating the pressure plates (see my challenge area setup description at the end of this chapter). Figure 16-7 shows the WAIT block I configured to use the Color sensor. I configured it to look for the Blue color range. The motors will keep spinning until this WAIT block is triggered by the Color sensor detecting the color blue.

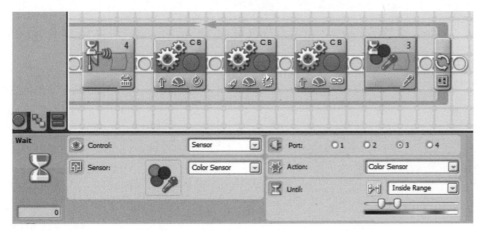

Figure 16-7. The Color sensor will look for the color blue.

After the Color sensor is triggered by finding the blue tape, the robot needs to move forward a short distance to push the statue over the tape and onto the pressure plate. Figure 16-8 shows the MOVE block I added that instructs the RampRider to roll forward one motor rotation with a Power setting of 40. (You may need to change these values if your pressure plate areas are not as wide as mine.)

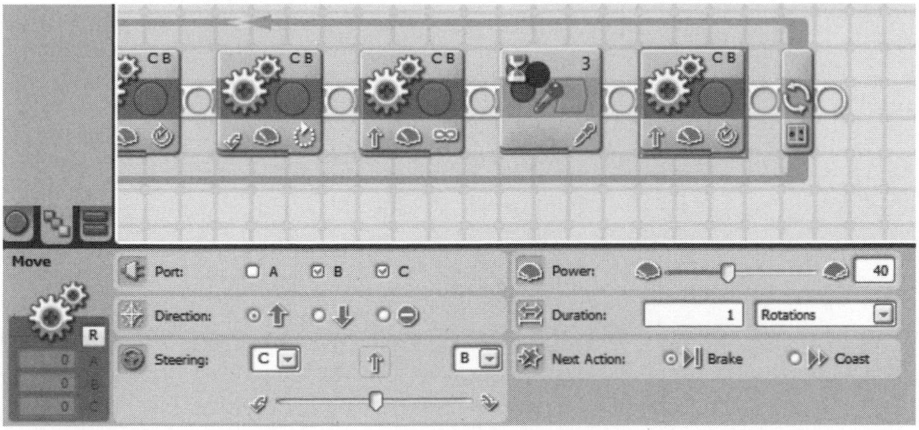

Figure 16-8. This MOVE block will move the robot forward a short distance.

Now the statue is on the pressure plate. At this point, the countdown has begun. If the robot does not trigger the pressure plate on the opposite side of the ramp within 10 seconds, a boulder (I used a basketball) will roll down the ramp and possibly crush the robot!

Rather than have the robot spin around, taking time, I'm going to have the RampRider simply roll in reverse… at a slightly higher speed than before. Figure 16-9 shows the MOVE block I configured that will get the robot to the opposite side.

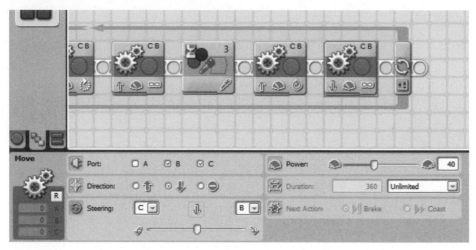

Figure 16-9. This MOVE block will have RampRider rolling in reverse at a higher speed.

I don't want the robot to roll off the edge of the ramp, so I'll use the Touch sensor mounted on the rear to detect when the robot is near the edge. When the Touch sensor moves off the ramp (over empty space), the button will be released. This button has, up to now, been pressed against the ramp's surface—the surface has been preventing the button from being released. Figure 16-10 shows the WAIT block I configured to test for the button's release.

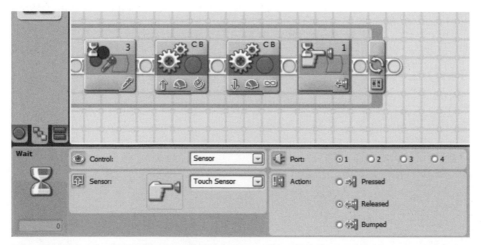

Figure 16-10. The WAIT block will check to see if the Touch sensor button is released.

Once the WAIT block is triggered (the Touch sensor button is released, indicating it's near the edge), the robot needs to stop immediately. Figure 16-11 shows the MOVE block that stops the motors.

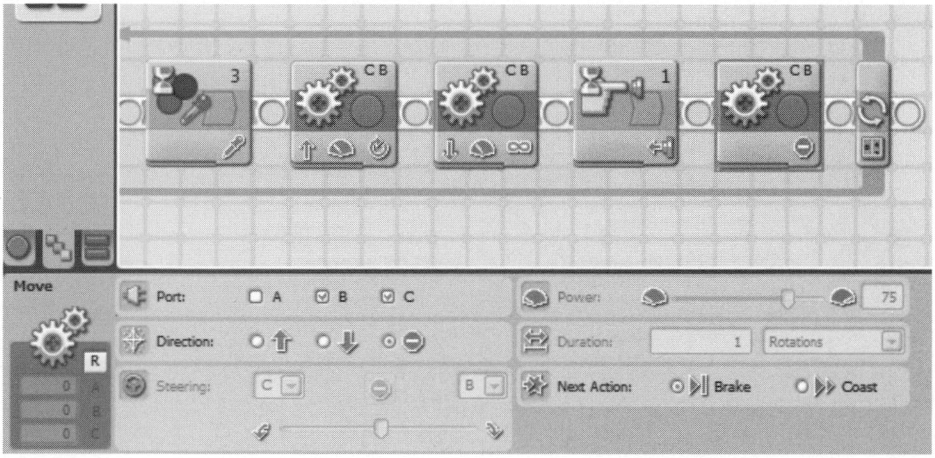

Figure 16-11. The robot will stop moving once it's reached the ramp's edge.

■ **Tip** If you find the WAIT block is triggering too early, it's possible that when the RampRider reverses direction, the pressure on the Touch sensor button is reduced enough to trigger a "Release" state. One solution I found for this was to add some weight to the back of the robot. I simply attached a third (unused) motor to the rear of the robot, which provided sufficient weight to keep the Touch sensor button pressed until it detected the ramp's edge.

Once the RampRider is sitting on the opposing pressure plate, it needs to wait for three seconds before any further movements. Figure 16-12 shows the WAIT block I added, configured for a three-second pause.

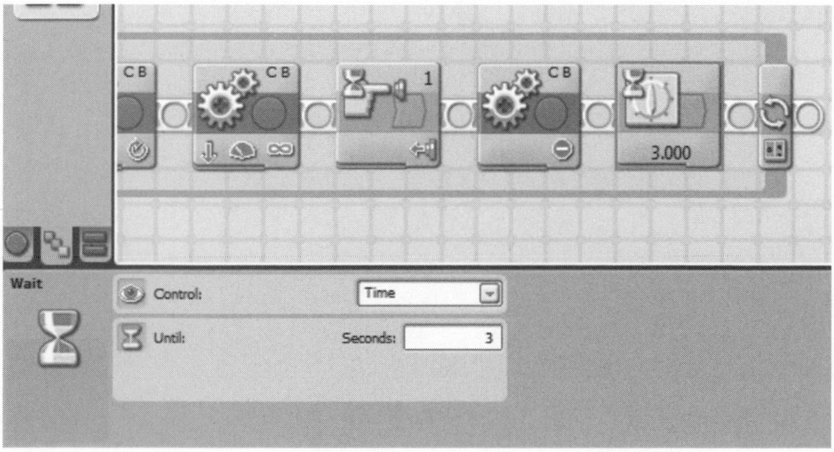

Figure 16-12. RampRider will wait three seconds before moving.

After the three-second wait, the RampRider must move to the center of the ramp, and then locate the second statue. Figure 16-13 shows the MOVE block I added to get the robot to the center of the ramp. (The Duration value may be different for you if your ramp is a different width than mine; change this value during testing to get your robot as close to the center of the ramp as possible.)

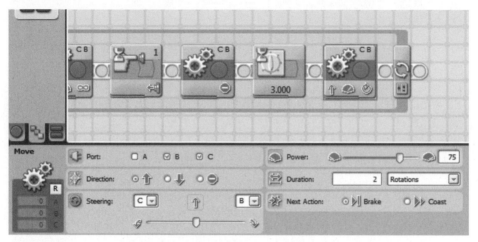

Figure 16-13. The robot will need to move back to the center of the ramp.

Once it's back to the center of the ramp, it needs to turn left 90 degrees. At that point, it will be ready to find the second statue. Figure 16-4 shows the MOVE block I dropped in to make the left turn. (Once again, this value will probably be different for you because of differences in ramp angle and surface material, so test and change this value to ensure the best possible 90 degree turn.)

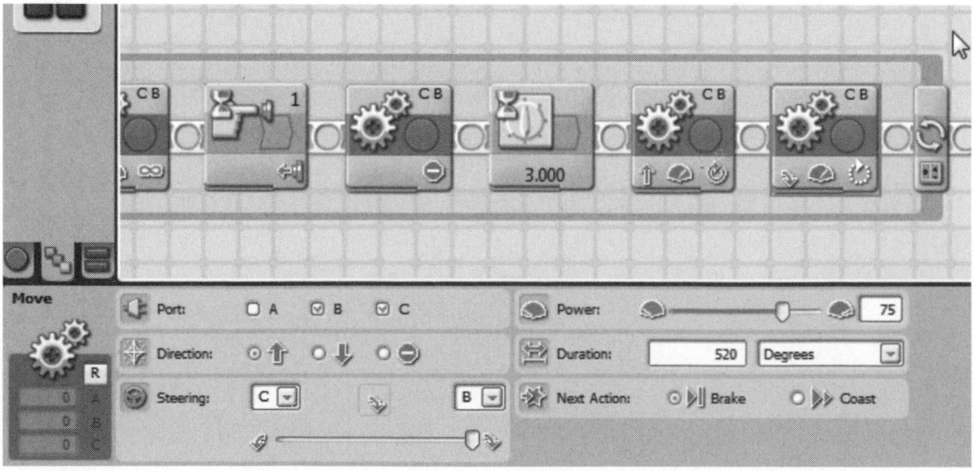

Figure 16-14. The robot will turn to the left and prepare to locate the second statue.

At this point, the RampRider will perform the identical steps for Statue 2 that it did for Statue 1. The LOOP block ended, but I configured it to loop twice, so it will execute all the blocks inside it one more time. When this has completed, the robot should be sitting in the center of the ramp, facing up the ramp. All that's left is to add a MOVE block to get the robot all the way back down the ramp. Figure 16-15 shows the MOVE block I added that will move the robot in reverse (no need to have it turn around).

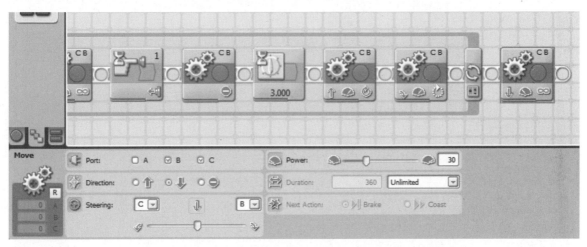

Figure 16-15. The robot will roll in reverse until it gets back to the start of the ramp.

Figure 16-16 shows a simple WAIT block added that waits for the orange select button to be pressed on the brick. This WAIT block is necessary so the MOVE block in Figure 16-15 will continue to execute. Without the WAIT block, the MOVE block would begin the motors spinning and then stop because the program has ended.

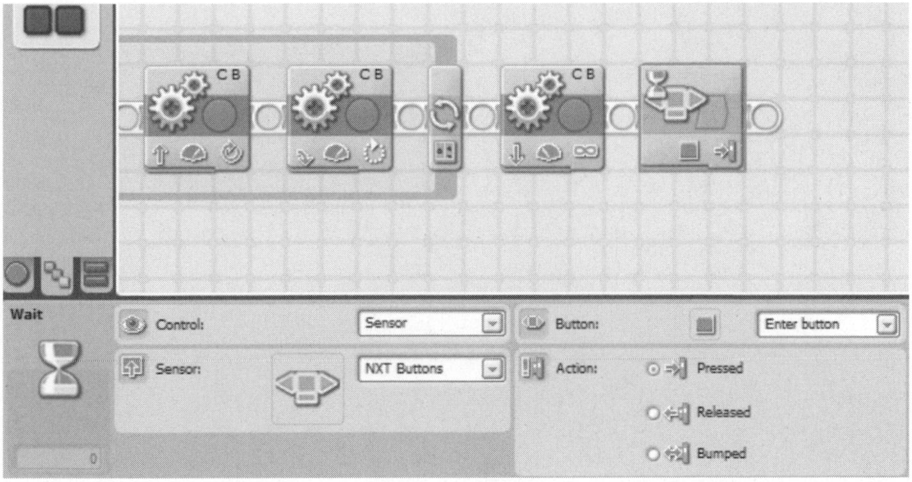

Figure 16-16. The WAIT block keeps the robot moving until the Enter button is pressed.

The Ramp Challenge Setup

This is a fairly simple challenge to set up. Keep in mind that you can make the ramp as short or long as you like and you can vary the width of the ramp. For my challenge area, I used a single piece of plywood with dimensions of 4 feet long and 2 feet wide.

I used blue painter's tape to mark off a few areas. First, I measured six inches from the ramp's left side and ran the tape down the complete length of the ramp. Next, I measured six inches from the ramp's right side and ran the tape down the complete length of the ramp. Finally, I used the tape to create the pressure plates by measuring 16 inches and 32 inches from the top of the ramp and using tape to create the sections shown in Figure 16-17.

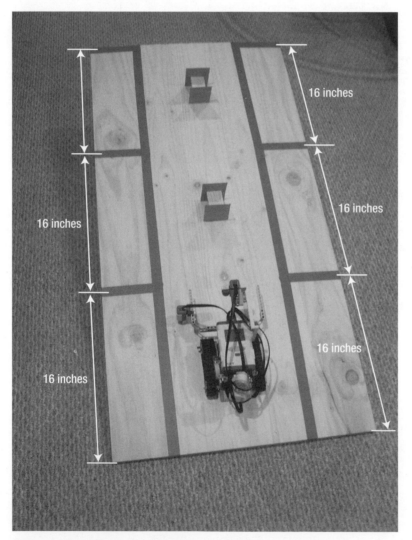

Figure 16-17. The ramp, with dimensions for the pressure plates

I used a box to raise the ramp approximately 12 inches, for an approximate angle of 30 degrees.

Next, I built two small "statues" by gluing small cardboard squares to the ends of small pieces of wood. The cardboard squares prevented the "statues" from sliding down the ramp. Feel free to create any kind of statue you like, but don't make them too heavy or your robot won't be able to push them. Also, keep the height of each statue less than the distance from your Ultrasonic sensor to the ramp's surface.

Locate two basketballs (or other type of ball) to serve as your boulders. A stopwatch can be handy, too—when the Color sensor detects the pressure plate (in this case, the blue tape), start the countdown from 10 seconds. When it reaches 0, have someone release the ball from the top of the ramp so it rolls down the centerline. Hopefully the RampRider makes it to the other pressure plate in time… or it could be messy.

After both statues are placed on their respective pressure plates, the correct stone slab should fall from the ceiling, indicating which tunnel leads to the final challenge.

■ ■ ■

CHAPTER 17

Grab and Release

Location: Southwest Guatemala

102 miles SW of Guatemala City

Coordinates: 14º 04' N / 90º 09' W

Weather Conditions: 97 degrees Fahrenheit, Humidity 82%

Day 7: King Ixtua's Treasure Repository, 8:41 a.m.

Evan couldn't believe his luck. His little robot's wheels had slipped on some sand or dust after pushing the second statue onto its pressure plate and had just rolled onto the matching pressure plate when one of the boulders released. It rolled down the ramp and towards the team standing in the doorway to the fourth chamber.

"Stand clear!" yelled Uncle Phillip. The boulder was only about the size of a basketball, but it still managed to make it all the way through the doorway and down the hall a few more feet.

Evan put his back against the wall with the rest of the team and let the boulder come to a rest.

Tag laughed. "That was close!"

Evan shook his head. "Too close. I think it may have actually knocked off a piece or two of the robot's frame."

A loud bang sounded from within the room. Evan saw his uncle quickly peer into the room then turn and smile. "The wood plaque over the door to the right fell off. I think we're in business. Everyone stay here, please."

Evan watched as his uncle slowly stepped into the room. Tupaxu had put enough traps along their way that Evan understood the caution. Even though the pressure plates in the room should have been disabled after the ramp challenge was completed, one really couldn't be certain.

After fifteen minutes examining the pressure plates, Dr. Hicks asked Tag and Erin to bring in the tripod lights and place them near the ramp. He and Evan picked up and moved the fallen plaque carefully out of the way of the right wall's door.

"Erin, will you get me some translations of the three plaques, please? And Tag, I'll need photographs of the entire room, plus measurements. Evan, let's take a look at the door."

Evan's uncle motioned for Evan to stand to the side to avoid anything that might be behind the door. Evan's uncle then attached a small piece of rope to the door's small handle, moved to the side with Evan, and pulled the rope.

The old wooden door opened with a loud creak. Evan raised his eyebrows and looked at his uncle. "All good?" he asked.

Uncle Phillip moved his head slowly around the side wall to take a look.

"Another hallway carved into the mountain," said Evan's uncle. "Take a look."

Evan joined his uncle. Another hallway ran approximately ten feet and then turned to the left. "Looks normal," Evan said. "That probably means traps."

Uncle Phillip laughed. "You're learning fast, Evan."

Uncle Phillip asked Evan to assist Tag with measuring and photographing the ramp room while he checked the hallway for more traps. Thirty minutes later, Uncle Phillip emerged from the hallway.

"Tag, I need you to photograph the new hallway," said Dr. Hicks. "I've marked six pressure plates with red tape, but do be careful stepping around them. And please take as many photos as you can of the next chamber, but watch the drop. You'll see what I mean when you get there. Where's Erin?"

"She had to go back for her books," Evan replied. "She said the plaques had some unusual glyphs."

"Yes, they did, "Uncle Phillip replied. "Some of them I've never seen before, not even variations."

Evan watched Tag shoot a photograph of the open door before turning on his flashlight and entering the hallway. "Will he be okay by himself?"

Uncle Phillip nodded. "Tag and Erin are careful, and I trust them. Tupaxu was tricky with his traps, but I'm confident I found them all."

"Did you see anything interesting in the next chamber?" asked Evan.

"It's dark but I think I saw enough to know it's going to be tricky. Let's head up to the camp site—I need to make a very important phone call."

Tupaxu's Story

Tag returned an hour later and found Evan alone in the command tent. "Where is everyone?"

Evan shrugged. "Uncle Phillip went to make a phone call and I saw Erin talking with some of the Guatemalan guides about twenty minutes ago. I've just been taking my robot apart."

Tag sat down in front of his laptop. "Well, come over and take a look. I've got some great photographs." Tag plugged his digital camera into the laptop and began downloading files.

"How big is the next chamber?" asked Evan. "Is it lit with torches?"

"Oh, yeah," replied Tag. "Opening the door most likely triggered some mechanism to light them, but we're going to need tripod lights anyway. The torches will be burned out by now."

"But how big is it?" asked Evan again.

Tag frowned. "You're not going to like this, Evan. It's like the second chamber—very high up."

Evan groaned. "Heights. Again."

"Sorry," said Tag.

Evan heard the tent flap open behind them. Erin ducked under the flap and entered.

"Did you get some good pictures of the next chamber?" asked Erin. "Please tell me you did."

Tag nodded. "I filled up my memory stick," he replied. "Why?"

"Because I'm not believing what I'm reading in these scrolls," said Erin, holding up a collection of rolls of parchment.

Evan pulled a chair over for Erin. "We were just getting ready to look over the photographs," he said.

"Here goes," said Tag, clicking a button to display the images as a slideshow.

Evan watched picture after picture dissolve on the screen. He was able to discern the hallway photographs, including many of the traps that Uncle Phillip had found and marked with red tape. More photos showed an opening at the end of the hallway that was completely dark except for the little light provided by Tag's flashlight.

"I moved one of the tripod lights all the way to the chamber's entrance," said Tag. "It was the only way I could get the next set of photos. I also drew a sketch of the room in my journal." Tag pulled out a leather journal from his bag.

Evan returned his attention to the laptop screen. Photos continued to appear for a few seconds before dissolving into more images. As the photos of the new chamber cycled on screen, Evan shook his head.

Erin patted Evan on the back. "Not a fan of heights, are you?" she asked.

Evan shook his head again.

The slideshow ended and Tag opened his journal. "Here's that sketch I drew of the chamber." (See Figure 17-1.)

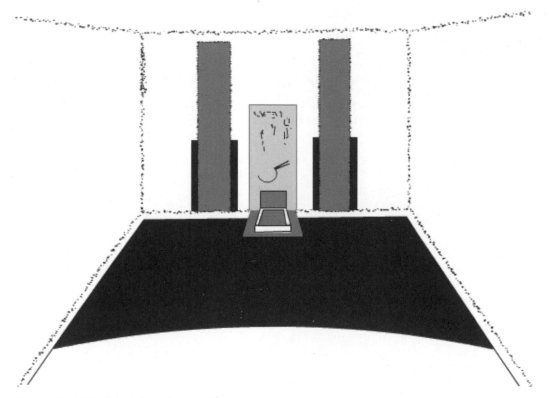

Figure 17-1. The final chamber sketch

Uncle Phillip entered the tent as Evan examined Tag's drawing.

"Any problems?" asked Erin. "Will they be here soon?"

"Tomorrow morning," replied Uncle Phillip. "Let's talk about the scrolls."

Evan was confused by his Uncle's change of subject, but he turned his attention to the scrolls that Erin was holding.

"This," she said, "is one of the scrolls we retrieved from King Ixtua's library. The glyphs on the plaque that fell from the door match the ones running along the top of the scroll. It's a story about Tupaxu."

Erin unrolled it and placed a few small stones at the corners to hold it down.

"Not the king?" asked Tag.

Erin shook her head. "No. According to these scrolls, Tupaxu died before the final chamber was completed. The final chamber was completed by his apprentice, Qau, and it's supposed to honor a legend about Tupaxu."

"This is getting interesting," said Tag.

Uncle Phillip smiled. "Yes, it is. You've all seen photos of the chamber?" he asked.

Everyone nodded.

"Good," replied Uncle Phillip. "So, what does the scroll tell us, Erin?"

"According to this scroll, while Tupaxu and his team of stonecutters were working on the first chamber it would take hours for Tupaxu to walk down the mountain to the nearby village. He had his team build a series of towers that held ropes that would allow workers to move items up and down the mountain. Supposedly, Tupaxu was known to take an occasional fast ride down the mountain on some sort of trolley. The scroll says no one else was brave enough to try it."

"Or crazy enough," said Tag.

"Well, the scroll states that Tupaxu died shortly after the fourth chamber was completed. Qau was given the task of completing the final chamber and he based it on Tupaxu's invention. This last scroll contains instructions for Qau's challenge but it's very faded, so I'm not completely certain about the translation. I saw Tag's photos, but I didn't see something mentioned in the scrolls and I'm a little worried."

"How about we all head down to the chamber?" asked Uncle Phillip. "I need another look and maybe Erin can figure out the challenge if she sees the room herself. Evan will need to see it, too, just in case we need his robotic expertise."

The King's Throne

"Wow!" exclaimed Evan. "Look at that."

Evan stood with Tag, Erin, and his uncle on the small stone entry in the fifth chamber. Across a large chasm was a simple golden throne. To the right and left of the throne, Evan could see two large wooden bridges leaning against the back wall. Each bridge also blocked what appeared to be a dark passageway reaching beyond the fifth chamber.

Uncle Phillip smiled. "Tupaxu and Qau were amazing, weren't they? All these challenges to protect the king's treasure."

"I don't see the trigger," said Erin. "But it has to be there."

During their journey back to the fifth chamber, Erin had explained that the scrolls mentioned a throne trigger that, when pressed, would lower the two bridges.

"It's behind the throne," said Evan's uncle. "It has to be."

Tag shrugged. "Well, how is it triggered then?" he asked.

Evan heard Erin giggle. "Now it makes sense," she said. She looked down at her notebook where her translation of the scrolls was written.

The team members all looked at Erin for an explanation.

"See, this glyph here?" she said, pointing to a small symbol in her notebook. "At first, I couldn't figure it out, but then I realized it was the symbol for throne but written at a ninety degree turn to the rest of the glyphs."

Uncle Phillip nodded. "Very smart. Without the scroll, you wouldn't be able to figure out how to trigger the release of the bridges."

Evan frowned. "I don't get it," he said.

"Neither do I," replied Tag. "I give up—how do we get the bridges to lower?"

"That hook just above the throne must have held a rope or vine at some point. See? There's a matching hook above our heads, up near the ceiling. My guess is the monkey could slide down the rope, crossing the chasm and triggering the bridges," said Erin.

"That makes sense," replied Dr. Hicks. "It would be easy enough to drop down on to the throne."

"Hey! Come on!" exclaimed Tag. "Tell us."

Erin laughed. "Okay, sorry. The back of the throne needs to be tipped over. Look carefully; the back doesn't seem to be attached to the rest of the throne. The trigger is behind it. The glyph turned on its side is the clue."

"Sneaky," said Evan. "Qau's just as tricky as Tupaxu."

"But the vine's gone," said Tag. "Unless Evan can build a robot that flies, I'm not sure how we're getting across there."

"And even if we did," said Erin, "I'm sure there's a trap or two waiting for us if we don't tip that throne over."

"Anyone up for a game of ring toss?" asked Uncle Phillip. "We could tie a piece of rope to a ring and try to hit the hook."

Evan looked carefully at the hook. It was small and it could take days for them to try and get a ring on to the hook. There had to be a better way.

"Is that stone or wood behind the throne?" asked Evan.

"Looks like wood," replied Uncle Phillip. "Why?"

Evan scratched his head. "Well, I saw a few of the Guatemalan guides hitting targets the other day with their bows. I'm wondering if we could get one of them to shoot a string across on an arrow?"

"Hmmm," said Uncle Phillip. "I hate to risk damaging the throne, but if one of them could hit just above it accurately, that might work."

"Why not just throw something across and knock the back of the throne over?" asked Tag.

"Because Qau probably thought of that," replied Erin. "I'll bet that the throne seat is a pressure plate that the monkey would have to be standing on when pushing over the back of the throne."

"Makes sense," said Uncle Phillip. "Evan, if we can get a string to the other side, what do you have in mind?"

Evan's Solution

Uncle Phillip and Tag had held a contest for the guides early in the afternoon to find the most accurate bow shooter. Evan had listened to the laughter and cheering as he wrote in his design journal and developed an idea for another robot.

A few hours later, Tag and Uncle Phillip entered Evan's tent and informed him that a guide had successfully shot an arrow across the chasm. With a string attached to the arrow, the team had recreated Qau's challenge.

Evan lifted his new robot off the table and showed it to his uncle. "What do you think?" he asked.

Uncle Phillip looked puzzled. "I have no idea what I'm looking at, but I trust you, Evan. If you think this robot can cross on the string and trigger the bridges, we'll attempt it after breakfast tomorrow. I'm expecting some important guests, too. Hope you won't mind the pressure of a few more observers."

"It'll work, Uncle Phillip. I've tested it and it's ready," Evan replied.

"Well, then," said his uncle, "tomorrow we tackle the final challenge and see what King Ixtua can share with the world."

The story concludes in Chapter 21...

■ ■ ■

CHAPTER 18

ZipLiner—Design and Planning

Once again, we find ourselves needing to build a robot that requires a different type of motion—in this case, zipping down a line to King Ixtua's throne! The robot must be designed in such a way that it avoids the risk of falling into the pit (or of falling from too high a distance above the throne). Before we begin building and programming a robot, however, we need to examine the challenge facing our little robot and develop a plan of attack. We are facing the final obstacle between us and King Ixtua's treasure—let's conquer it, shall we?

The ZipLiner

For the Robot Name box, I've selected ZipLiner as my robot's name. Zip lines are gaining popularity around the world as a fun way to cross great distances (at slow and fast speeds). You are strapped into a harness, way up high—when released, gravity takes control and you zip down the line through trees, over rivers, and even across canyons! Zip line obstacle courses must be safe for people, but our robot also needs to be kept safe from falling.

■ **Note** There are blank Design Journal worksheets in the back of this book. If you need more pages, feel free to make photocopies of the Design Journal worksheet or visit the Apress Web site to download the page in PDF format.

The Robot Description

For the Robot Description, you may find as I have that there's not much challenge to completing this section. My robot will need motors and possibly a sensor or two, but I'm not going to worry about those decisions right now. Instead, what I need to concentrate on is writing out a basic explanation of what ZipLiner must do to trigger the release of the bridges and let the team access the king's treasure room. I've done this in Figure 18-1.

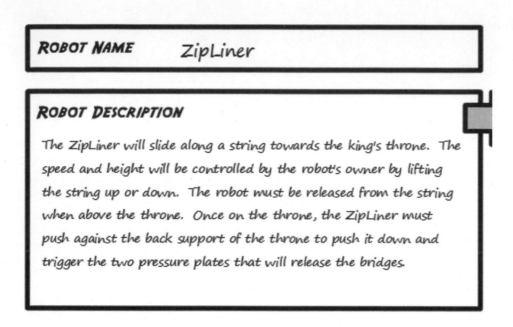

ROBOT NAME   ZipLiner

ROBOT DESCRIPTION

The ZipLiner will slide along a string towards the king's throne. The speed and height will be controlled by the robot's owner by lifting the string up or down. The robot must be released from the string when above the throne. Once on the throne, the ZipLiner must push against the back support of the throne to push it down and trigger the two pressure plates that will release the bridges.

Figure 18-1. *The ZipLiner's Robot Description*

Notice that I haven't explained how the robot will slide along the string; that's a construction detail that I don't need to worry about just yet. Likewise, I haven't figured out how I'll get the robot to release itself from the string once it's over the throne, but I imagine I'll use one of the sensors. The final job the robot must perform will be to push against the back support of the throne until it tips over; this will require motors, obviously, as well as some pushing power on the robot's part.

I've got plenty of thinking to do about the specifics of this robot's design, but for now, I believe I've captured the basic concept of the ZipLiner's challenge.

Now, it's time to break down my description into discrete tasks for the Task List.

The Task List

I still have a few unknowns after completing my Task List (shown in Figure 18-2).

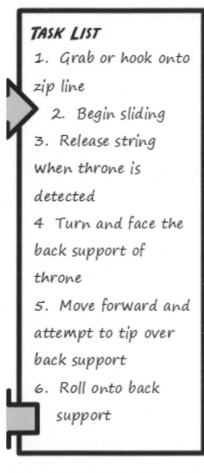

TASK LIST

1. Grab or hook onto zip line
   2. Begin sliding
3. Release string when throne is detected
4 Turn and face the back support of throne
5. Move forward and attempt to tip over back support
6. Roll onto back support

Figure 18-2. The Zipliner's Task List isn't long, but there are still some unknowns.

The Task List isn't extremely long or complicated, but you may notice that it still has some actions that aren't explained in detail. For example, Task #1, "Grab or hook onto zip line," doesn't explain how the robot will move along the string, only that it will use some sort of grabbing or hooking design. And that's exactly when this decision will be made—during the design phase.

Task #3, "Release string when throne is detected," doesn't explain how ZipLiner will find the throne or how it will release the string, but by including it in the list, I at least acknowledge that some sort of method must be developed for this extremely important task.

Once the Zipliner is on the throne seat, it's going to need to locate the back support. That probably won't be too difficult, but it does indicate that I'll need my robot to have some method of movement other than using the string—wheels are a likely solution here. With the wheels and maybe a sensor or two, my robot should be able to finish the final tasks of tipping over the back support. That will trigger the hidden plate behind the throne.

Remember, during this challenge, the ZipLiner is facing some serious risks. First, it's going to be sliding down the string over a deep pit. Release too early? No more ZipLiner! Second, it's got to be balanced enough not to tip over once it reaches the throne's seat. Keep these in mind during your testing phase. (Hopefully you won't be attempting this challenge over a real pit—the worst you may need to worry about is your robot breaking apart on impact, but there are ways around that problem. I'll discuss them in Chapter 20.)

Limitations and Constraints

Because ZipLiner will be using a non-traditional method for getting to the throne, we don't have to deal with common limitations such as the steep slope of a ramp or a height limitation imposed by a tunnel. But ZipLiner does have some of its own constraints, as you can see in Figure 18-3.

Figure 18-3. The Zipliner has some limitations that must be considered during its design.

As you can see, the issue of the ZipLiner's weight must be considered. If the robot is too light, it will be difficult to get it to slide down the string. If it's too heavy, it will either hang low on the string, preventing it from sliding… or it will slide too fast to control!

Another issue that I think will come into play is the balance of the robot. As it hangs from the string, if it's too heavy in front or back, the robot will tilt. A serious tilt may have serious side effects when it comes time for the robot to release the string; it might tip over on a side or prevent any sensor we may use from detecting the throne properly.

Mindstorm

The task list and the constraints on this robot have certainly got me thinking. While I don't yet have a firm idea of this robot's final design, I am starting to get a few ideas on how I might get it safely to the throne. I've written down many of my initial thoughts in the Mindstorm section that you can see in Figure 18-4.

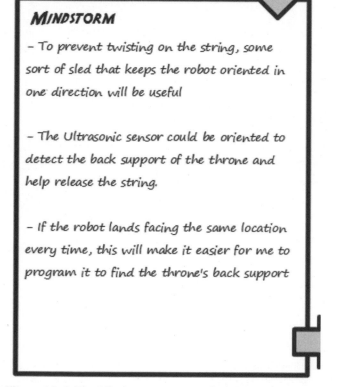

MINDSTORM

- To prevent twisting on the string, some sort of sled that keeps the robot oriented in one direction will be useful

- The Ultrasonic sensor could be oriented to detect the back support of the throne and help release the string.

- If the robot lands facing the same location every time, this will make it easier for me to program it to find the throne's back support

Figure 18-4. The Mindstorm section is helping me to get a better idea of the robot's design.

I don't think I have the proper parts to give ZipLiner hands so it can cross the string like a monkey, but I do have NXT motors that I can use to create fingers or grippers that can grab and release. I know I can get a more stable robot on the string if it has at least two points where it grabs or hooks on to the string. This will prevent the robot from spinning in place; if the robot spins, I cannot be certain that a sensor will be able to detect the throne. So, I'm going to try and develop something that will keep my robot oriented in one direction as it moves down the string.

If I'm successful in designing a method for moving down the string without spinning, I can also consider adding a sensor to look for the throne. The throne's back support is high and the string ends just above it, so I could possibly use the Ultrasonic sensor to detect the back support in time for a motor to release the string and allow the robot to fall or land gently on the throne seat. If I'm good, I may even be able to move the string up and down so I can place the robot on the throne seat or maybe a few millimeters above it, reducing the chance of damage from a fall. I'll definitely try to use the Ultrasonic sensor to trigger the string's release.

Have you noticed how success with one task can make the next task easier? If I can get my robot moving down the string without twisting, I give the Ultrasonic sensor a good chance to detect the throne. And if the Ultrasonic sensor detects the throne and allows the robot to land in a consistent manner during testing, I can use this to program it to find and tip over the throne's back support. And that's exactly what I plan to do—I'll assume I can get the robot to land in the same manner consistently, because I can then program its movements from that landing position to turn and push down the throne's back support!

Now it's time to take some of my ideas and see if I can put together a rough sketch of a robot that can complete this challenge.

Sketches

Once again, here's a list of the things that I know (or suspect) will give this robot a greater chance of success:

- The Ultrasonic sensor will be used to detect the throne's back support

- I can prevent my robot from twisting on the string by using two (or more) contact points

- I need to design a symmetrical robot to keep its weight balanced for a smoother ride on the string and to prevent tilting

Using these ideas, I drew the rough sketch of the Zipliner shown in Figure 18-5.

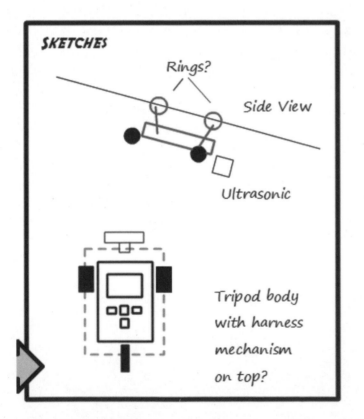

Figure 18-5. The Zipliner has a lot of sensors and a different method for movement.

For me, one of the simplest designs for a robot is a tribot body—two wheels and a caster. You've seen this design plenty in this book and with other NXT robots, so rather than try to reinvent the wheel, I'm going to go with a tribot body so I can spend more of my design time trying to come up with a useful system for moving down the string.

First, I plan on using some sort of sled system that uses two rings—these rings will help keep the robot pointed in the same direction as it moves down the string—no twisting! But I've still got to come up with some mechanism that will hold on to this sled and release it at the appropriate time. The mechanism will be attached to the robot's top; because it will most likely require a motor, I'll need to design it so it keeps the motor centered with respect to the tribot body.

The Ultrasonic sensor will be placed at the front of the robot; of course, "front" can mean different things. If the robot moves down the string with the wheels and caster pointed towards the throne's back support, then I won't have to program the robot to make any turns; it will simply move forward to tip over the back support. But if the sled-release motor has to be attached in such a way that the wheels are not pointed at the back support, I'll have to add some additional programming steps to rotate the robot so it can tip the throne back over.

This is a challenging robot! You can follow along with my instructions found in Chapter 19 or attempt to build your own. Maybe you have your own ideas for how to get the robot to the throne? Don't be afraid to test them!

And, of course, whether you build my version of the ZipLiner or your own, you're going to need to program it (Chapter 20) to get the job done. Only then will you be able to enter King Ixtua's treasure room and make the final discovery.

CHAPTER 19

■■■

ZipLiner—Build It

My version of the ZipLiner can be seen in Figure 19-1. Yes, it's an unusual-looking robot!

My robot body is somewhat symmetrical (i.e., the Tribot base body), but the sled mechanism is not. If you have difficulty figuring out where a part goes from a given figure, take a look at the next few figures; it's likely that a later image will show the placement of the part in question.

Figure 19-1. Evan's version of the ZipLiner.

■ **Note** If you modify or try to create your own version of the ZipLiner (or any other bot in this book), please take a picture and e-mail it to me. I would enjoy seeing your final bot in action. I've included my e-mail address in the Introduction.

And now, on to the construction of the ZipLiner!

Step by Step CAD Instructions – ZipLiner

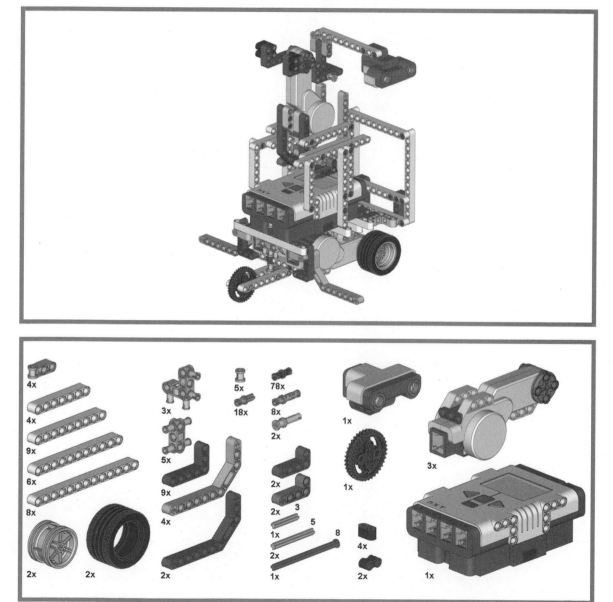

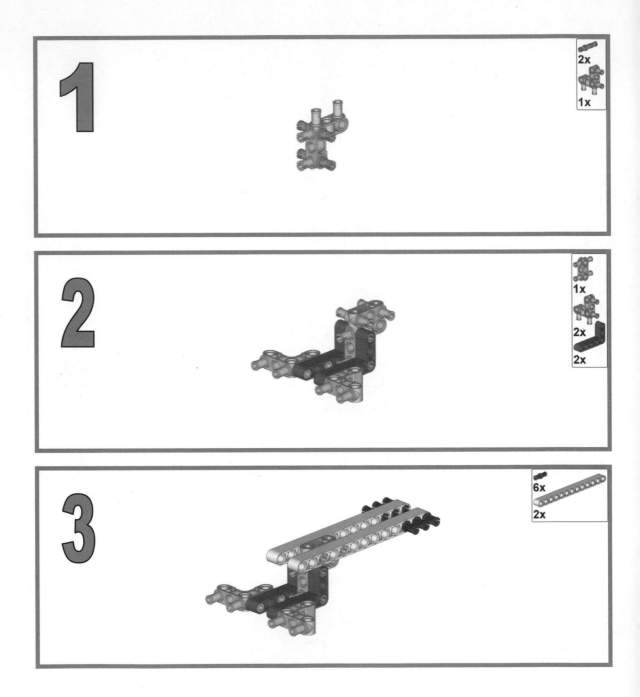

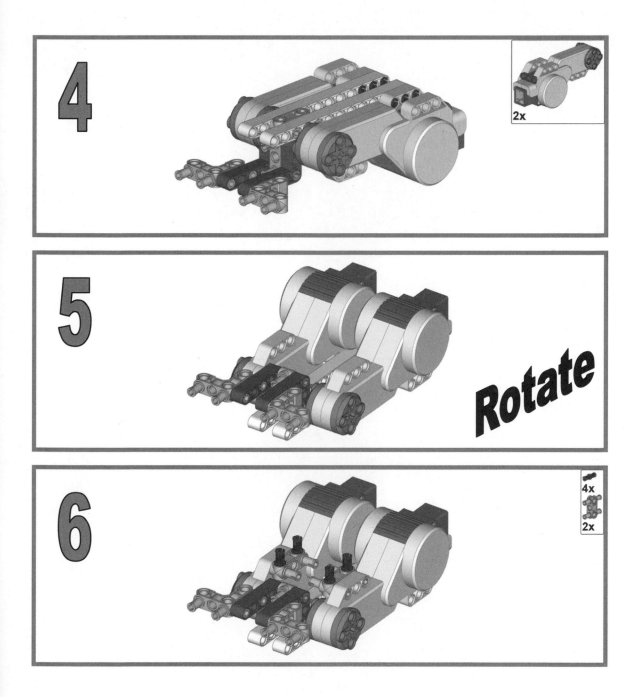

Rotate

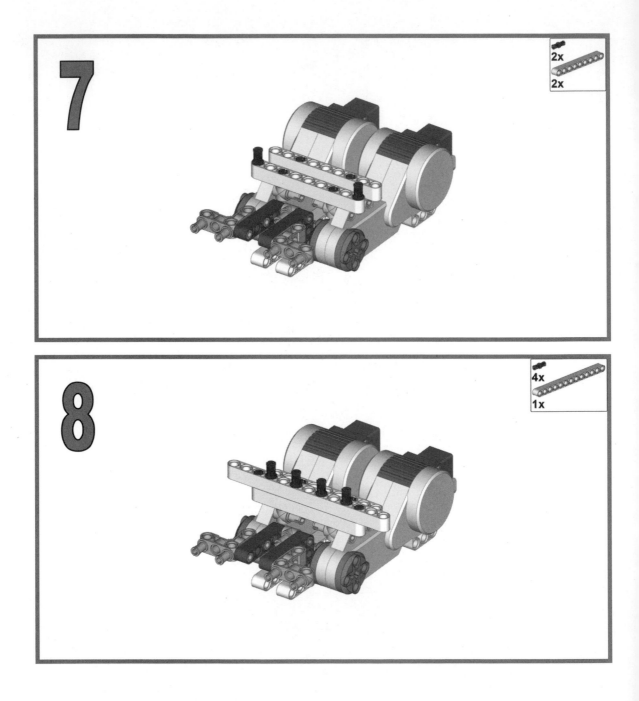

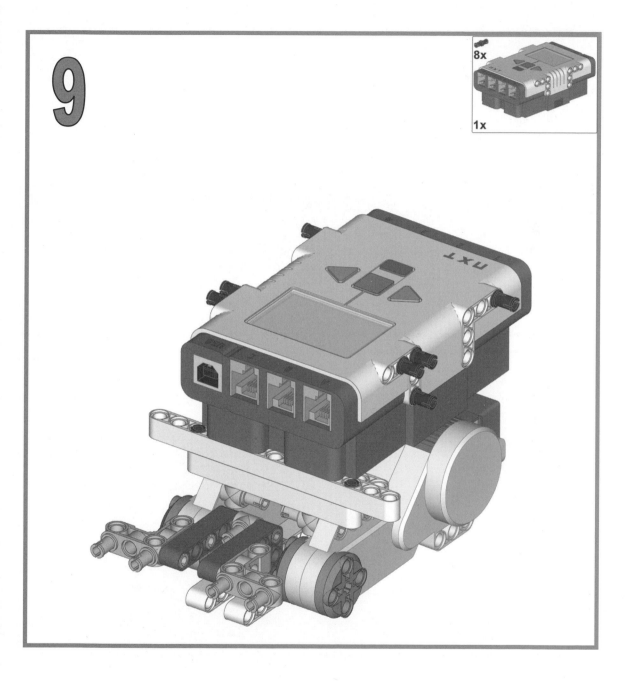

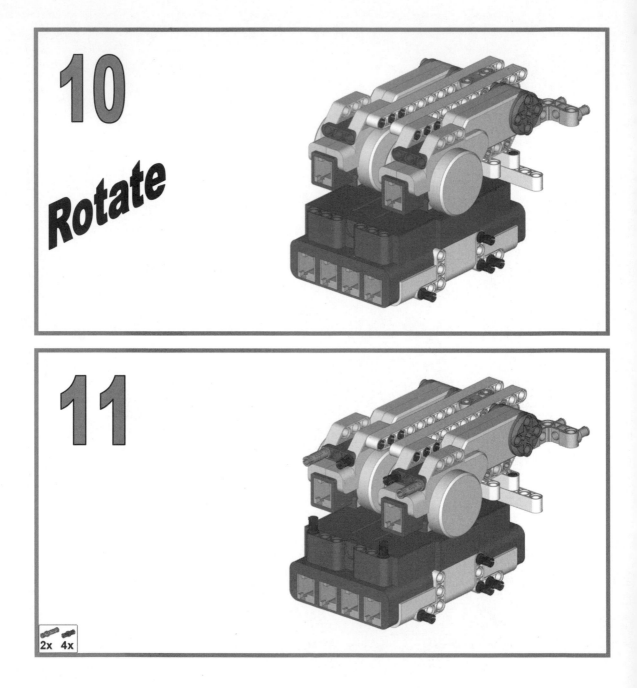

10

Rotate

11

2x 4x

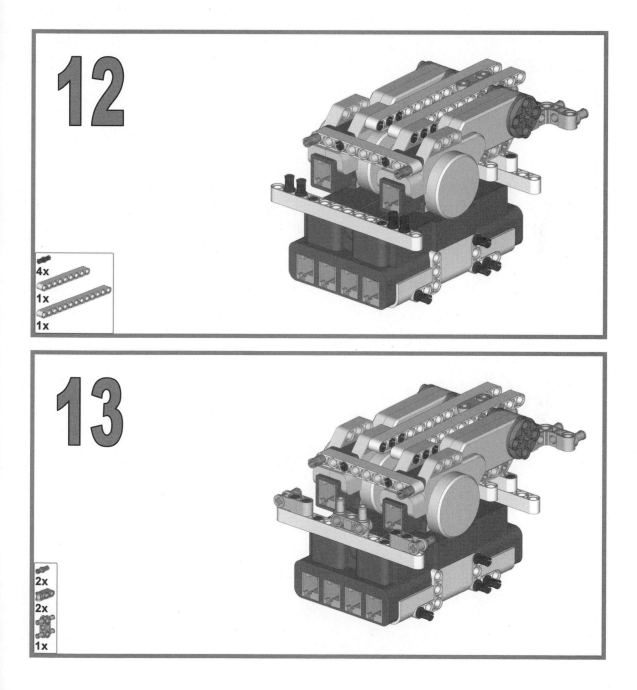

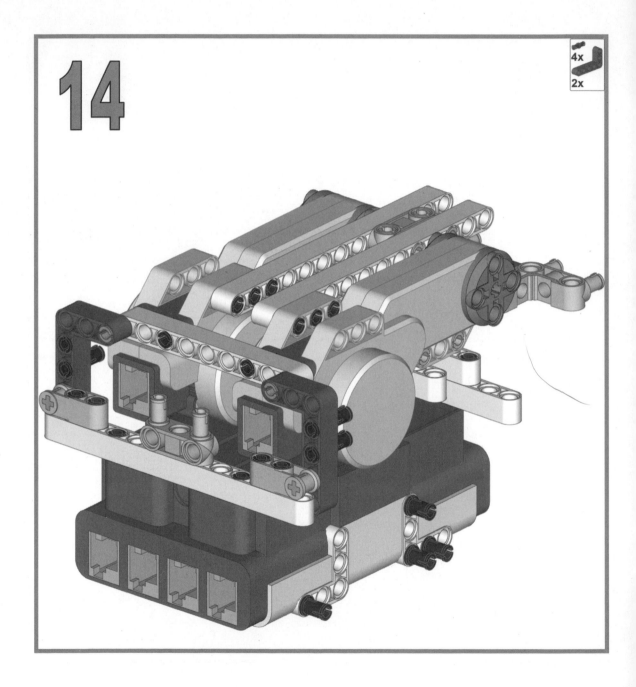

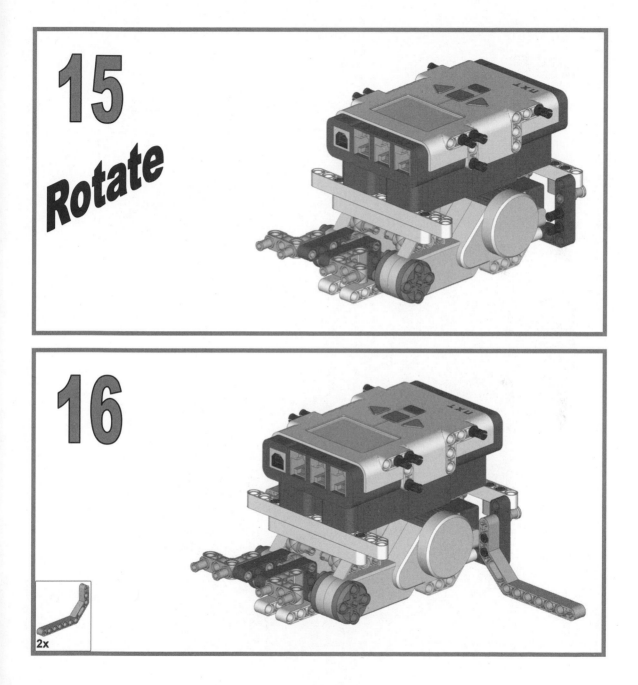

15

Rotate

16

2x

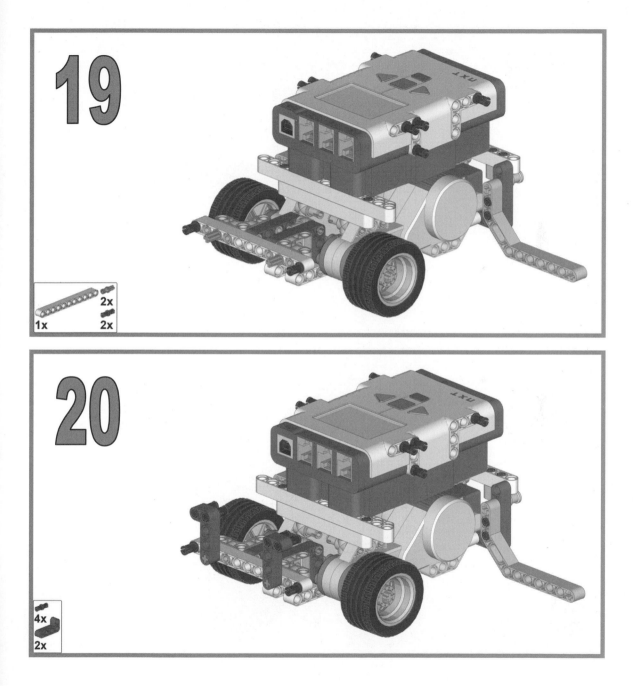

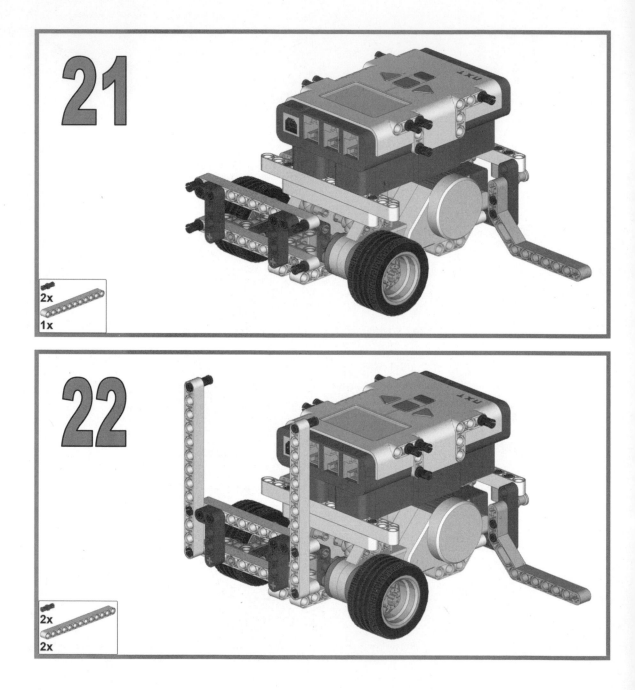

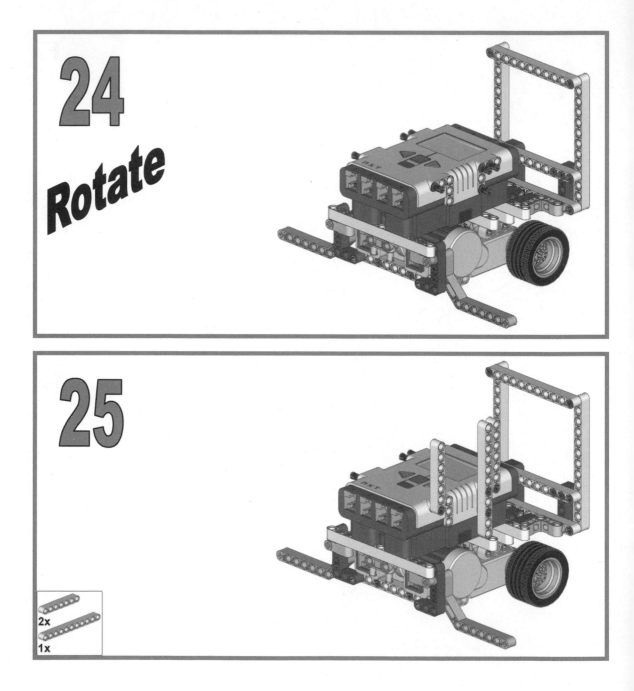

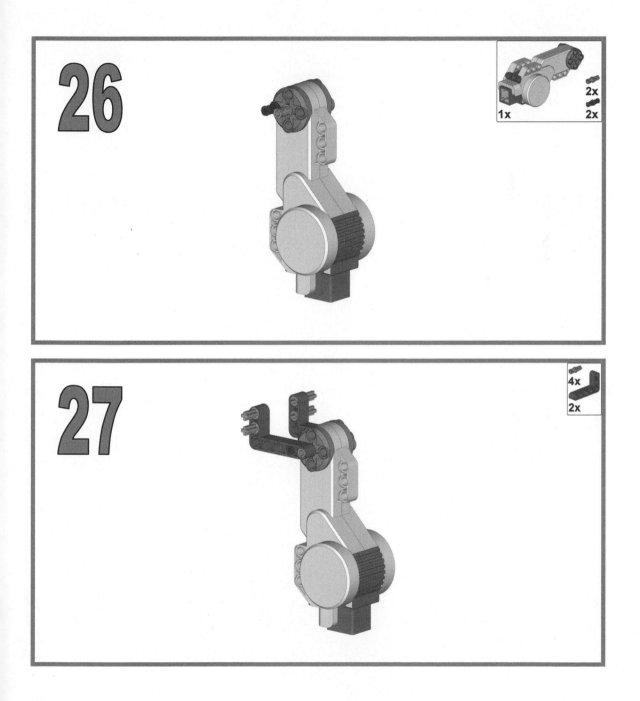

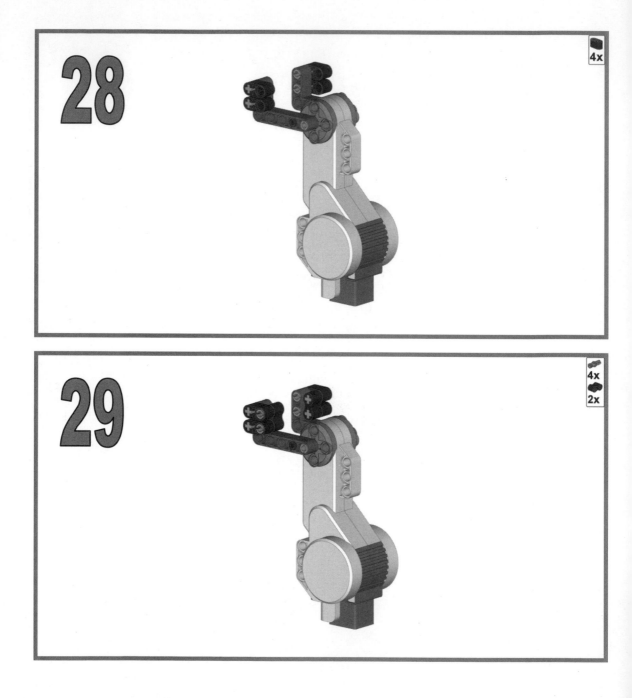

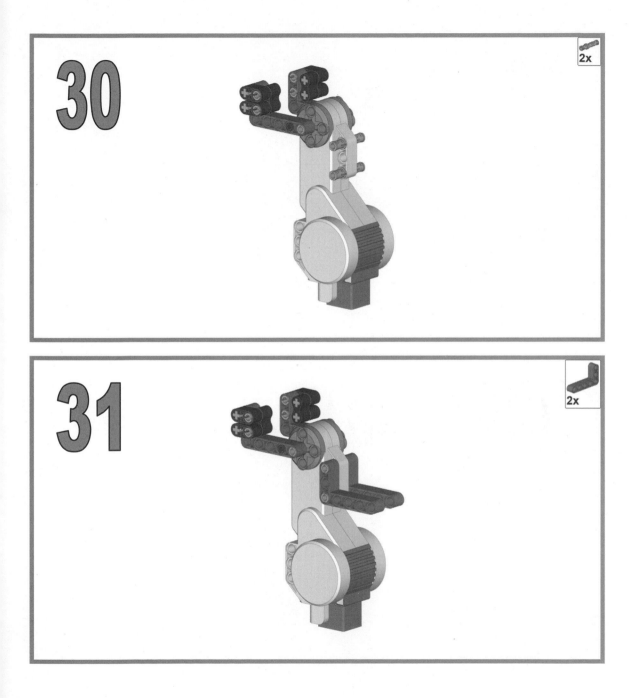

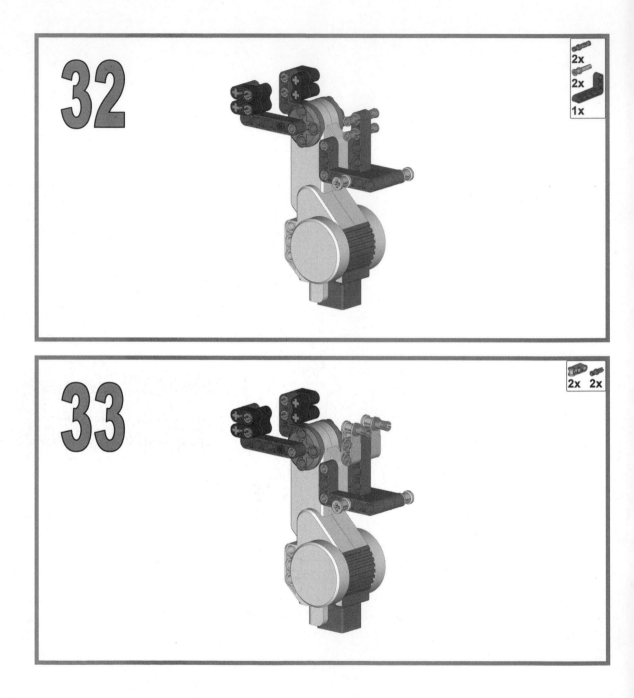

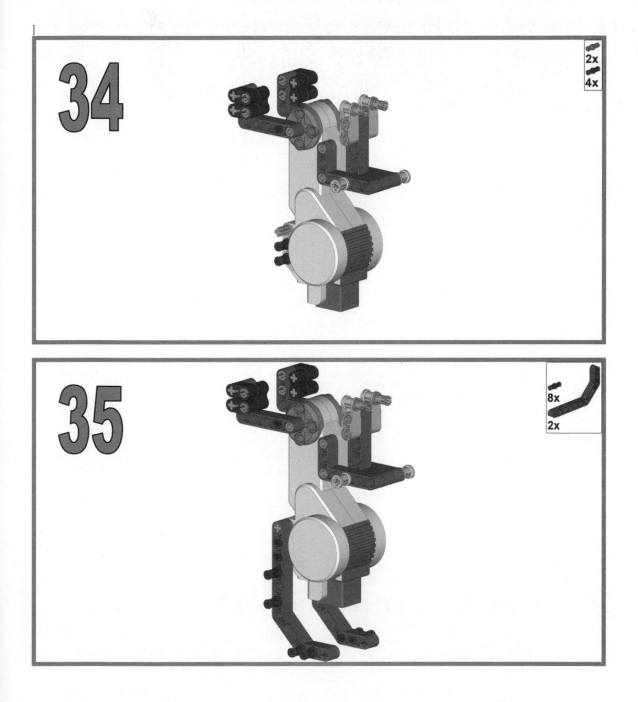

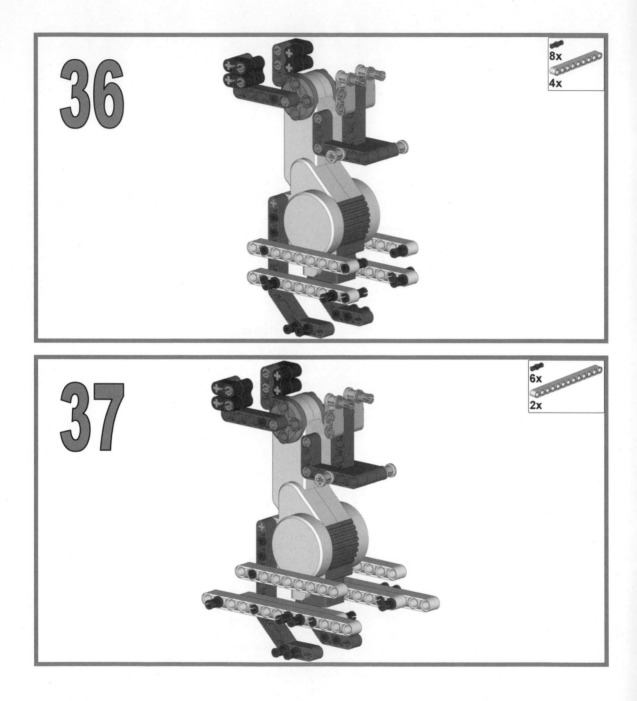

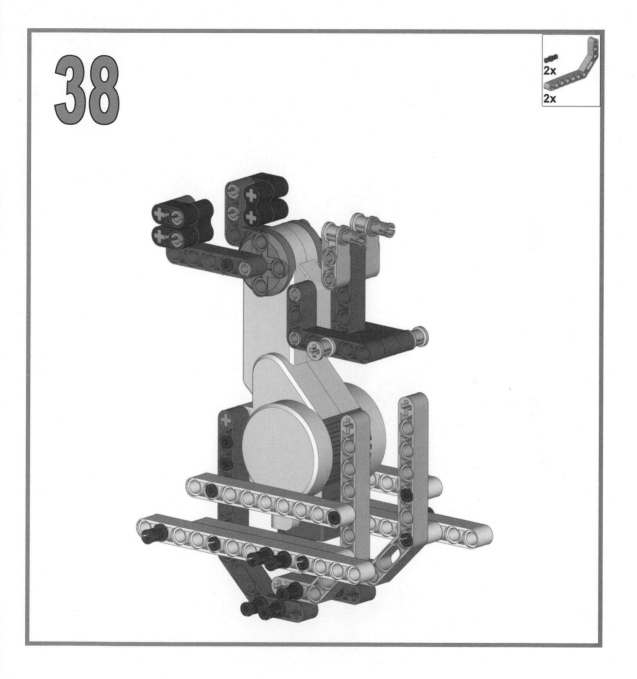

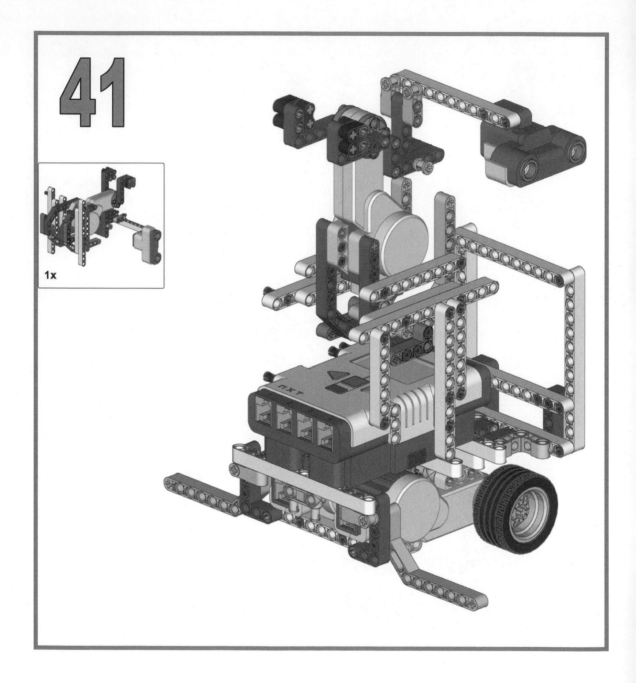

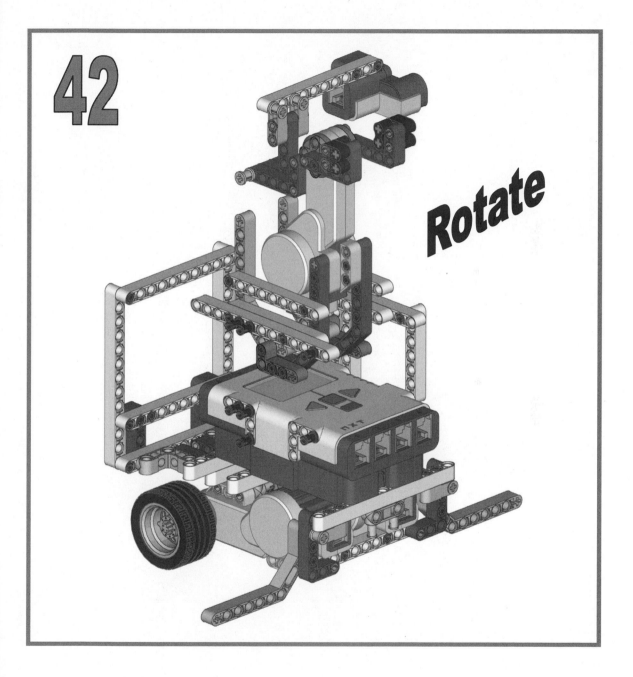

42

Rotate

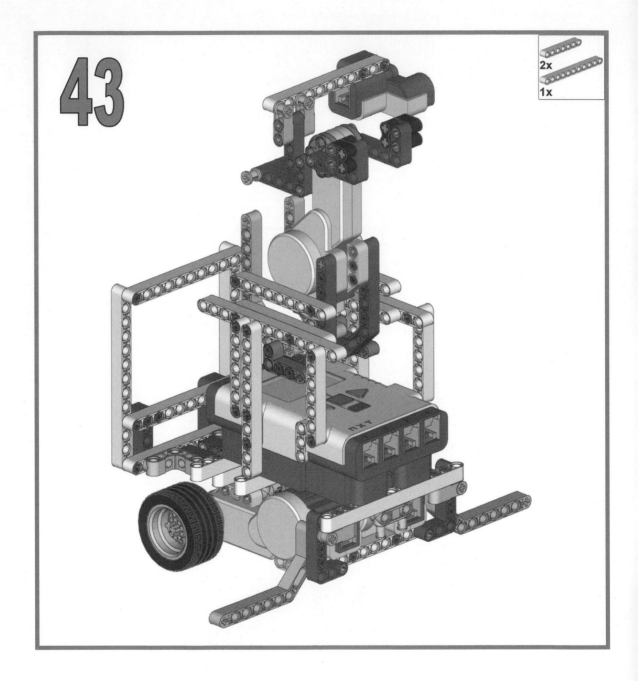

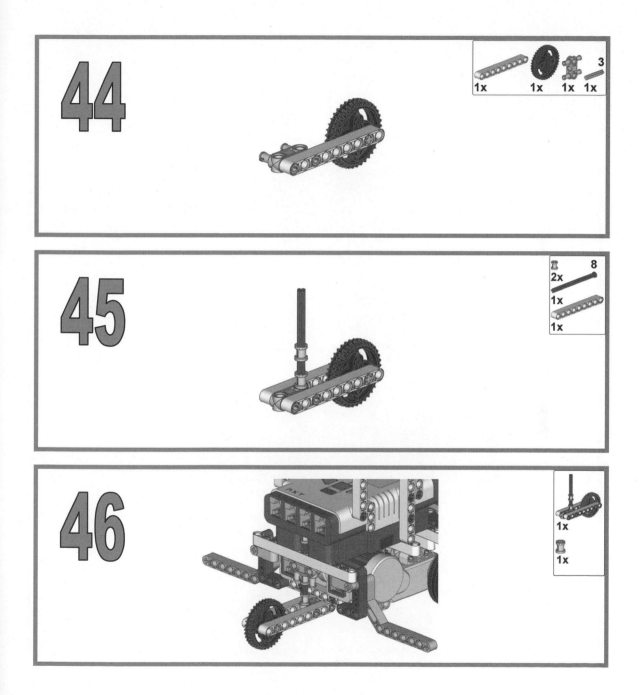

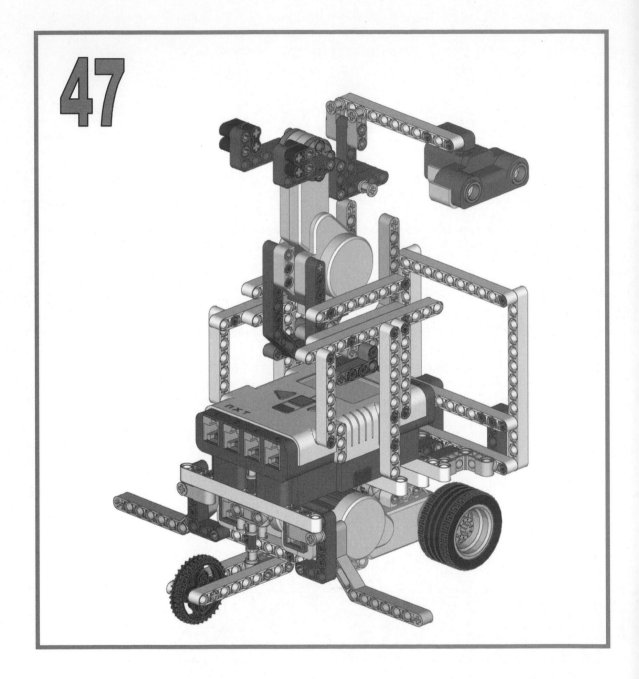

■■■

ZipLiner—Program It

The ZipLiner's success is all that stands between you and King Ixtua's treasure! It's not a complex robot—much of the trickiness with this robot is involved with moving the string up and down to get the ZipLiner safely to the king's throne. When it's at the throne, however, you have some programming to do. It needs to find the throne, release itself from the string, and find and tip over the throne's back support.

We'll get started by opening our NXT software and placing the proper blocks needed to make certain the ZipLiner grabs and holds on to the sled!

Hold On!

For the early part of this challenge, the ZipLiner's main goal is to hang on tight. If you examine the robot I built in Chapter 19, you'll notice that it uses Motor A to latch on to something. What is that "something?" It's a single 15L beam (15 holes) acting as a sled. As long as Motor A is exerting a small force, it should be able to hold on to the sled until it's time to release. I'll provide more details on how to build that sled later in the chapter.

Figure 20-1 shows the first block in my program. This MOVE block is configured for Motor A—I had to experiment to find the best settings.

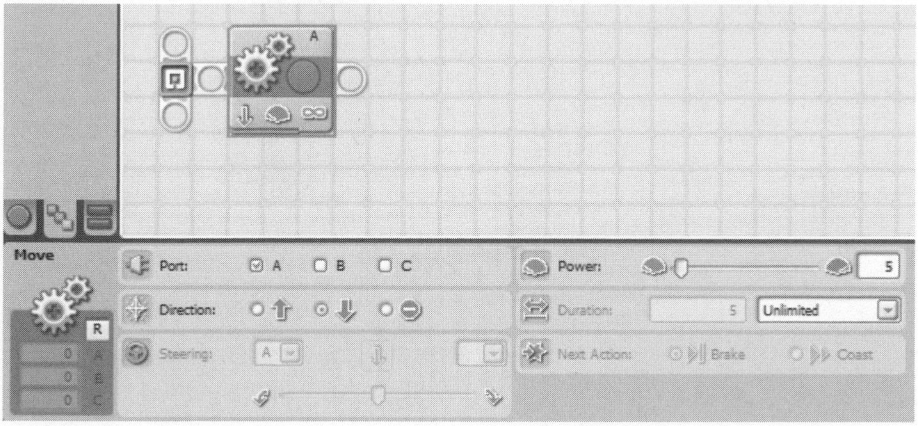

Figure 20-1. This MOVE block will let the ZipLiner hold tightly to the string.

Notice that I've configured it to run for an Unlimited duration. Normally this would keep the motor spinning, but because I've set the power at 5, it's only exerting a small force—just enough to hold on to the sled. Motor A will continue to exert this force until another MOVE block stops Motor A or the program ends.

Okay, now that the ZipLiner is holding tightly to the sled, you (the human) must raise and lower the string to allow it to slide towards the throne. For my challenge, I have a throne back support made of foam board that is approximately 12 inches in height. My robot's design has the Ultrasonic sensor facing the direction of the throne. Once the Ultrasonic sensor detects the throne's back support, it should trigger Motor A to release the string. Figure 20-2 shows the WAIT block I've configured to help with this action.

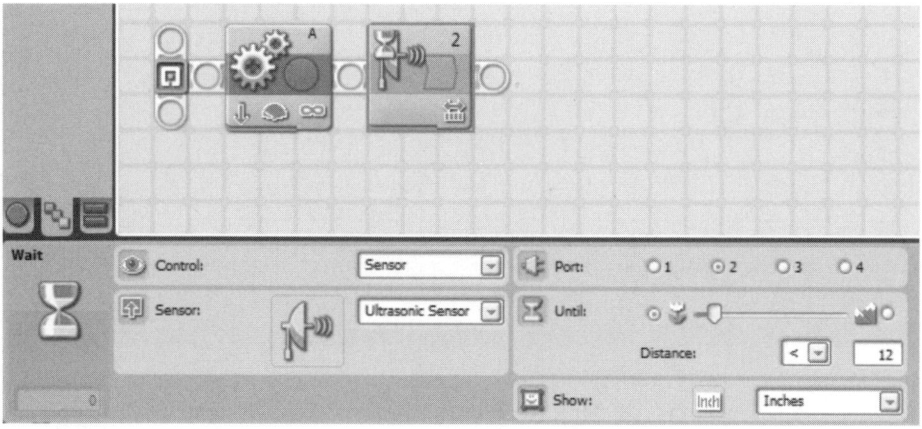

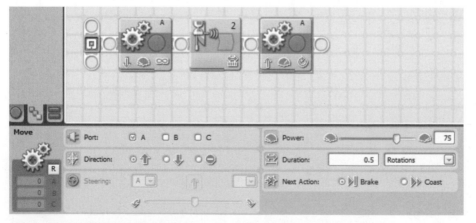

Figure 20-2. A WAIT block will trigger the release of the string.

As you can see, I've configured a WAIT block to pause the program until the Ultrasonic sensor is triggered. Once again, you'll want to test different values for the Distance setting.

Once the Ultrasonic sensor is triggered, Motor A needs to release the string. This is accomplished using another MOVE block, as shown in Figure 20-3.

Figure 20-3. The MOVE block will reverse Motor A to release the string.

After the string is released, ZipLiner is facing left (or 90 degrees counterclockwise from the rear of the throne). Because the robot has just dropped from the string, I want to wait a few seconds just in case the robot may be rocking back and forth slightly. I'll drop in a WAIT block as shown in Figure 20-4.

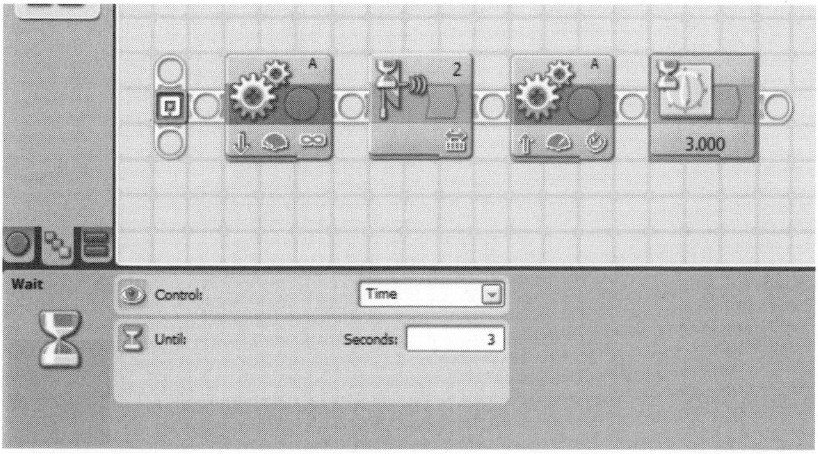

Figure 20-4. The WAIT block will pause for 3 seconds.

After pausing briefly, I need the robot to turn 90 degrees clockwise. This will have my robot facing the throne's back support. (If you've designed your own robot, you may have to change the next MOVE block to match the direction your robot will be facing.)

Figure 20-5 shows the MOVE block I've configured.

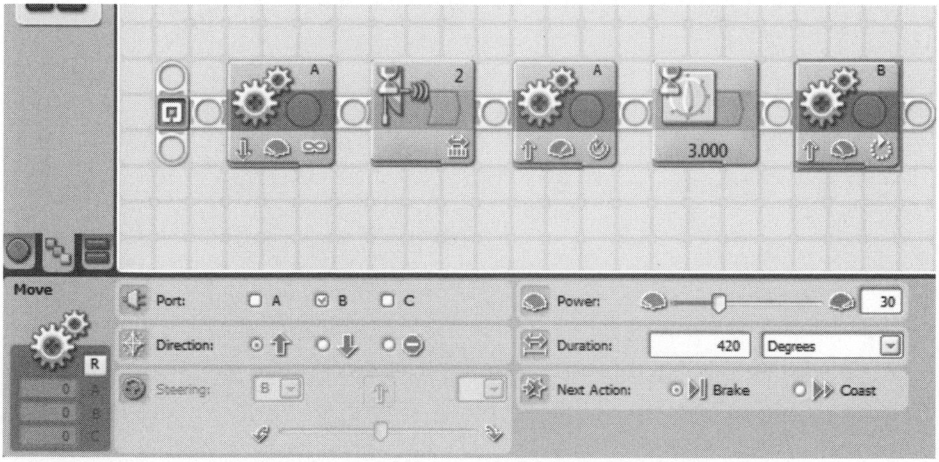

Figure 20-5. The MOVE block will rotate the robot 90 degrees clockwise.

You'll want to experiment with the Duration value; factors such as the floor's surface or the speed of the rotation can all affect how far the robot turns. You need your robot to turn as accurately as possible, so test frequently with different values until you get the closest 90 degree turn possible.

And now the robot needs to move forward quickly and tip over the throne's back support! I don't want my robot moving at the fastest speed, so I've configured it to run at a Power of 75 for a short distance (as shown in Figure 20-6). The value you use for the Duration may be different than mine; test various values until you find the proper one for hitting and tipping over the back of the throne.

■ **Tip** You may wish to add a little complexity to your robot by adding the Color sensor to allow it to scan for the color of the throne's back support. This will also allow you to perform a proper search for the throne's back support no matter how the robot lands on the throne seat.

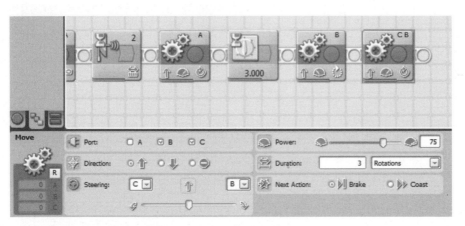

Figure 20-6. The robot will begin to move forward again.

Once the throne's back support is tipped over, I just need the robot to roll up on top of it and wait for me to retrieve it! To do this, I'll add the final block, a MOVE block, to the program as shown in Figure 20-7. Be sure to test to obtain the best value for Duration so your robot doesn't roll off the throne's back support!

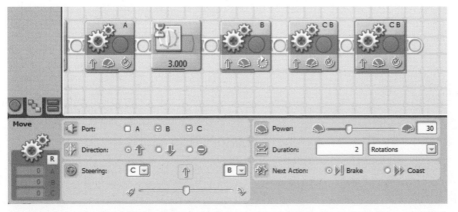

Figure 20-7. The final MOVE block will move the robot on top of the throne's back support.

And that's it! Not an extremely complicated program, is it? As I stated earlier in the book, sometimes the most complicated robots end up with the simplest programs.

The Zip Line Challenge Setup

For this challenge, I purchased two sheets of ¼" foam board (one gold and one blue) and built the throne as seen in Figure 20-8. In addition to the foam board, I also used 20 feet of string and blue painter's tape, and I purchased two small rings from a hobby shop—the total cost for the challenge was less than $12.00.

Figure 20-8. The throne is easy to make from foam board and painter's tape.

To build the throne's sides, use a box cutter or other sharp blade to cut six pieces of the gold foam board with dimensions of 4" tall by 24" long; scissors will work, but the edges might be a little rough or ragged. Figure 20-9 shows the cut foam board (with two extra pieces, just in case).

Figure 20-9. The throne's sides are made from pieces of the gold foam board.

Glue up three sides—two pieces per side, with the gold facing outward. Use a hot glue gun to join the three sides and then use painter's tape to strengthen the joints and add some nice color to the king's throne. Figure 20-10 shows the sides glued and taped.

Figure 20-10. *The throne's sides are glued together and tape added for strength.*

Finally, cut a piece of the blue foam board (for the throne's back support) with dimensions of 12" tall by 24" wide. Do not glue this to the sides; simply place it so it leans against the back of the left and right side pieces. Figure 20-11 shows the final assembly.

Figure 20-11. The throne's back support leans against the sides.

You'll want to attach a small eyehook to the wall (or to a scrap piece of wood) behind the throne. Attach the eyehook 14-16" from the floor. Figure 20-12 shows the string, robot, and throne.

Figure 20-12. The completed challenge area.

Now, all that's left to do is to attach the robot to the sled and begin testing. Figure 20-13 shows a close-up of the sled, and Figure 20-14 shows how the robot attached to the sled. Insert the string's end through both rings first. Then, place the sled as shown in Figure 20-14 and run the program. Motor A should close its clamps slowly and grab on to the sled.

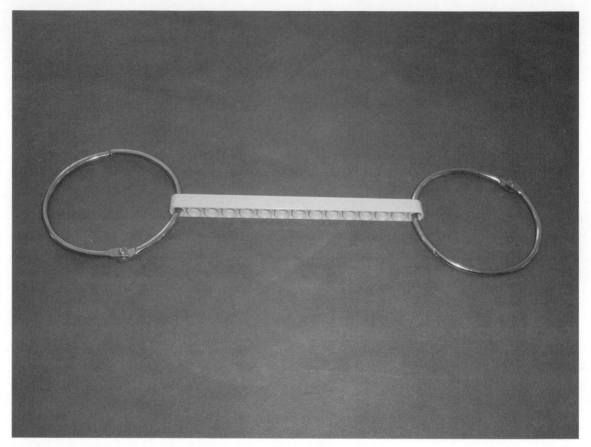

Figure 20-13. A closeup of the 15L beam with rings attached

Figure 20-14. The robot grabs on to the sled using Motor A.

After tipping over the throne's back support, the ZipLiner rolls up on top of it and the challenge is completed (see Figure 20-15).

Figure 20-15. *The challenge is complete and the treasure room is opened.*

And now it's time to open and enter King Ixtua's treasure room... congratulations!

CHAPTER 21

■ ■ ■

Treasure and Discovery

Location: Southwest Guatemala

102 miles SW of Guatemala City

Coordinates: 14º 04' N / 90º 09' W

Weather Conditions: 87 degrees Fahrenheit, Humidity 84%

Day 8: King Ixtua Treasure Repository, 7:02 a.m.

Evan was awakened at 7 a.m. by the sound of vehicles and a helicopter. He rushed out of his tent and was surprised to see two military trucks and four police cars a few hundred feet from the camp site. Overhead, a helicopter continued to hover.

"It's okay, Evan!"

Evan turned to see his uncle running in his direction.

"I wasn't expecting them this early. Sorry for the noise," yelled Dr. Hicks.

"Are we in trouble?" aked Evan loudly. The helicopter had apparently found a landing spot and was moving away from the camp but dropping in altitude.

"No, we're not in trouble," replied Evan's uncle. "I called a contact yesterday about our progress and asked for some assistance. I have a feeling we'll need some more security from this point forward."

"The treasure," said Evan.

"Yep," replied Uncle Phillip. "Everything we find... everything we've discovered... is property of the Guatemalan government. We have to be careful to protect their national treasures."

Evan saw Tag and Erin shake hands with a couple of the soldiers who exited one of the military vehicles. He also watched as the helicopter landed carefully in a clearing on the other side of the camp. The engine whine began to drop in pitch and the blades slowed their spin.

"Come on, Evan. I want to introduce you to someone," said Uncle Phillip.

Evan weaved through the dozens of tents set up in the camp site and followed his uncle to the helicopter. Two men in suits had already exited the helicopter and were waving at them as they approached.

"Dr. Hicks!" exclaimed a man in a light tan suit. "Good to see you again!"

Uncle Phillip shook hands with the man. "And you, Dr. Azurdia. And Dr. Cabrera, it's been a long time."

Evan watched as the second man, dressed in a darker suit and grinning widely, shook his uncle's hand.

"My friends, let me introduce you to my nephew, Evan," said Uncle Phillip.

Evan shook hands with both men.

"Evan, Dr. Azurdia and Dr. Cabrera are from the archaeology department at the Universidad de Guatemala. They have been assisting my team with the inventory of King Ixtua's tomb."

Evan smiled. "It's nice to meet both of you."

Uncle Phillip patted Evan on the back. "Evan's the reason for my phone call to both of you yesterday. We've reached the final challenge room, and I believe his robot is ready to go."

"I cannot wait to see your robot," said Dr. Cabrera. "Your uncle has told us how critical your work has been to accessing these ruins."

"And we're anxious to speak to you about adding robotics as a course of study for our students," replied Dr. Azurdia. "Dr. Hicks has convinced us that archaeological teams could benefit from this technology."

"Uh, sure," said Evan. "I'll try to help you with that."

Uncle Phillip looked over his shoulder and saw Tag and Erin entering the command tent. "It's going to be a long day, so we better get started. Let's go meet the rest of the team and we'll fill you in on what we'll be doing today."

Qau's Challenge

A few hours later, Evan was standing with his uncle's team and the guests in the final chamber before the treasure repository. Evan noticed that the visiting archaeologists had changed into more suitable clothing. *A good thing*, thought Evan, looking at his dusty jeans with their numerous rips and tears.

Evan's robot was halfway over the chasm and sliding slowly down towards the throne. Evan lifted his left hand; with the string raised, the robot started to move forward at a faster rate. Even though he'd practiced this dozens of times in his tent, he only had one chance to get it right here in the final chamber.

Behind Evan, Dr. Cabrera was videotaping the events. Dr. Azurdia had taken a few photographs before the robot was placed on the string, but he was worried the flash would startle Evan. Instead, he stood to the side of the chamber with Uncle Phillip and the other team members to give Evan plenty of room.

Evan lowered the string and the robot's movement slowed. It was hanging approximately one foot above the throne. Evan carefully lowered the string further until the robot was just a few inches above the throne's seat. The Ultrasonic sensor on the robot hadn't yet triggered, so Evan raised the string a few inches... and the robot released the string and dropped onto the seat. It wobbled back and forth slightly but did not tip over.

"Almost done," said Evan.

No one spoke, but Evan heard Tag take a deep breath and hold it. He squinted his eyes at his robot, waiting for the program's final instructions to complete. Slowly, the robot rotated clockwise and then stopped.

"Here we go," Evan said in a hushed voice.

The robot suddenly rolled quickly forward, startling the group. It hit the back support of the throne head-on and stopped suddenly. Evan breathed in deeply—please work, he thought. And then the back support fell away from the robot, triggering the pressure plate.

"Yes!" yelled Tag, making Evan jump.

They all heard a loud creaking, followed by the pop of warping wood. Slowly the two bridges began to lower, and Evan could see that rotting rope was barely keeping the bridges from falling.

Uncle Phillip walked forward and put his hand on Evan's shoulder. "Nice work, Evan. Nice work."

The King's Legacy

Evan's uncle had used most of the afternoon working with various guides and other members of the team to strengthen and secure the two bridges crossing the chasm. Although the bridges were sturdy enough, measurements had found the chasm to be over 200 feet deep. Multiple harness systems had been bolted to the ceiling to aid those people crossing over and prevent anyone from falling.

Even with the harness on, however, Evan's palms were still sweaty and his heart raced. He didn't look down as he crossed the bridge to the left of the throne to join his uncle in the left hallway. Tag and Erin were in the hallway to the right of the throne.

Dr. Hicks had already examined the hallways that had been obscured by the raised bridges and found no traps. It appeared that the team had proven itself to Tupaxu and Qau and earned the right to enter King Ixtua's treasure room. When he returned to ask his team to cross the bridges, he informed them that there was a chamber but said nothing else.

The visiting archaeologists watched from the other side of the fifth chamber as Dr. Hicks and his team moved slowly down the two hallways.

The hallways angled down slightly as Evan walked forward, his uncle close behind him. Both of them held their flashlights in their hands; the bright beams gave off a strong white light.

Evan saw the hallway opening up twenty feet ahead of him. Unable to see anything in the next chamber, he began to walk faster.

Uncle Phillip laughed. "I know the feeling," he said.

As Evan reached the end of the hallway, he could hear Erin and Tag whooping and laughing. He could see beams from their flashlights moving up and down quickly, then to the right and left. He walked forward a few more feet, pointed his flashlight into the room, and smiled.

The treasure chamber was everything he imagined it would be. Golden, full-sized statues of Mayan warriors encircled stone tables in the center of the chamber. The tables were spilling over with gold jewelry and carvings. Gems twinkled as the flashlight beams moved around the room. At the back of the chamber, large holes had been chiseled out of the stone walls; dozens of scrolls poked out from each hole.

Evan's uncle walked forward and motioned for Tag, Erin, and Evan to join him.

"Congratulations to all of you," Dr. Hicks said. "Outstanding work."

Tag smiled at Erin and Evan. "I can't believe it's over."

"Over?" asked Dr. Hicks. "We've got years of work ahead of us. Everything in this room and the previous chambers will have to be documented, inventoried, and examined again and again. There's a lifetime of work here. The two of you could build your entire careers on this discovery."

Erin smiled. "That sounds pretty good to me," she said. "Look at all those scrolls to translate!"

Uncle Phillip laughed. "I think it's time to invite the rest of the team to take a look."

Evan looked at Tag and Erin. "Um… can we wait a few more minutes?" he asked.

"I agree," said Tag. "There's no rush, is there?"

"Not a bit," said Uncle Phillip. "I think we've all earned a little rest. How about we take a minute or two and just look at what we've found; enjoy it, team." He sat down on the stone floor and motioned for the others to join him.

Qau's Teacher

Evan got a surprise the following day. He watched as a new truck arrived and the two occupants got out.

"Max! Grace!" he yelled. He ran over to the truck and hugged them both. "What are you doing here? Uncle Phillip told me you were away on your own expeditions."

"Are you kidding?" asked Grace. "First King Ixtua's tomb and now his treasure chamber? We drove all night to get here. And your uncle found something in the treasure chamber he wants me to check out."

Max and Grace had been Uncle Phillip's student assistants for the opening of King Ixtua's tomb two years ago. Since then, Grace had focused her studies on Tupaxu and the scrolls he left behind in the king's library while Max had done more research on King Ixtua. Although they had graduated and moved on with their careers, Evan was happy to hear that they still wanted to be part of his uncle's team.

"Over here!" Evan turned to see his uncle waving the group to the command tent.

"It's so cool to see you guys," said Evan.

Max nodded. "I'm glad to see your interest in history and archaeology has grown. I'm sure your uncle was glad to have you here this week."

Evan followed Max and Grace into the tent. Uncle Phillip introduced his former students to Erin and Tag and then asked everyone to have a seat. A tour of the treasure chamber would have to wait for a few minutes, he said.

"Take a look at this," said Uncle Phillip, turning his laptop. The group leaned forward to examine the photo displayed on the screen.

"That represents Tupaxu," said Grace, pointing to a large necklace placed around a stone statue's neck. "That's his glyph right there."

"Notice anything else?" asked Uncle Phillip.

Grace leaned closer. "The scroll?" she asked.

Evan looked; sure enough the statue was holding a scroll in its left hand.

Dr. Hicks smiled. "We found this statue in the far left corner of the treasure chamber. Erin translated the scroll. It's a note from Qau, Tupaxu's student and the builder of the fifth chamber."

"What does it say?" asked Max.

"It doesn't really say much," replied Erin. "But it does contain a map."

Evan sat up straight. "A map?" he asked.

Uncle Phillip nodded and smiled. "Grace, you're the expert on Tupaxu, so I wanted you to hear the news before the rest of the world gets it."

Grace looked at Erin and then to Dr. Hicks. "Okay," she said.

Uncle Phillip took a deep breath and let it out. "I'm going to be busy here for the next year or two, and I'm going to need someone to take the lead on a very important expedition. I think that person should be you."

Evan was confused. "What expedition?"

"Qau left us a scroll showing the location of Tupaxu's tomb. I would like Grace to put together a team and find it."

Evan looked over at Grace, who was grinning from ear to ear. Max gave her a hug and a nod and then Evan saw Grace shake hands with his uncle and exchange a few words. Uncle Phillip nodded, and Grace turned to look at Evan.

"Evan… care to join my team?"

DESIGN JOURNAL

☐ ☐ ☐ ☐ ☐ ☐

ROBOT NAME

ROBOT DESCRIPTION

TASK LIST

LIMITATIONS/CONSTRAINTS

MINDSTORM

SKETCHES

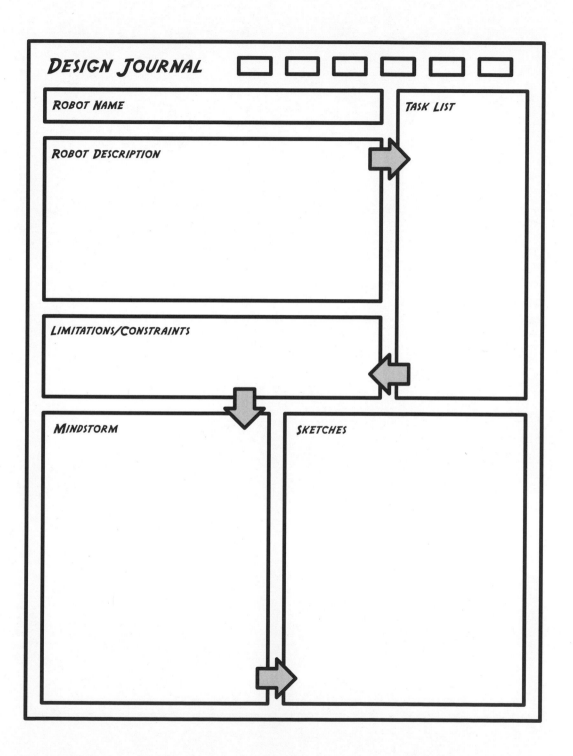

DESIGN JOURNAL

ROBOT NAME

TASK LIST

ROBOT DESCRIPTION

LIMITATIONS/CONSTRAINTS

MINDSTORM

SKETCHES

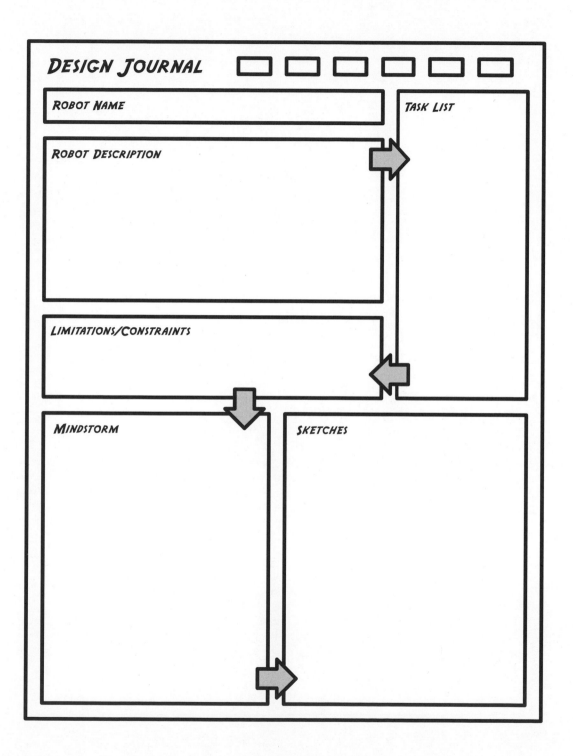

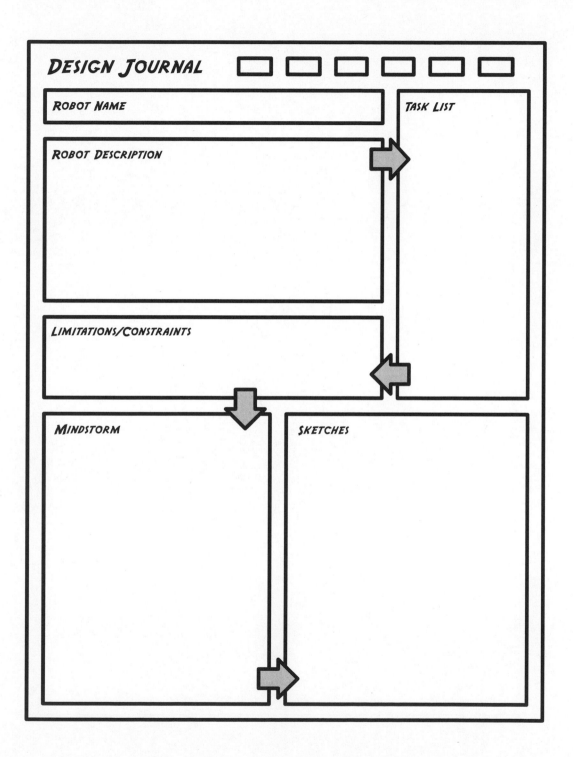

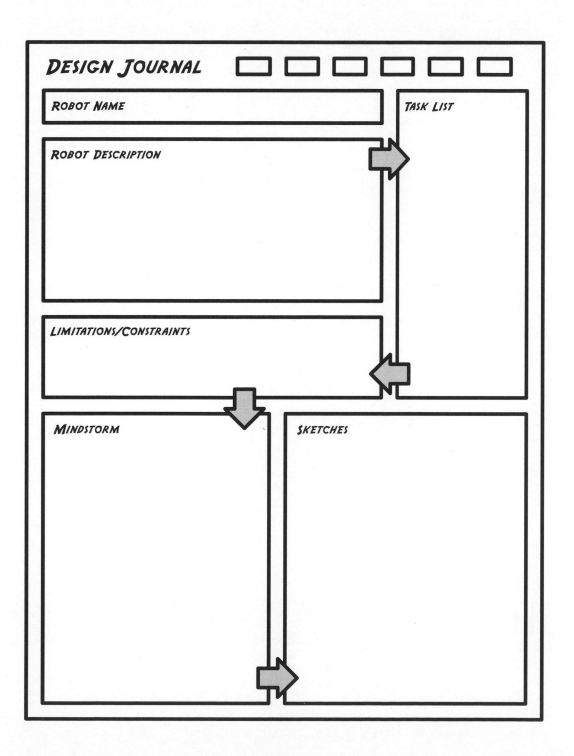

Index

◼A,B,C

CAD instructions
for building MazeBot, 20
for building RampRider, 216
for building RingTosser, 142
for building RopeSwinger, 74
for building ZipLiner, 262
challenge area setups
for testing MazeRunner, 59–60
for testing RampRider, 244–246
for testing RingTosser, 187–201
for testing RopeSwinger, 117–122
for testing ZipLiner, 295–302
Color sensors
for MazeRunner, 12–13, 18, 48, 50–51, 54
for RampRider, 212–213, 239
for RingTosser, 138, 182–183, 198
for ZipLiner, 294
COMMON palette, 44
COMPLETE palette, 44

◼D

design and aplanning process, 9
Design Journal worksheets
downloading, 10–11
using to program, 41
downloading Design Journal worksheets, 10–11
Duration values, obtaining during testing, 54

◼E,F,G,H

experimenting
with MazeRunner construction, 20
with RopeSwinger construction, 74

◼I,J

Intelligent Brick
defined, 7
as main body (MazeRunner), 18
sketch of, 18

◼K

King Ixtua's treasure repository
crossing the bridge, 125–126
entering long hallway, 126
final chamber, 247–250
four Mayan warriors, 128–129
hooks and doors, 129–131
king's legacy discovered, 304–305

king's throne, 250–251

maze challenge, 4–6

Munala's door, opening, 201–202

preparing to enter, 1–4

press-and-release trap, 127–128

Qau's challenge, 304

ramp of the warriors, 203

ramp room, 205–206

robot kit, 6–8

story wall of Mayan glyphs, 202

Tupaxu's tomb, 305–306

uphill challenge, 202–203

■L

left/right turn calculations (MazeRunner),
58–59

LEGO MINDSTORMS NXT 2.0

kit, 13

*LEGO MINDSTORMS NXT: The Mayan
Adventure* (Kelly), 9

software, creating new program in, 42

software, tutorials for, 41

lever model, constructing (RopeSwinger),
117–122

Light sensor for RampRider, 212–213

Limitations/Constraints

MazeRunner design, 13–15

RampRider design, 210

RingTosser design, 136

RopeSwinger design, 68

ZipLiner design, 256

logic signals, defined, 50

LOOP blocks

basics, 45

for MazeRunner, 49–53, 55–57

nesting, 49–52

for RampRider, 208, 235–236

■M

maze challenge (King Ixtua tomb), 4–6

MazeRunner

building, 19–20

Design Journal worksheets, 10–11

Limitations/Constraints, 13–15

Mindstorm, 15–17

overview, 9–11

programming. *See* programming
MazeRunner

Robot Description, 11

sketches, 17–18

Task List, 12–13

Mindstorm (Design Journal worksheet)

for MazeRunner, 15–17

for RampRider, 210–211

for RingTosser, 136–138

for RopeSwinger, 68–70

for ZipLiner, 256–258

motors for turning, 16, 18

MOVE blocks

basics, 43–44

for MazeRunner, 46–48, 50, 52, 54, 56–
57

for RampRider, 236–240, 242–243

for RingTosser, 179–187

for RopeSwinger, 114–115

for ZipLiner, 291–295

Munala's door, opening (King Ixtua tomb),
201–202

■N,O

nesting with LOOP blocks (MazeRunner),
49–52

■P

planning and design process, 9

press-and-release trap (King Ixtua tomb), 127–128

programming MazeRunner
Color sensor, 48, 50–51, 54
creating new program, 42
Design Journal worksheet, 41
left/right turn calculations, 58–59
LOOP blocks, 45, 53
LOOP blocks, nesting, 49–52
MOVE blocks, 43–44, 46–48, 50, 52, 54
removing from maze, 55–58
Task List, grouping, 46
testing with blue tape, 59–60
Ultrasonic Sensor, 47–48
using Task List for, 43
WAIT blocks, 46–47

programming RampRider
challenge area setup, 244–246
Loop blocks, 235–236
Move blocks, 236–240, 242–243
Statue Movements, 235–243
WAIT blocks, 236–237, 239–241, 243–244

programming RingTosser
challenge area, building, 187–201
MOVE/WAIT blocks for rolling/turning/stopping, 179–187
overview, 179

programming RopeSwinger
constructing lever pull challenge, 117–122
MOVE blocks, 114–115
testing lever pull, 123
Ultrasonic sensor, 113–114
WAIT blocks, 113, 115–117

programming ZipLiner
Color sensor, 294
MOVE blocks, 291–295
Ultrasonic sensor, 292
WAIT blocks, 292–293

■Q

Qau's challenge (King Ixtua tomb), 304

■R

ramp of warriors (King Ixtua tomb), 203
ramp room (King Ixtua tomb), 205–206

RampRider
building, 215–216
Design Journal worksheet, 207
Limitations/Constraints, 210
Mindstorm, 210–211
programming. *See* programming RampRider
Robot Description, 207–208
sketches, 212–213
Task List, 209–210

right-angle turns, 14–15

right/left turn calculations (MazeRunner), 58–59

RingTosser
building, 141–142
Design Journal worksheet, 133
Limitations/Constraints, 136
Mindstorm, 136–138
programming, see programming RingTosser
Robot Description, 133–134

sketches, 138–139

Task List, 134–136

Robot Descriptions (Design Journal worksheet)

    for MazeRunner, 11

    for RampRider, 207–208

    for RingTosser, 133–134

    for RopeSwinger, 65–66

    for ZipLiner, 253–254

robots

    kit, 6–8

    symmetrical, 19

RopeSwinger

    building, 73–74

    Design Journal worksheet, 65

    experimenting with building of, 74

    Limitations/Constraints, 68

    Mindstorm, 68–70

    programming. *See* programming RopeSwinger

    Robot Description, 65–66

    sketches, 70–71

    Task List, 66–68

■S

sketches (Design Journal worksheet)

    for MazeRunner, 17–18

    for RampRider, 212–213

    for RingTosser, 138–139

    for RopeSwinger, 70–71

    for ZipLiner, 258–259

story wall of Mayan glyphs (King Ixtua tomb), 202

surface conditions, wheels for, 15

symmetrical robots, 19

■T

Task Lists (Design Journal worksheet)

    grouping tasks, 46

    for MazeRunner, 12–13, 43

    for RampRider, 209–210

    for RingTosser, 134–136

    for RopeSwinger, 66–68

    for ZipLiner, 254–256

testing challenges. *See* challenge area setups

Touch sensor

    for MazeRunner, 18

    for RampRider, 211, 213

    for RingTosser, 137–138, 180, 184–185

    for RopeSwinger, 68

True logic signals, 50

Tupaxu's tomb (King Ixtua tomb), 305–306

turning

    calculations for (MazeRunner), 58–59

    right-angle turns, 14–15

    and rotating, motors for, 16, 18

tutorials for software, 41

■U,V

Ultrasonic sensor

    for MazeRunner, 18, 47–48

    for RampRider, 211–213, 236–237

    for RopeSwinger, 68, 70–71, 113–114

    for stopping, 12–13

    for ZipLiner, 259, 292

uphill challenge (King Ixtua tomb), 202–203

■W

WAIT blocks

for MazeRnner, 46–47

for RampRider, 236–237, 239–241, 243–244

for RingTosser, 179–187

for RopeSwinger, 113, 115–117

for ZipLiner, 292–293

Won't Work strategy, 69

■X,Y,Z

Zamor spheres, 19

ZipLiner

building, 261–262

challenge setup for, 295–302

Limitations/Constraints, 256

Mindstorm, 256–258

overview, 253

programming. *See* programming ZipLiner

Robot Description, 253–254

sketches, 258–259

Task List, 254–256

You Need the Companion eBook

Your purchase of this book entitles you to buy the companion PDF-version eBook for only $10. Take the weightless companion with you anywhere.

We believe this Apress title will prove so indispensable that you'll want to carry it with you everywhere, which is why we are offering the companion eBook (in PDF format) for $10 to customers who purchase this book now. Convenient and fully searchable, the PDF version of any content-rich, page-heavy Apress book makes a valuable addition to your programming library. You can easily find and copy code—or perform examples by quickly toggling between instructions and the application. Even simultaneously tackling a donut, diet soda, and complex code becomes simplified with hands-free eBooks!

Once you purchase your book, getting the $10 companion eBook is simple:

❶ Visit **www.apress.com/promo/tendollars/**.

❷ Complete a basic registration form to receive a randomly generated question about this title.

❸ Answer the question correctly in 60 seconds, and you will receive a promotional code to redeem for the $10.00 eBook.

THE EXPERT'S VOICE™

233 Spring Street, New York, NY 10013

Offer valid through 4/10.